For Monica with all love from Ann Stokes

Ann Stokes: Artists' Potter

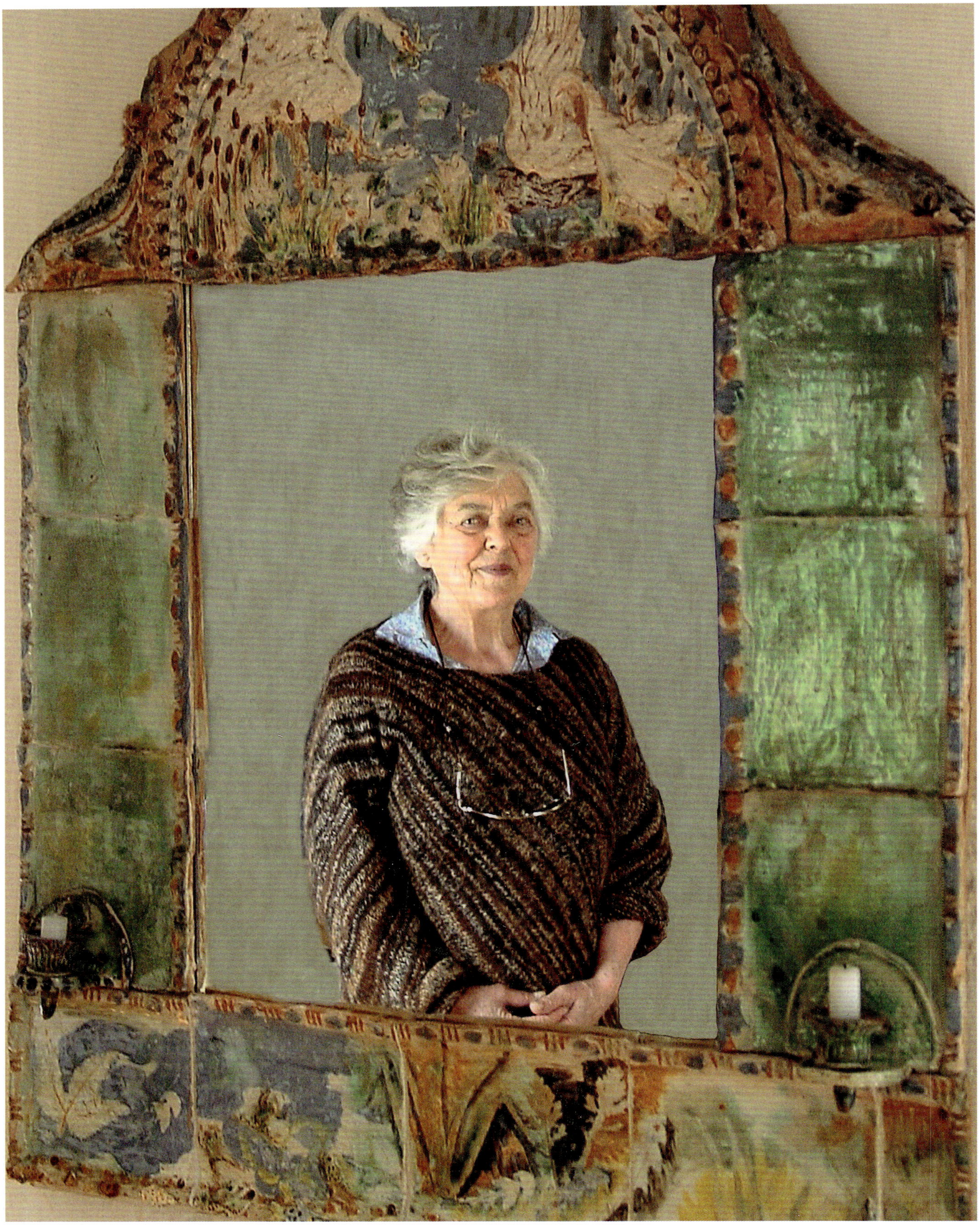

Ann Stokes: Artists' Potter

Edited by Tanya Harrod

Contributions by

Grey Gowrie, Richard Morphet and Hilary Spurling

Lund Humphries

frontispiece:
Ann Stokes in her mirror, 2007
Used as an invitation card for the exhibition To Cage a Peacock, *2007.*
Photo: Philip Stokes

First published in 2009 by Lund Humphries

Lund Humphries
Wey Court East
Union Road
Farnham
Surrey GU9 7PT

Lund Humphries
Suite 420
101 Cherry Street
Burlington
VT 05401-4405
USA

www.lundhumphries.com

Lund Humphries is part of Ashgate Publishing

British Library Cataloguing-in-Publication Data:
Ann Stokes
1. Stokes, Ann - Criticism and interpretation 2. Stokes, Ann 3. Women potters - Great Britain - Biography 4. Potters - Great Britain - Biography
I. Harrod, Tanya
738'.092
ISBN: 938-1-84822-007-2

Library of Congress Control Number: 2008938584

Edited by Clare Farrow
Designed by Studio Gossett

Printed in Singapore

Contents

Foreword

Grey Gowrie

(mantelpiece, left to right)
1 Omega plate, marked Omega back stamp, c.1915
Earthenware, white tin glaze
29 cm (11.5 in)
2 Fish tureen, unmarked, mid 1990s
Modelled
20 x 52 cm (8 x 20.5 in)
3 Bird, unmarked, 2003
Modelled
16 x 19 cm (6.3 x 7.5 in)

(above mantelpiece)
Roger Hilton, Untitled, 1971
Oil on canvas

(foreground, left to right)
1 Table, unmarked mid 1990s
Thrown moulded, slab built, pierced
33 x 26 cm (13 x 10 in)
2 Gordon Baldwin, Strange Vessel, *marked GB 2006*
Stoneware, coiled,
42 x 53 cm (16.5 x 21 in)

Collection: Lord and Lady Gowrie
Photo: Stephen Brayne

THIS BOOK, WHICH LUND HUMPHRIES has produced in collaboration with The Derek Hill Foundation, is both welcome and overdue. Ann Stokes is an original and inventive artist. Yet she is not widely known and she is not easy to classify. Being widely known is not the same thing as being well known. Ann Stokes' work is, nonetheless, very well known indeed to many of the individuals, critics and practitioners who have influenced modern British art over the last fifty years.

You can judge artists by the company they keep, or rather the company their works keep. Ann Stokes' work has been owned, cherished, used and, as she would approve, sometimes abused by such makers and arbiters as Richard Wollheim, David Sylvester, Nikos Stangos, David Plante, Sonia Orwell, William Coldstream, Lawrence Gowing, Derek Hill, John Fowler, John Golding, Catherine Lampert, John Craxton, Barry Flanagan and Nigel Greenwood. Hilary Spurling, biographer of Matisse and a contributor to this volume, is a collector and a fan.

You have to be many times a millionaire to buy a Matisse or Monet nowadays but if, like me, your home is hung with Ann's mirrors and plates, you enter a world congenial to Monet and Matisse and fill the darkest chamber with sunlight and joy. Ann works part of the year in Italy and it shows. She has, too, something in common with Picasso, without sharing any visual kinship with him. It is the ability, in her three-dimensional pieces, to worship the god of things as they are. She sees the fishiness of fish, the movement of boats and horses, and perceives that our eyes are often humorous, our minds drawn to visual puns and metamorphoses. Also

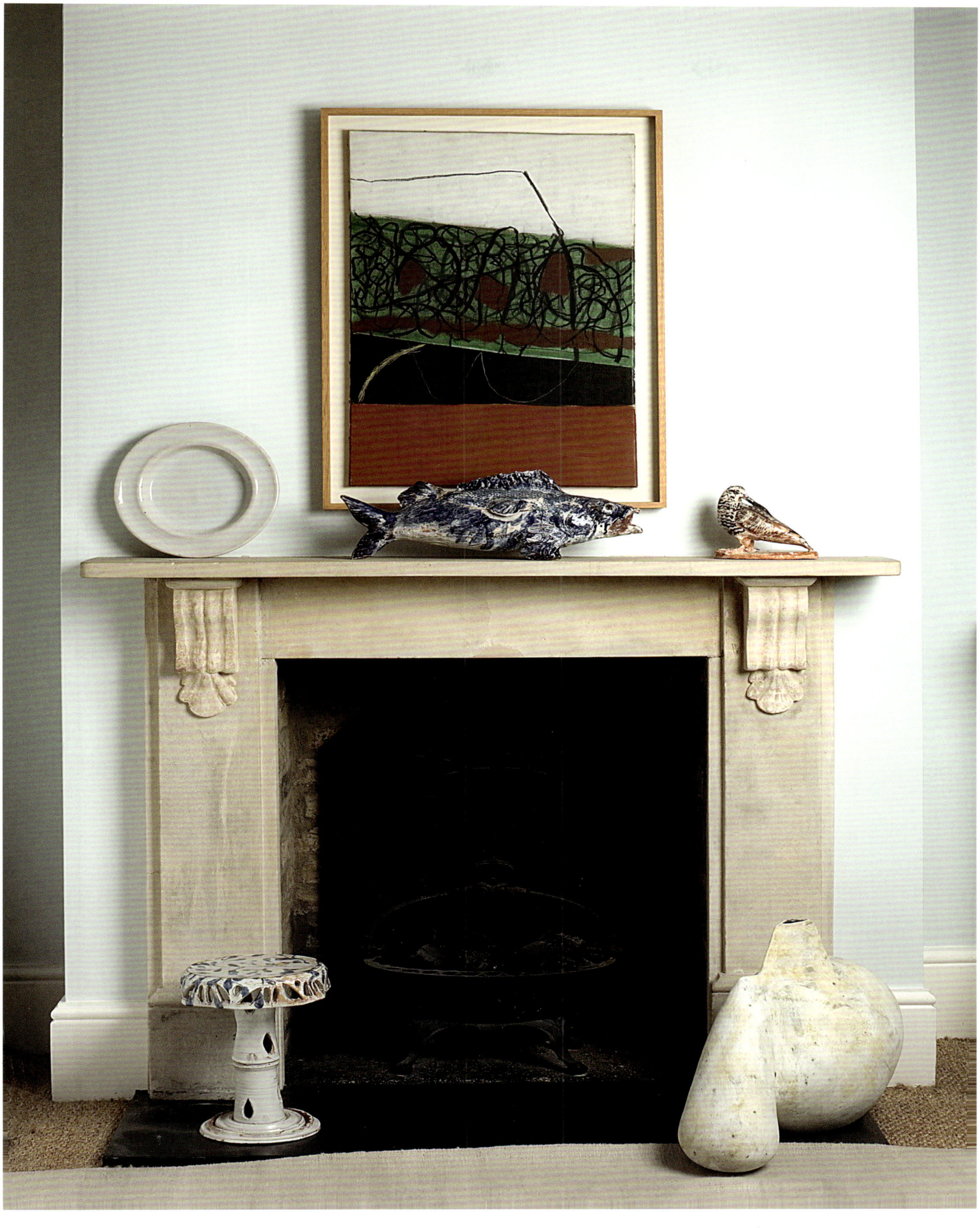

Picasso-like is the difficulty, when you find yourself confronted by a significant piece of Stokes, to concentrate on anything else in the room, however fine.

I was introduced to Ann and her work by Mary Day Wollheim, a potter and a former pupil of Ann's, her husband, the philosopher and aesthetic theorist Richard Wollheim, the art critic David Sylvester and, above all, by my wife. For an outlay of a few hundred pounds our rooms have been transformed ever since. All good art, even good gloomy or tragic art, must in the end give pleasure. It has to provide a kind of elation. Ann Stokes' work begins and ends with the pleasure principle. You look at it; it gives light generously back; you can use it to store things in or eat and drink from. It is entirely and eminently there. When you move a piece or break one your environment seems altered in some way, or bereft.

Ann's work is hard to classify but it has affinities with the painters of Ann's generation or a little older, Roger Hilton especially. I doubt that Hilton is an influence exactly. It seems that Ann took to his late gouaches after his death in 1975. But there is shared sensibility: zest, humour, movement – no other ceramicist, not even Picasso, is more kinetic. Above all, Roger Hilton and Ann Stokes share a belief in Blake's innocent eye. If you wish to see, and make things new, you must employ adult technique and guile to recover an unedited childhood perception.

I have for over twenty years now lived mainly among Ann Stokeses and Roger Hiltons. I bought my first Hilton as an undergraduate; my wife bought her first Stokes in the mid 1980s. The pianist Alfred Brendel has written about humour in music. Also a Hilton admirer, he is a connoisseur of humour in pictorial, mainly Eastern European art. Stokes and Hilton are not comic artists, but they do share a strong sense of the place of comedy in art. Their paintings, on canvas or on clay, are not jokes, which you get and then move on from. But they do provide a kind of governing happiness, a fortress of sensuous pleasure from which you sally forth to face the world. They both love birds and animals: Stokes for what they look like and for what they are, Hilton for their connection with the animal life of men and women.

In our sitting room, high above a large farmhouse fireplace, there stands a range of plates that glow like late Monets; nearby, a mirror; beside it, two jugs and three boxes. In the kitchen, more plates on a dresser; a huge dish in the form of a spatchcocked turkey; a little soup tureen in the shape of a turbot; many soup plates, some of them chipped. Presiding household gods are a face of an owl (his outstretched wings got broken) and a bas-relief of a Homeric battleship, oars apparently trembling in a rough cobalt sea. In the study, a letter-rack of galloping horses; in the bedroom, one of Ann's Moroccan and very Matisse-like night-lights, always left on at night. It was a proud day, twenty years ago, when the late David Sylvester told us that our round, blue and white small ceramic side table was Ann's masterpiece. I am not sure that it is, but was in no mood to cavil.

Richard Morphet is absorbingly informative about Ann's career and connections. His essay is as clear about her place in modern British art as Tanya Harrod is about Ann's relation to ceramics in our time. Hilary Spurling's prose poem is, I feel, coloured, literally, by years of living among Stokeses. I know that the late Derek Hill, who so admired her, would be pleased that his foundation is helping to bring her work to a wider audience than friends and fans. Like Prunella Clough, another original, Ann Stokes for many years effectively subsidised her admirers by selling her work direct and without promotion. Those who pick up this book will see how lucky we were.

Introduction

Tanya Harrod

This is a remarkable book about a remarkable artist, whose work is not easy to categorise. She defies standards set by the institutionalised avant-garde within the worlds of both fine art and studio ceramics. For that reason, writing about Ann Stokes has proved challenging and rewarding. As her chroniclers we have had to set aside taxonomic preconceptions and confront a creativity that has flourished with informal power. This has resulted in three very different essays.

Hilary Spurling provides what amounts to a phenomenological response to the work of Ann Stokes, with descriptive writing of empathetic perception. Some passages are so powerfully evocative that they seem to outface the photographic images in the book. She combines this with a wry, sympathetic assessment of the influences on a career that was to reach fruition as the artist approached her sixties and which, in her eighty-seventh year, shows no signs of diminution.

Richard Morphet peoples his deeply researched essay with an array of artists, art historians, psychoanalysts and intellectuals who form Ann Stokes' world. They are like rocks around which the stream of her creativity flows. Never seeking to challenge their high achievements or taste, Stokes just got on with the business of making. They in turn appreciated her work – keeping it, however, for themselves, as a private passion. The art world, to which Morphet himself belongs, found it difficult to situate her work and, until recently, it seemed destined for a literal interiority – loved, yet housebound.

Meanwhile, the world of contemporary studio ceramics found her pottery transgressive, being earthenware instead of stoneware, taking on representation as opposed to pure form, mixing media, embracing variousness, and apparently careless of all the hard-won conventions of the twentieth-century studio pottery movement. As a ceramics 'outsider', she is in good company. Status in ceramics is hotly contested, but Stokes has created her own territory, made up her own rules.

The late twentieth century and neophyte twenty-first century have proved liberating for the work of Ann Stokes. She now shows with a dealer and there are new theoretical tools with which to analyse and position her work. The extraordinary nature of her story is just beginning to emerge.

Notes on Technique and Captions

Plates, cups and saucers (flatware and hollow-ware) are usually marked with Stokes' *sigma*, the month (though this is sometimes omitted) and the year, scratched into the leather-hard clay. Modelled pieces and mirrors are often not marked or dated. The captions include these marks where given, and provide the date (when known) of unmarked works.

All work is earthenware, with both biscuit and glazed wares being fired to 1,080°C, often in the same kiln.

Ann Stokes only occasionally gives titles to her works; in most instances they are descriptions only.

The dimensions given in the captions are as follows, unless otherwise indicated: pots (height), sculptural pieces (height by width, or height by width by depth), plates (diameter), cups (height by diameter), paintings, mirrors and tile reliefs (height by width).

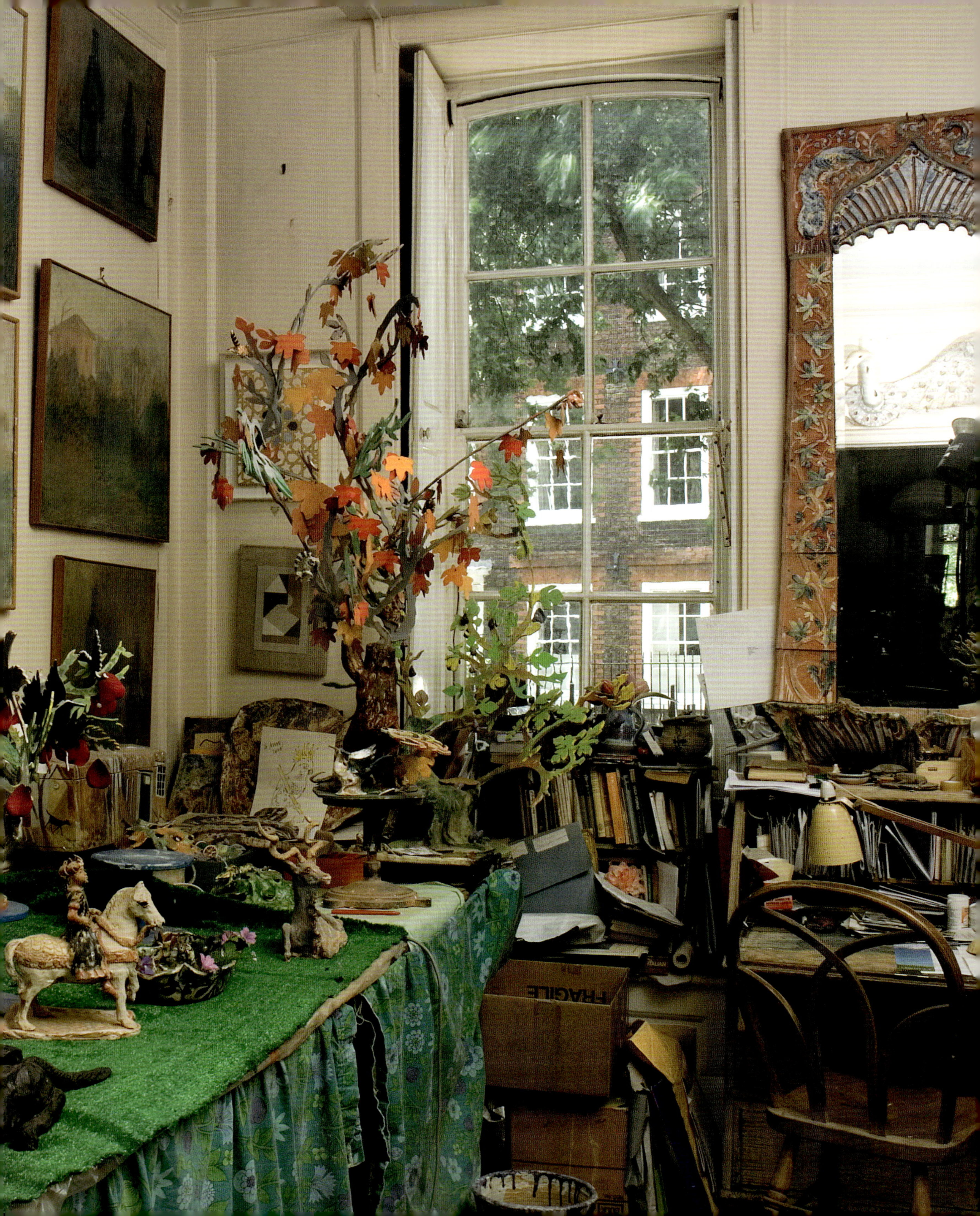

ONE

Potter as Painter and Sculptor

Hilary Spurling

1 *The Church Row end of Ann Stokes' studio, June 2008: paintings by Adrian Stokes hang on the left wall*
Photo: Stephen Brayne

Of all the artists whose careers I watched take shape in London in the 1970s, Ann Stokes is probably the strangest. For one thing she belonged to an earlier generation than the painters and sculptors who were my own contemporaries, nearly all of them galvanised initially by American Abstract Expressionism, subsequently branching out into Op art, Pop art and their multiple derivatives, when what felt like a mass jail-break in the 1960s finally put paid to decades of British insularity, nostalgia and restriction in the arts.[1] Stokes' trajectory was different. For a long time it hardly looked like a career at all. She had no gallery, no dealer, no reviews and no public exhibitions. She showed her work once a year in her Hampstead basement kitchen. I came across it by chance when a friend commissioned a set of mug, jug, egg cup and pudding bowl for each of my first two children, born in 1972 and 1974. Looking back now at those fat-bellied child-sized pots decorated in sober, semi-abstract, almost monochrome designs, the gilt lettering scraped and faded, the piecrust rims cracked and glued back together after much use, there is nothing – apart from a single minute blotchy sky-blue frog with gilded spine and fingers clambering up a cup-side – to suggest the explosion of imaginative energy that followed.

The first I knew of it was a blue-green fish dish given to us by the same friend, an exuberant rococo invention ridged like a shell with wavy edges and stubby fan-shaped tail, the whole opened out flat so as to represent both a gutted bream or mullet and the plate that holds it. The dish itself is a ceramic pun in the form of a fish dinner, its baleful eye and mouth-slit incised at one end, its undulating sides conveying the muscular thrust of fin and bone slicing through water, its puckered bottom and streaky turquoise surface mimicking the sea it swam in. That fish dish was the first of many *(fig.2)*. Relatively static to start with, predominantly blue, scalloped or spotted with mottled scales, they rest firmly on flat-bottomed keels or, in the case of lidded fish tureens, on chocks of fluke and flipper.

Stokes' zoomorphic experiments – fish, frogs, pigs, crocodiles, birds above all in the form of bowls, lamps, fruit-stands, cooking pots, wall-tiles, mirrors, chandeliers – became on their own terms as inventive as the imperial grand services created in porcelain by eighteenth-century ceramicists, or the exquisitely observed and executed Napoleonic bronze or silver table-pieces of animals slaughtering their prey by Antoine Louis Barye. But Stokes' work is at least in origin essentially domestic. She belongs as firmly to the unpainted pinewood dressers, scrubbed worktops and sturdy kitchen tables of a particular intellectual subsection of twentieth-century urban living, as

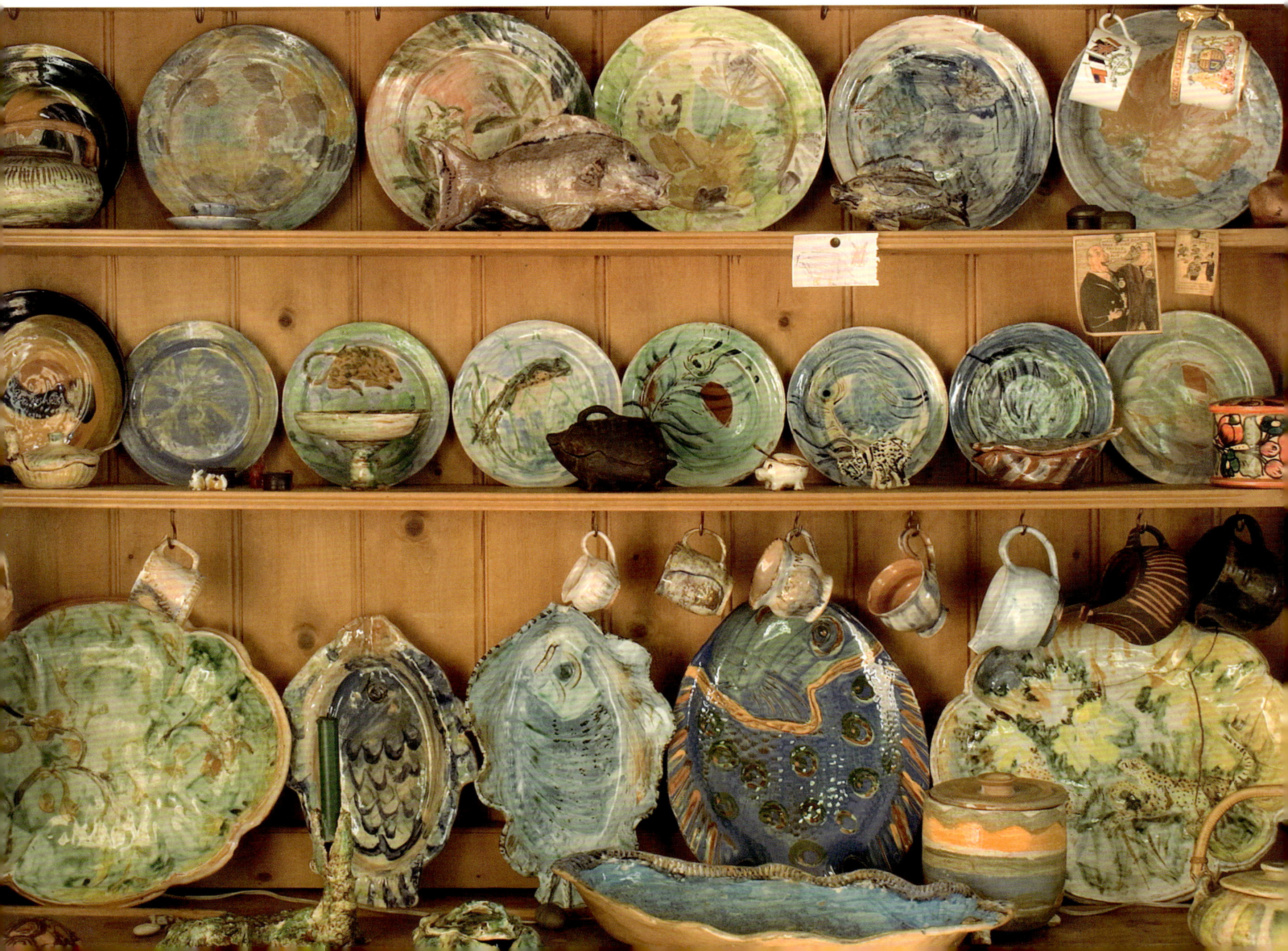

2 *A dresser with fish dishes and tureen, 1970s and 1980s*
Collection: Hilary and John Spurling
Photo: Stephen Brayne

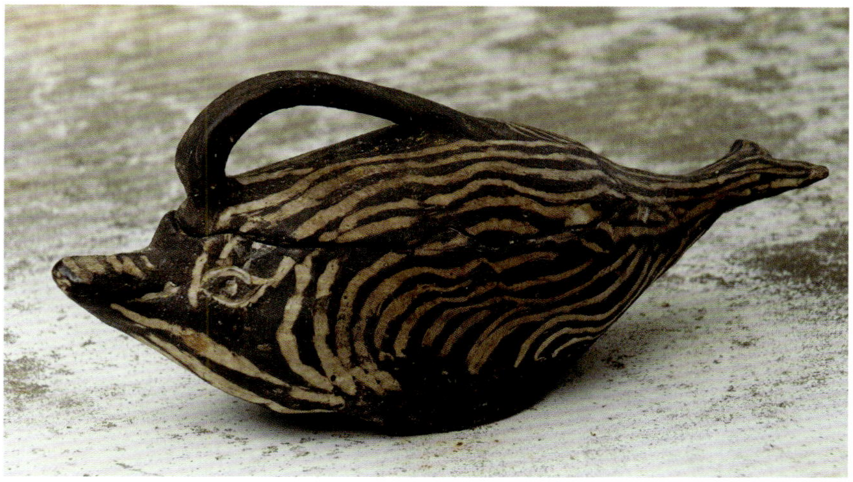

3 Lidded salt pot in the form of a porpoise, marked Σ 11/73
39 x 12 cm (15.4 x 4.8 in)
Collection: John Craxton
Photo: Stephen Brayne

eighteenth- and nineteenth-century French *animaliers* to the dining conventions of their own time and place. In spite of her instructions to the contrary, Stokes' collectors are generally reluctant to let their purchases lead the humble, expendable working life of earthenware with chipped edges, cracked spouts and missing handles leading almost inevitably to breakage in the long run. Her own position is uncompromising. What matters is to exploit and explore to their limits the properties of clay, its fragility and transience as much as its fluidity and extreme versatility.

For Stokes the function of any given object is, in the expressive phrase of Stephenie Bergman, 'a path to invention'.[2] A lid in the form of a whole flounder lies lightly on a small shallow butter dish, like a hollowed-out flat stone. More often the lids of her fish pots project as curving fluted or zigzag fins. One is the hoop-handled hump, balanced at either end by flange-shaped snout and tail, of a small porpoise salt pot *(fig.3)*. Decorative stripes are streamlines indicating the flow of water against a sleek compact hull. A cruising predator with a mouthful of uneven teeth appears to glide by virtue of the wavery purplish reflections on its scaly flanks, and its bulbous black eyes magnified as if seen close up through water.

Form contains movement in her work. Colour is intrinsic. 'I pot in order to paint,' is the formula by which she differentiates her output from the studio potters who are her contemporaries. When Stokes started potting, and for years afterwards, she stuck to a palette weighted towards blue and the soft earth colours of clay itself: buff, cream, grey, sludge-green, warm shades of tan and bistre. Over the last three decades her handling of both colour and form has increasingly ignored accepted boundaries. Richer blues, emphatic yellows, amber, purple and plum-pink infiltrated and

4 Hoopoe light, 1990, Pergo, Italy
The artist's collection
Photo: John Ross

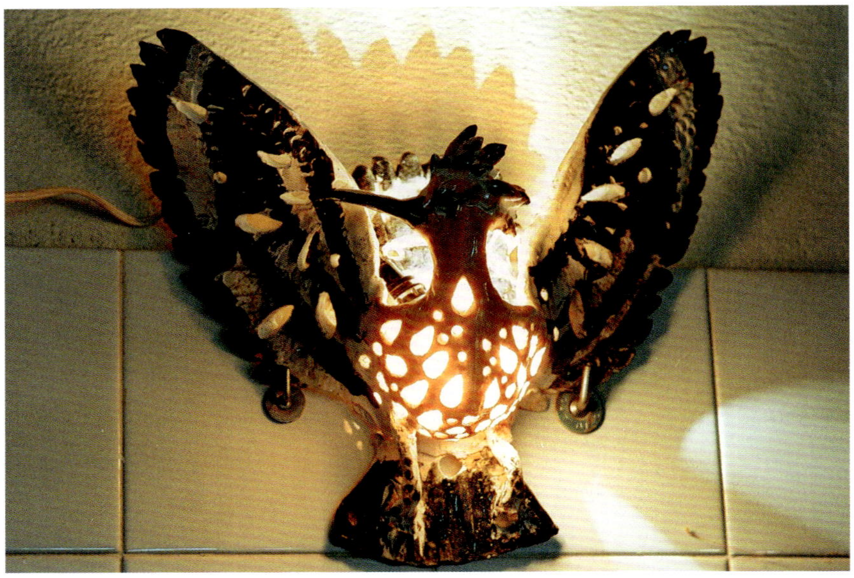

overthrew conventional potting disciplines of understatement and restraint. She infused kinetic energy into her birds and fish in ways that defy the earthiness of clay. The perforated lamp-bowl of a dramatic hoopoe wall light outlines the bird's serrated crest, blade-like beak and dark striated wings within the penumbra cast by its illuminated breast *(fig.4)*. Holes pierced in the wings of a swan, itself reduced to minimal abstract notation (a tubular head-and-throat surmounting the wingspan's inverted 'W'), somehow convey both the flimsiness of the hollow wing structure, and the rush of air streaming past in flight *(figs 5–6)*. The long series of fish platters culminated in a majestic, high-glazed, canary-coloured banqueting dish, one of several made in 2001, each nearly three-quarters of a metre long and half a metre wide. The dish takes the shape of a plaice, intact, indeed vibrantly alive, slightly concave rather than convex, as if resting momentarily in a depression on – or perhaps, given the faint dips and runnels in its gleaming yellow surface, just under – the sand of the sea floor. Like many of Stokes' recent pieces, it is a poised and confident twenty-first-century variant of an archaic fusion between the creature represented and the clay vessel it inhabits.

This kind of transmutation grew from homely beginnings still apparent in Stokes' annual exhibitions when I first started going to them round about 1974. A saucepan-lid holder made of painted plywood horses hung beside the kitchen stove *(fig.8)*. There was a small kiln next to the sink, crockery stacked high all along the dresser, and on the table always a selection of crested nesting birds, each the size and shape of a cupped palm, which turned out to be lidded bowls with cocked heads and fan-tailed spoons. You

5 Swan, 1973, Ann Stokes' first swan, c.1978–9, bought by Chris Dromedous for Melanie's Banqueting Suite, Hendon Way, London (now destroyed)
Photographer unknown

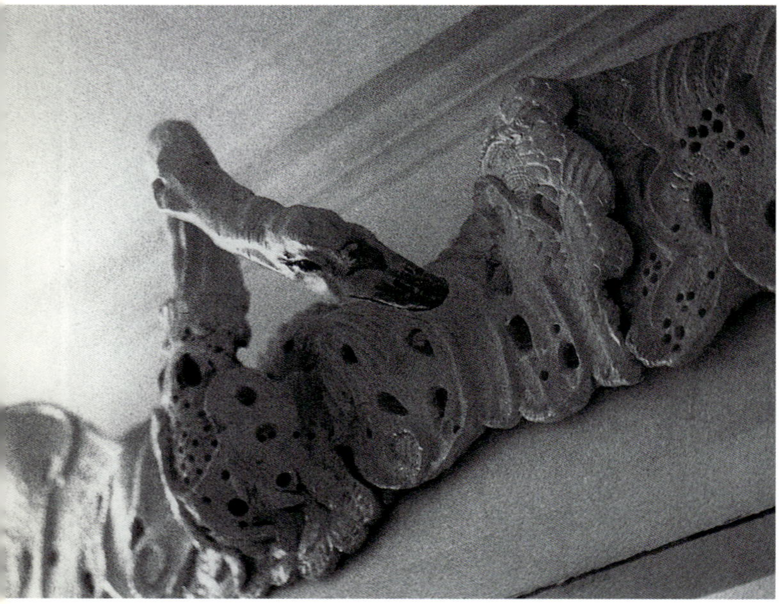

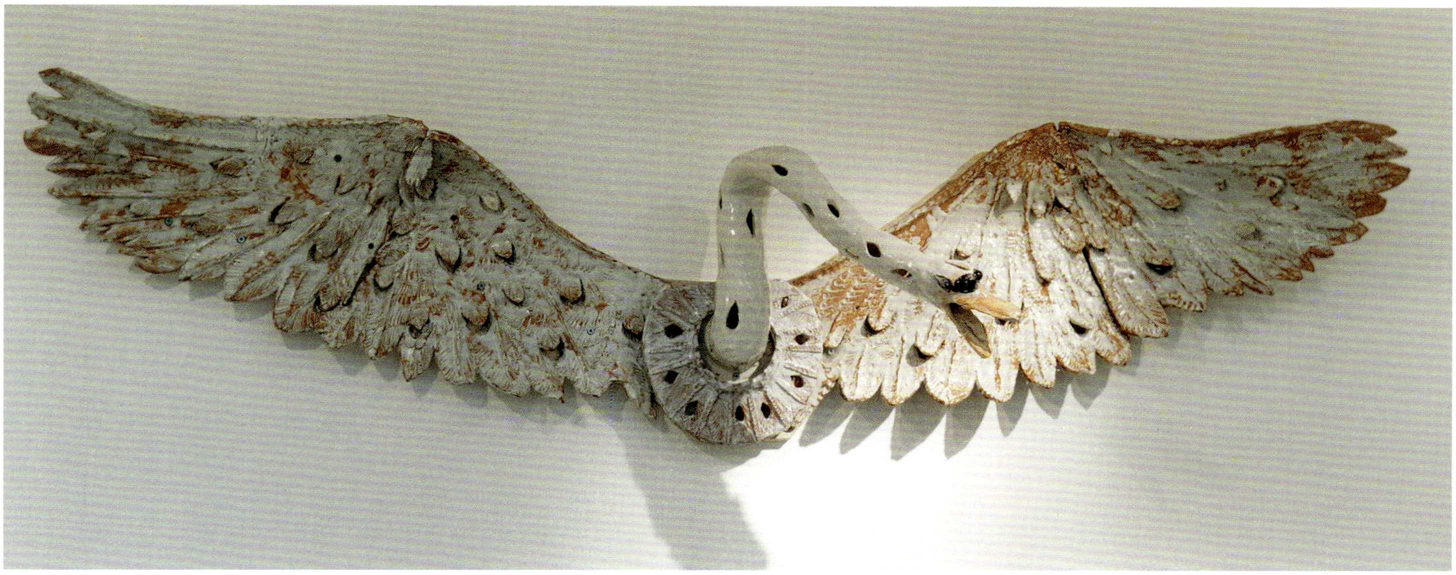

6 Swan, 1995, modelled and assembled (wingspan) 200 cm
The artist's collection
Photo: Rebecca Hossack Gallery

7 Ann Stokes hanging from a tree, Church Row, 1973, one of a series of photographs of his friends commissioned by Jim Dine
The artist's collection
Photo: Godfrey Argent

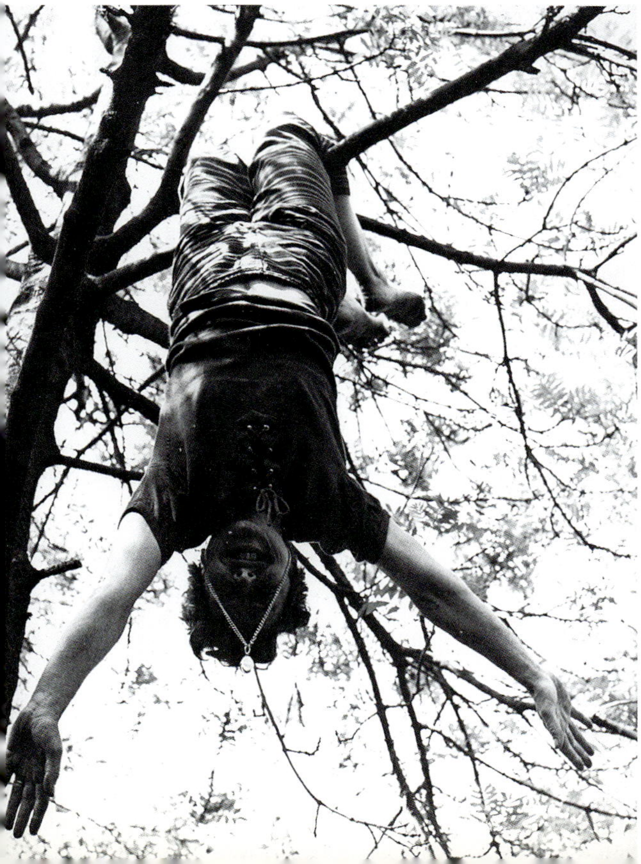

found containers everywhere – under the shell of a tortoise, inside a parturient brown sow, beneath the small male partner clamped on top of a corpulent, copulating female frog. The people crammed into that small basement kitchen in those early years gave off an unmistakable low humorous hum, something I'd only ever heard before at the Tate's Picasso retrospective in 1960, when for the first time the British public stopped feeling collectively aggrieved and started to recognise Picasso as Modernism's prime joker.

It was obvious, the second or third time I went, that a marked change was taking place, signalled by sharper greens, flashes of chrome yellow, a palpable sense of imaginative stretching and expansion. A photograph taken in 1973 shows Stokes swinging upside down from the poplar tree in her back garden, silhouetted twenty feet up against the sky with legs hooked over a slender branch and arms outflung *(fig. 7)*. It is an image of liberation paralleled by an accelerating momentum in her work. The same year, or the year after, she made a rhinoceros, one of several, all solidly planted on stocky legs, all with an air of comical self-deprecation – the overlapping armoured plates protecting the bull-like hump and barrel-shaped upper body are detachable, coming away to form the domed lid of a soup tureen *(fig. 9)*. The original was commissioned as a present for the art historian Ernst Gombrich, whose qualities the beast embodies. But at some point an element of self-portraiture seems to have invaded this particular low-slung ruddy-brown rhino with its unexpectedly tentative, enquiring horn, small observant eyes and delicate leaf-like ears. For all its mild absurdity there is deliberation in the lowered head, strength and purpose in the long supple

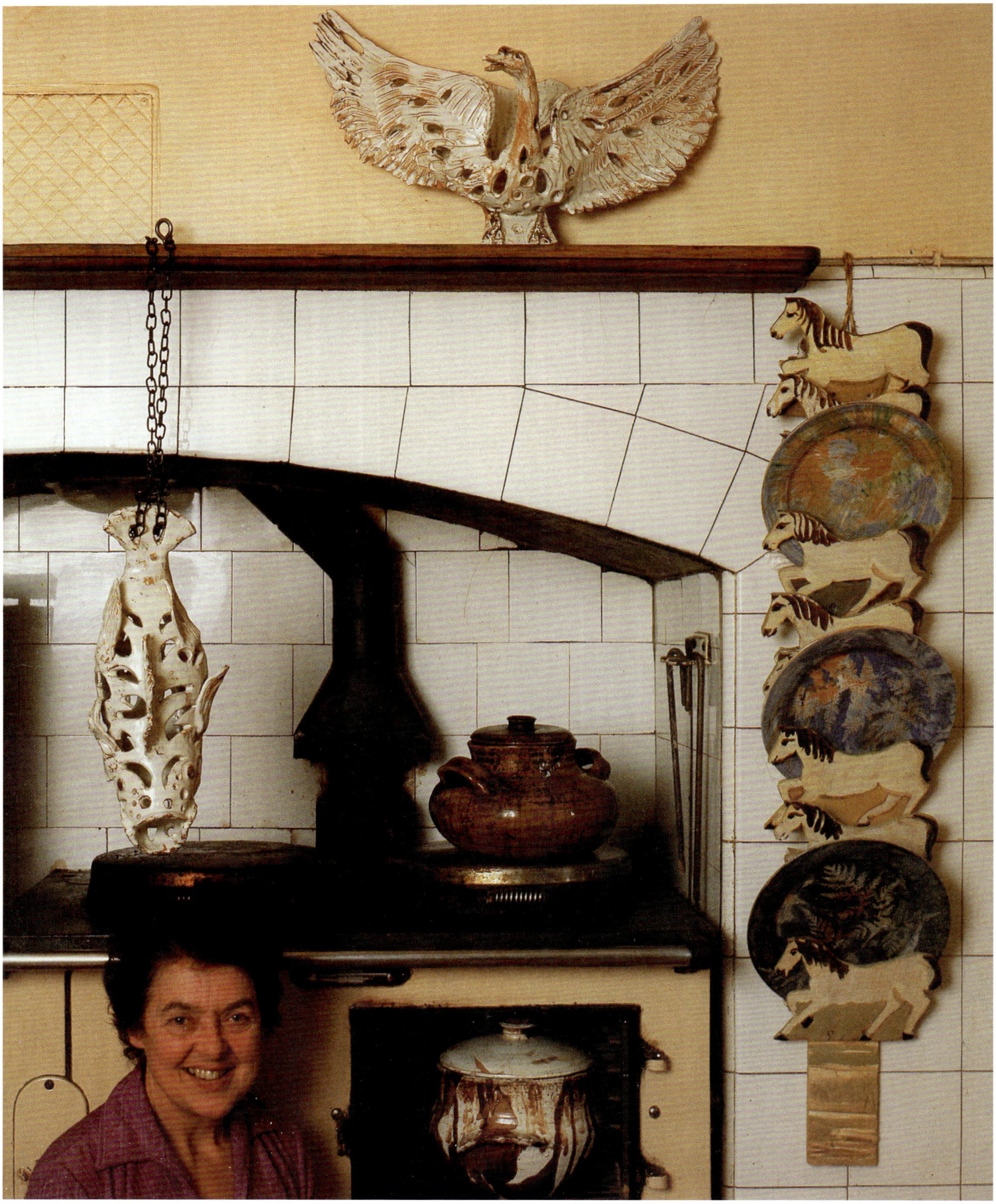

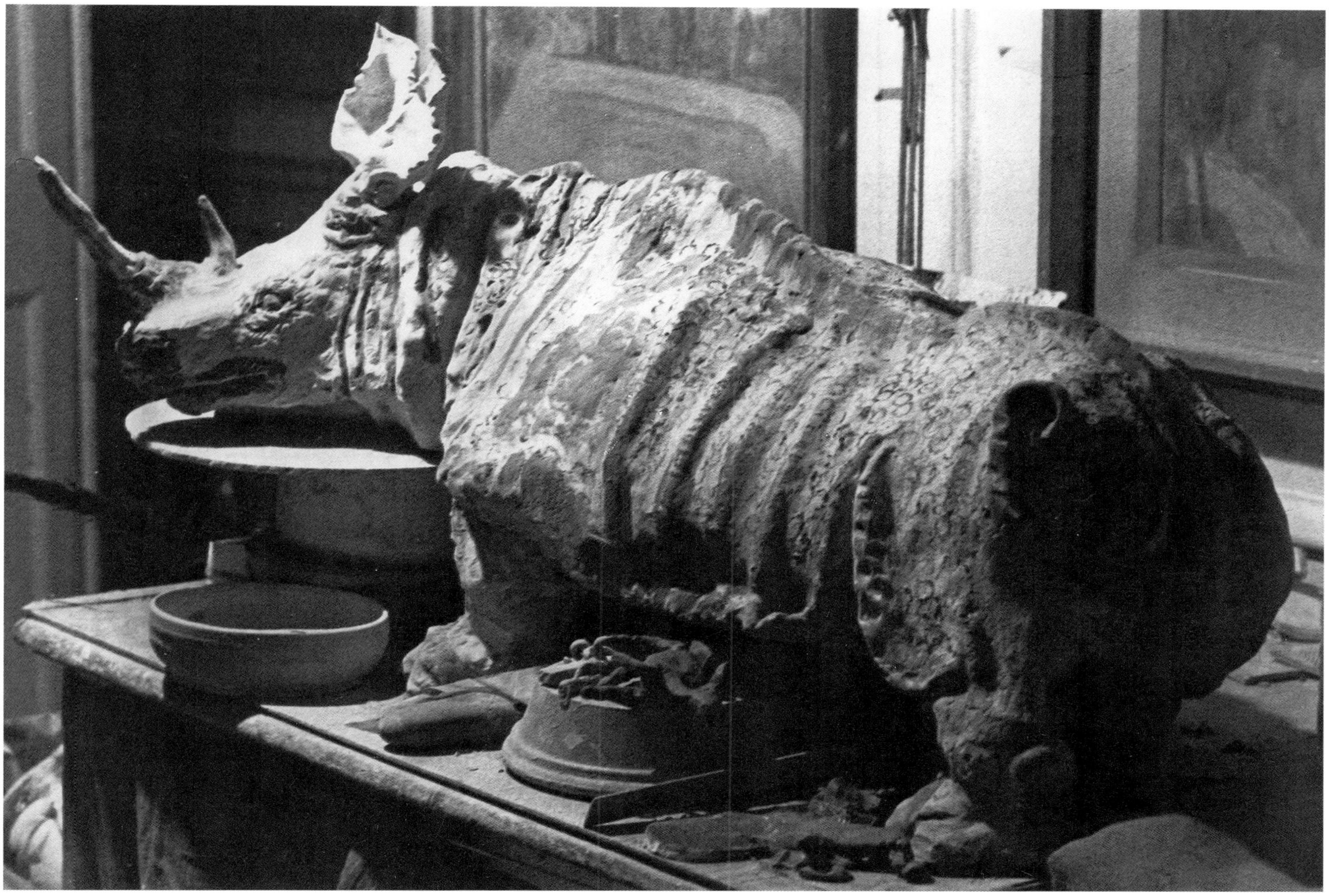

9 *Rhinoceros being modelled in Ann Stokes' studio, c.1974*
The artist's collection
Photo: Ann Stokes

8 *The artist in her kitchen at Church Row, 1985: a swan, a fish, casserole dishes and a plate and saucepan-lid holder constructed from fret-sawed plywood by Ann Stokes*
Photo: Ben Rice

curving spine braced as if preparing for a charge.

Sharply increased production rates over the next three decades and more were matched by heightened creativity. Stokes improvised tools, equipment and techniques, ignoring standard procedures and testing basic rules to breaking point. For all the wit, economy and precision of her sculpted animals, the core of her work was, and remains, the painted plates that poured out of her studio in a steady flow of variety, brilliance and profusion. New colours, experiments with temperature, accidents in firing put even the plates at risk. 'You had to keep guessing, you had to try it out,' said Stokes, describing the constant tension of working without preconceptions. '*That* keeps you interested.'[3] Her spontaneity in these years had more in common with the openness and lack of inhibition of contemporary painters half her age than with the studio output of other potters. Up until the early or mid 1970s Stokes' pots were still recognisably related to a rigorous Modernism that attaches prime importance to clarity of shape emphasised by rhythmic

10 *Side plate, marked Σ 8/81*
19 cm (7.5 in)
Collection: John Golding
Photo: Stephen Brayne

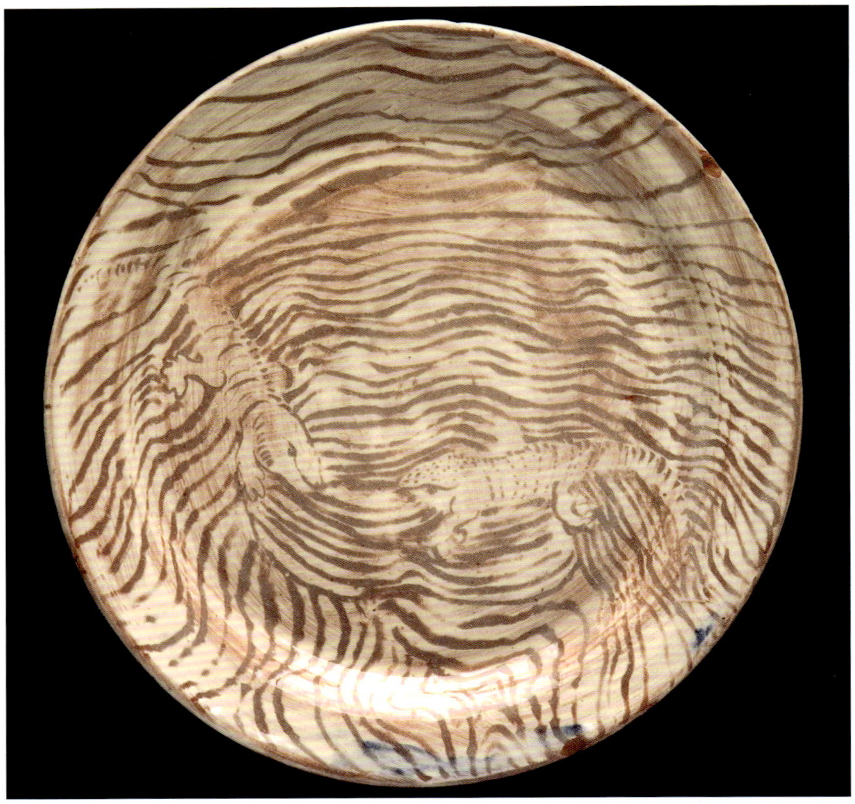

lines in muted colours, but their elegant plainness remained comparatively anonymous. The difference is immediately apparent in a beautiful austere group of plates she made in 1981, recording small aquatic disturbances, the passage of newt or frog through water deducible only from bands of concentric or concurrent lines incised freehand in white slip glaze over pinkish clay *(fig.10)*. The means could hardly be simpler, or the end result more unmistakably imprinted with Stokes' distinctive signature.

Pieces like these mirror the preoccupations of Op artists (Bridget Riley, for instance, in linear black and white acrylic studies of the early 1960s), who also looked closely at ripples, waves, and the impact of sun or rain on water. Stokes' frame of reference is eclectic. Echoes of the ancient world – especially Etruscan, Cretan, Greek – sit alongside bang-up-to-date allusions. She says she took the central yellow and brown checkerboard terrace in *Odysseus Finds His Father* – an early clay panel illustrating a scene from Homer, complete with authentic architectural detail and furnishings *(fig. 11)* – from a tiled floor at Delos, 'as an excuse to do the pop-art pavement that jumps in your eye'.[4] That checked pavement was a relatively crude pointer to more complicated games she went on to play later with colour, light and space on plates. In theory, limitations of scale, shape and texture should have been

11 Odysseus Finds His Father,
unmarked, 1970
Tile relief
39 x 41.5 cm (15.4 x 16.3 in)
The artist's collection
Photo: Stephen Brayne

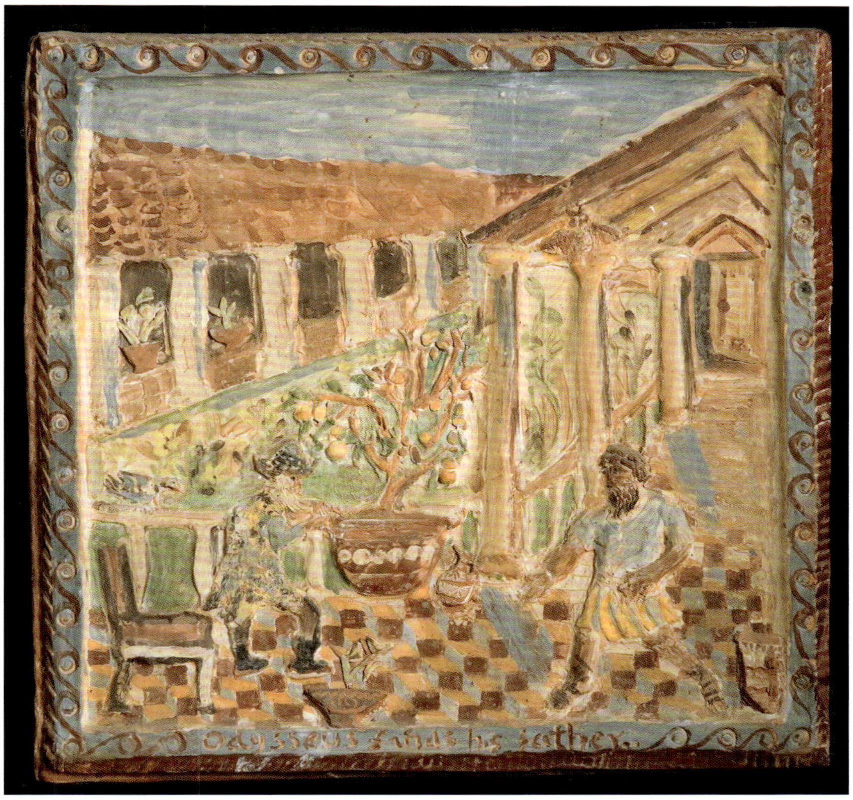

insurmountable. In practice, the restricted format generated ideas, nearly always sparked off by natural phenomena almost wholly inaccessible to the abstract painters working on canvas in the 1970s and 80s, whose aesthetic sensibility in many ways Stokes shared. 'Painting is what I pot *for*,' she has said,[5] explaining that for her the plate itself was indissoluble from its painted surface.

Leaves, flowers, increasingly exotic fish, birds and animals heighten and intensify flat expanses of pure or orchestrated colour in her work. One year there was an elaborate cycle of dinner plates focused around emphatic big white daisy-heads *(fig.56)*. Another time it was a set of shallow peacock-feather-patterned bowls and side dishes in luxuriant Pre-Raphaelite blue-greens *(fig.55)*, pale lime or lemon yellow. The concentration and the naturalist's exactitude required to abstract movement and transpose it to ceramic surfaces serves (like the function of a pot) to stimulate invention. Plant-stems, strands of weed, drifting filaments of feather repeat, disrupt, fit into or arc out from the curves of edge or rim. Irregularities in the smoothness of the glaze sharpen the overall decorative effect like a jarring note in music. The glaze itself accentuates shifts and glints of light on the flat shiny surface of a watery plate bisected by a leaping frog, a narrow curved

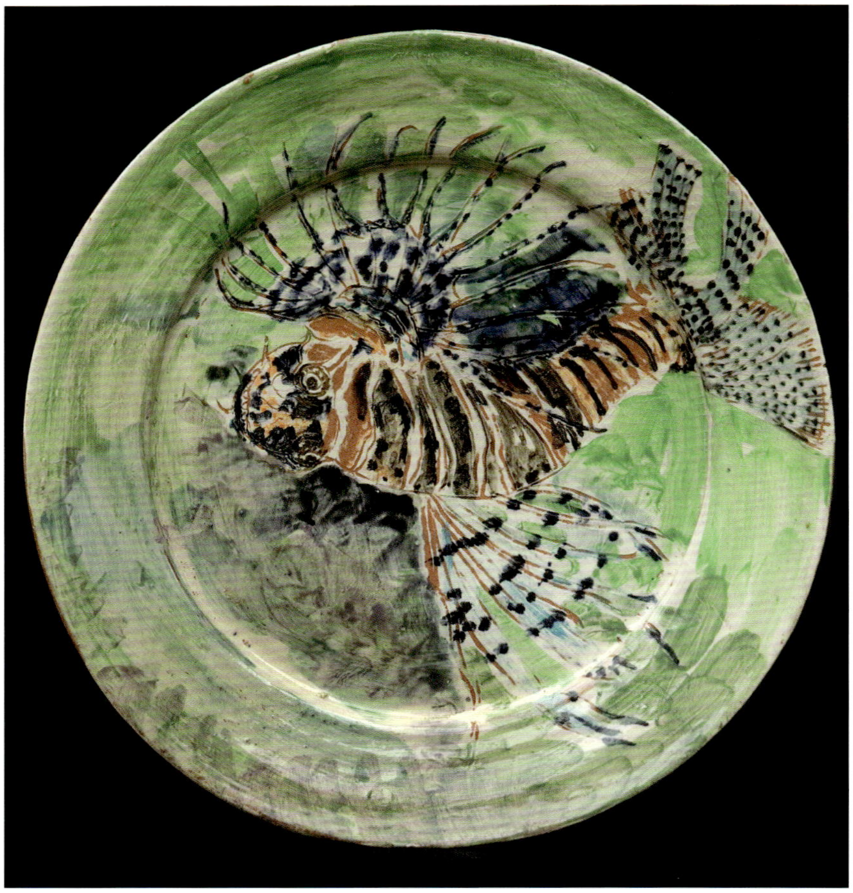

12 Plate with scorpion fish, marked Σ10/95
26 cm (10.2 in)
Collection: John and Hilary Spurling
Photo: Stephen Brayne

projectile launched across straight slanting green lines of reed against a central patch of cloudy pink.

A long-running series of storm plates maximises every surface dent, scratch and scuff in swirling currents of wind or water with their debris of tattered plumage, skeletal leaves, sprays of slime or spume. It is not always easy to make out pinions and tail feathers scudding across a plate that contains within its animated compass the faint outline of a goose taking off, or a herring gull landing in a high wind against banks of blue-flared, wind-shredded, rust-coloured cloud. Some come close to the ambiguity of abstraction. Others exploit a single extravagant motif, a scorpion fish trailing inky-blue and ochre veils and tail fans across a grass-green ground *(fig.12)*, or the dark lashing backbone of a balletic sturgeon tightly confined within the rim of a turbulent sea plate. Leaves are a recurrent theme, traced onto the clay or pressed into the slip before firing – floating pink silhouettes of sycamore or papery white ghosts of ivy, each with its characteristic script (ragged, feathery, spiny, denticulate or spatular), subsumed within the identity of the plate.

When Stokes became the first potter ever to be shown at London's Hayward Gallery, in a Hayward Annual exhibition in 1985 chosen by Nigel Greenwood, her plates bewildered both the contemporary art world and the pottery establishment. Few people on either side had ever heard of her before. Each put her firmly in the other camp. 'It gave potters a shock,' wrote Tanya Harrod at the time.[6] Plates no more uniform in size than in decoration stack lumpily, and are in any case too thick to nest smoothly one inside another. An earthenware art that embraces surface blemishes made no sense to formalists who saw 'accident' as the province of stoneware. Stokes' unorthodoxy produced in potters the same sort of dismay as the output of artists like Matisse and Picasso in the opening years of the last century, when highly trained, technically skilled and disciplined fellow painters found themselves obliged, in spite of outrage and revulsion, to admit that this new stuff, crude, garish and childishly incoherent as it demonstrably was, nonetheless made their own work look lifeless and insipid. Raw energy always comes at the expense of polish and refinement. Stokes' formal training was late and patchy. 'He's quite perfect,' she said of a fellow potter generally accepted as a master of the art of throwing. 'And it just shows that you do not want perfection. It's not interesting.'[7]

'In her pottery she is both painter and sculptor,' wrote John Golding, himself a painter as well as an outstanding teacher who trained a whole generation of Modernist art historians at London's Courtauld Institute in the 1960s and 70s. 'She is a purely instinctive artist. She pots as others might sing or hum to themselves, or as we all – quite simply – breathe.'[8] Bloomsbury's house critic Clive Bell used almost identical words to describe Matisse's method in the 1930s.[9] Golding knew and worked with Stokes almost from her beginnings as a potter. His choice of words suggests the emotional and intuitive assent coupled with intellectual reservations that her work has commonly provoked from the art world, an ambivalence at least in part explained by the unusual pattern of a career that did not reach fruition until the late 1970s, by which time Stokes was already approaching sixty.

At this point her natural affinity lay not so much with the painters in her own circle, mostly identified when young with the Euston Road School, as with a succeeding generation which rejected the relatively narrow and inward-looking Euston-roaders for broader transatlantic allegiances. The contemporaries shown alongside Stokes at the Hayward mixed show (*A Journey Through Contemporary Art with Nigel Greenwood*), headed by Henry Moore and Francis Bacon, included Bridget Riley, Richard Long and Tony Cragg. But, unlike the younger artists whose careers ran parallel with her

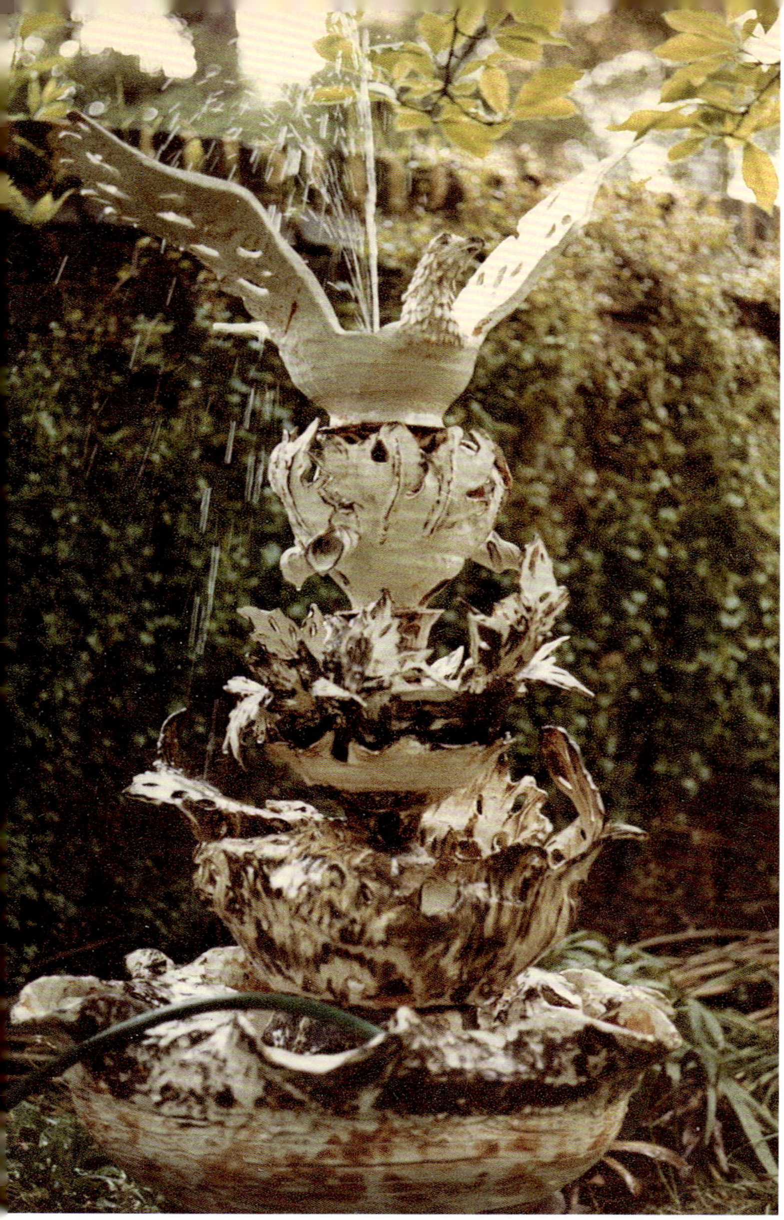

13 *Large fountain shown at the Chelsea Flower Show, c.1978*
Thrown and modelled (note hosepipe hydrology)
Photo: Philip Stokes

own, Stokes had been directly exposed at a formative stage to Modernism in its purest and most potent form. She was a seventeen-year-old school-leaver with an impressive athletic record (she would go on to train as a ballet dancer) when she joined the movement's British wartime headquarters at St Ives in 1940. Its leaders were Ben Nicholson, Barbara Hepworth and Naum Gabo who, with various acolytes and followers, would maintain its forward momentum against all odds over the next few years. They had set up their base at the start of the Second World War in a house belonging to the movement's leading theorist and spokesman Adrian Stokes, newly married to Ann's elder sister, the painter Margaret Mellis. Rarely can so many powerful egos have been shut up together at close quarters with virtually all outlet to the outside world cut off by the threat of imminent invasion. The artists competed in hotly disputed games of tennis, croquet and poker, relieving aesthetic tensions in serial disputes over the matchsticks they used as gambling counters, and the distribution of hens' eggs.

Ann Mellis, recruited to take charge of the Stokes' new baby, Telfer, was the only member of that combative community with no creative identity of her own to assert or defend. 'I was no competition of any sort', she said, 'but I was good at looking after their children.'[10] Nicholson and Hepworth had with them their six-year-old triplets, previously farmed out to other people pretty much since birth. The Stokes' son was taken care of throughout his first eight months by his aunt, who was well placed to observe at first hand the heavy pressures brought to bear on any woman attempting to pursue a purpose other than marriage and childrearing in the patriarchal world still universally accepted as the norm at that time in Britain. Hepworth and Mellis, born respectively in 1903 and 1914, were two of the very few female artists who refused to let their careers be cramped by gender in these years. Ann Mellis herself reverted to a more conventional role as wife and mother in 1947, when her brother-in-law divorced her sister to marry her instead. The marriage, eminently successful in personal terms, effectively blocked any serious professional life she might have led in her own right for a quarter of a century.

It was her husband's death in December 1972 that gave Stokes for the first time the opportunities she had given him – 'opportunities, in particular of solitude, of detachment, of suitable leisure'[11] – to concentrate on her own artistic development. She used them to produce work that on the face of it repudiated everything he stood for, in particular his trenchantly expressed contempt for the 'formless mud' of clay.[12] The principles underlying her pottery ('I love earthenware because of its colours')[13] could hardly be further from the doctrines so eloquently expounded by her husband in favour of an abstract art that distils maximum expression from minimal components, painting that aims always to reduce human experience 'to the scantiest visual terms',[14] sculpture that eschews the slackness and laxity of clay for the cold, hard, exacting and essentially colourless severity of stone.

But one of the engines that drive Adrian Stokes' writing is the friction between his doctrinaire controlling impulses and his overpowering response to the visual world. Ann Stokes' creative energy, finally released by his death, centred on a shared preoccupation – as essential to his writing as her potting – with movement, force and feeling. 'Living is ceaseless expression,' he wrote.[15] His books are full of crisp and lively descriptions of trees, birds and the *quattrocento* fish celebrated so abundantly in *Stones of Rimini*: 'Fish slither and wriggle ... The stone is alive with them.'[16] There is something of her exhilarating intensity of observation in virtuoso passages like his account of watching the fountains turned on in Kensington Gardens:

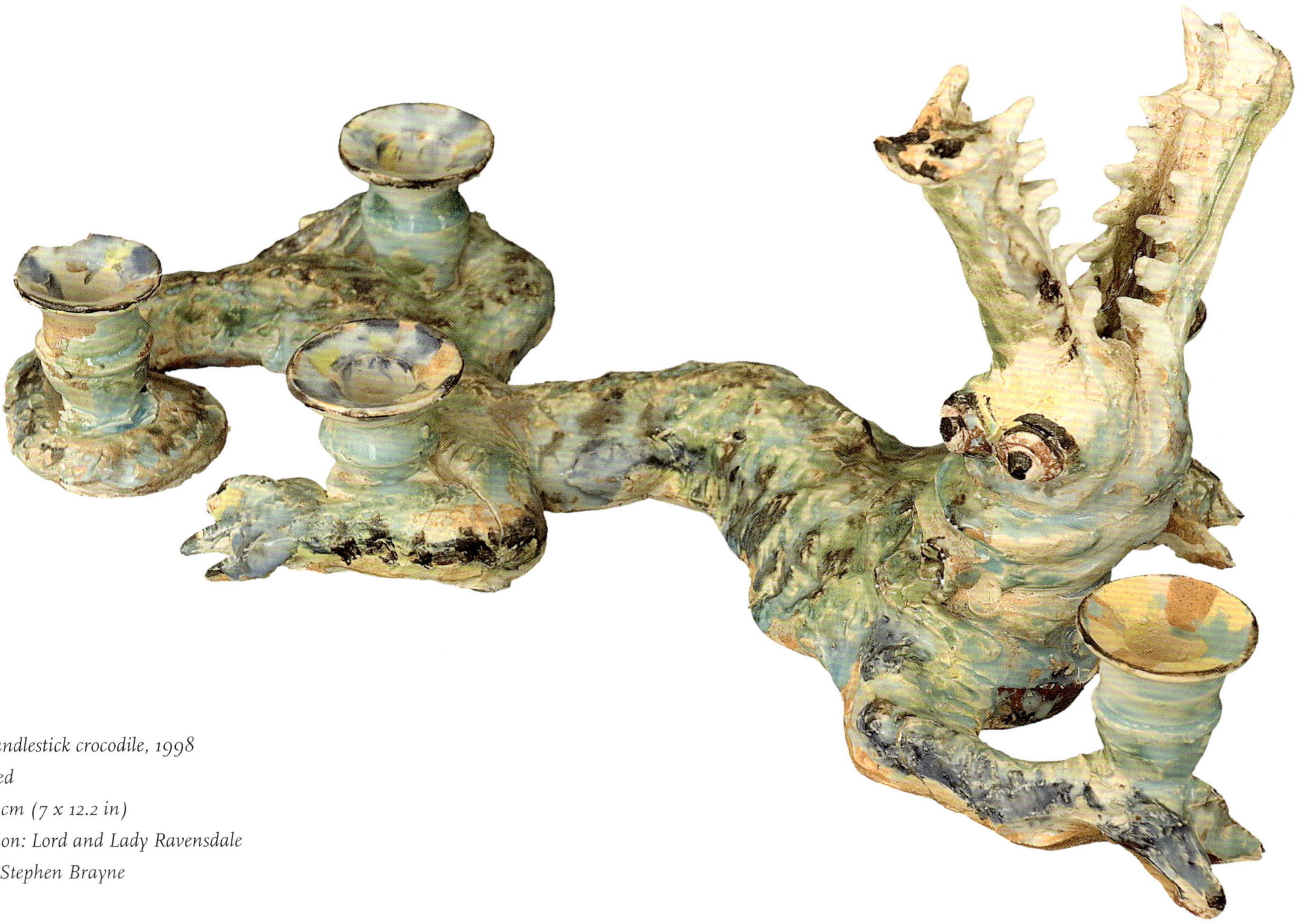

14 Candlestick crocodile, 1998
Modelled
18 x 31 cm (7 x 12.2 in)
Collection: Lord and Lady Ravensdale
Photo: Stephen Brayne

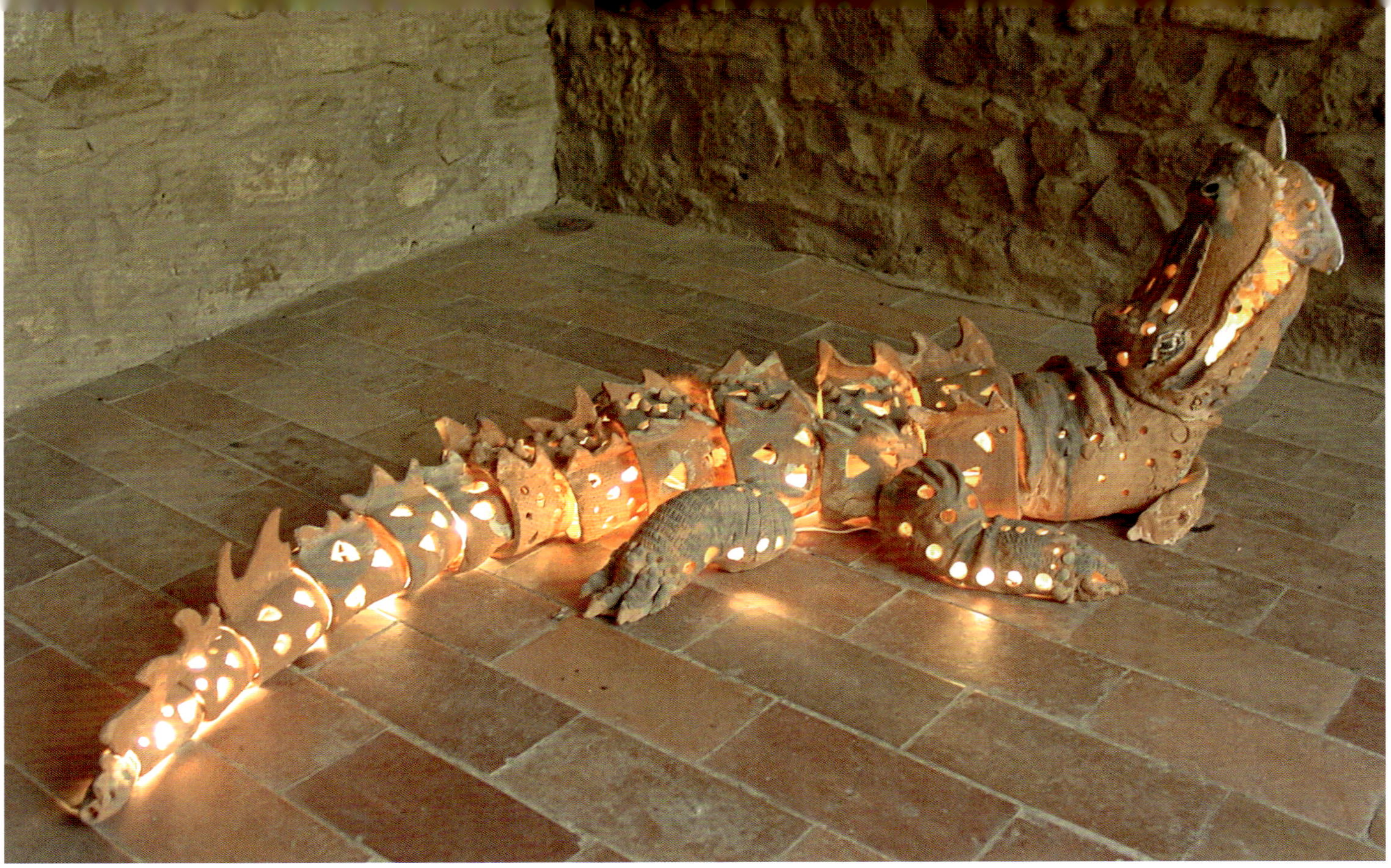

15 Crocodile shown at Castle Malatesta, Montefiore Conca, Rimini, 2002, at an exhibition to celebrate the publication in Italian of Adrian Stokes' Stones of Rimini
Internally illuminated by Philip Stokes. Photo: Philip Stokes

> ... the spouts grew from a trickle to an inch, to a foot, to a yard, finally reaching a great height, sustained there by an eager pumping pulse; at the summit, rainbow colours could be discerned; a thin elegant summit sometimes torn by the wind but formed again immediately. The wind might tear off the whole summit or bend the column like a tree, but the compensating power returned in the end.[17]

Perhaps Ann Stokes thought of these lines when she, too, turned her attention to the audacious, many-layered fountains whose water-spouts and sprays seem to echo the pottery plumes, foliage and lacework from which they are constructed *(fig. 13)*.

Increasingly her inventions set out not simply to extend but to transform or perhaps, more accurately speaking, to re-imagine the properties of clay. On the one hand she capitalises on its elemental, earthy nature in a procession of solidly ground-based crocodiles that started out as candlesticks *(fig. 14)* – vigorous, spiky little creatures designed to hold candles in their upturned open jaws – and ended up life-sized with massive snouts and stumpy, slime-crusted claws, their furrowed, ridged and pitted skin, monolithic bulk and minatory presence suggesting the kind of monster more familiar from primeval myth or cinematic special effects than in a potter's studio *(fig. 15)*. On the other hand, she activates air and water in

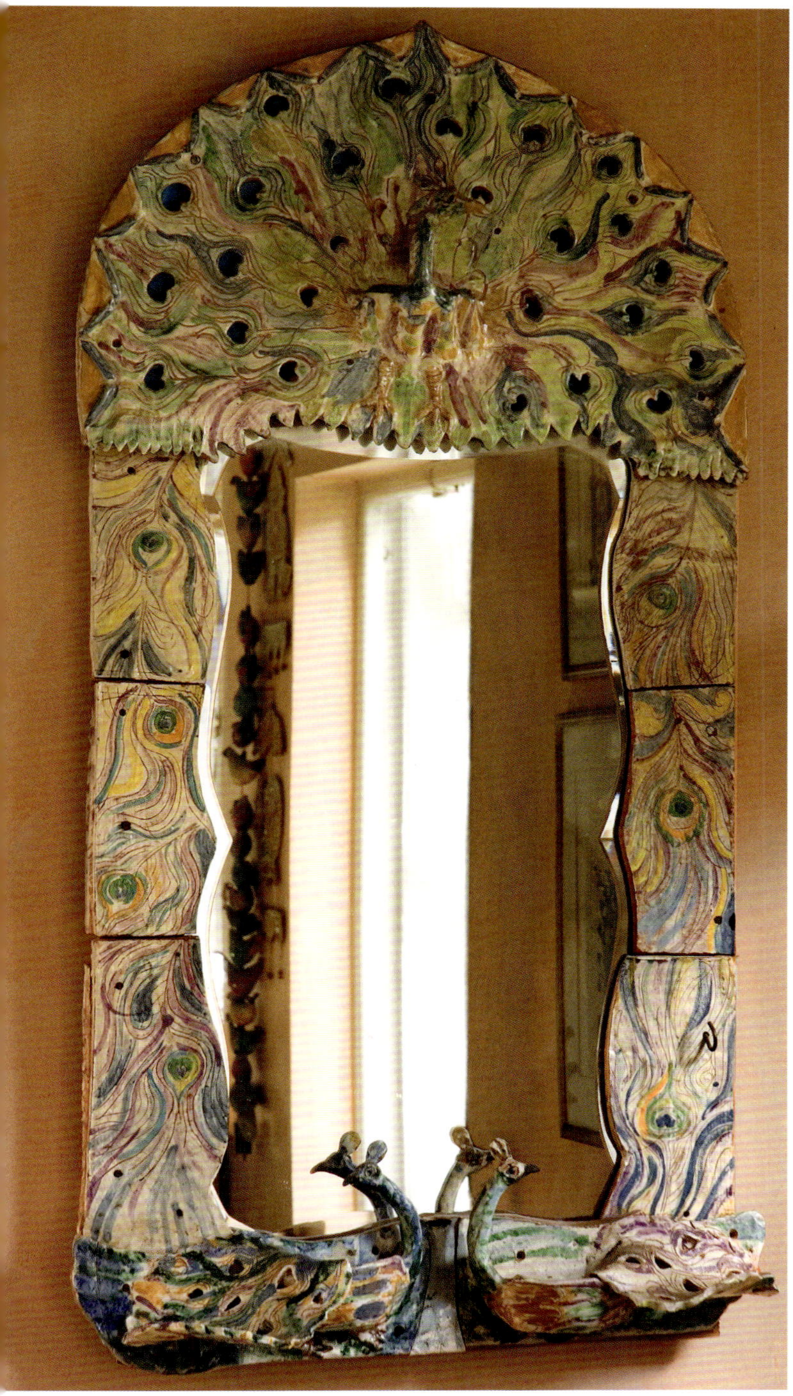

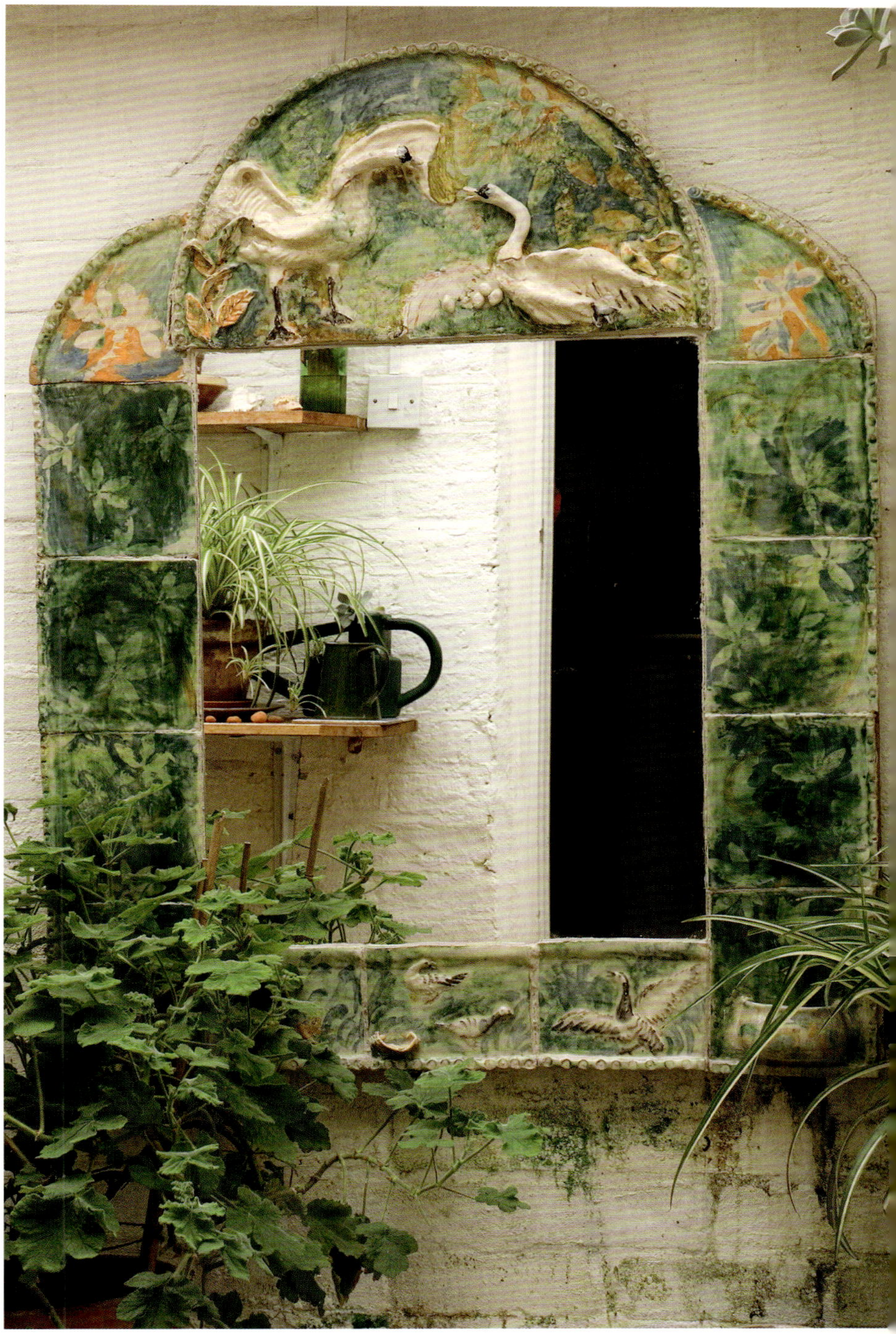

16 Peacock mirror, 1990
Tiles, modelled birds, mirror glass on board
106 x 58 cm (41.7 x 22.8 in)
Collection: Lord and Lady Ravensdale
Photo: Stephen Brayne

17 Mirror with swans, 1980s
Tiles, modelled birds, mirror glass on board
107 x 90 cm (42.1 x 35.4 in)
Collection: John and Hilary Spurling (former collection: Bryan Robertson)
Photo: Stephen Brayne

18 Lyre-shaped mirror with birds, 1992
Tiles, modelled birds, mirror glass on board
70 x 48 cm (27.6 x 18.9 in)
The artist's collection
Photo: Stephen Brayne

her fountains, and appropriates light and space in a remarkable series of eighty or so mirrors made over two or three decades. These range in scale from diminutive early try-outs, not much bigger than a sheet of writing paper, to tall, stately looking-glasses well over a metre high. Each has its live inhabitants – hoopoes, peacocks, bluebirds, swallows, swans, hens, even an unexpected crew of pugnacious goats – and its own distinctive character. Swans nest in the semi-circular tondo at the top, or swoop rhythmically in pairs around the frame, partnering their own reflections in the glass *(figs 17, 83)*. A peacock fills the spacious curved pediment with the spread fan of its tail, framed on either side of the glass by a long sweeping fall of tiles depicting the bird's furled and trailing feathers *(fig.16)*. A lyre-shaped mirror *(fig.18)* in pale spring-greens and blues musically repeats the instrument's swelling, gently rounded shape, and classical modesty of scale.

In mirror after mirror the medium acquires an airy grace and lightness not readily associated with clay. A courtly white-glazed swan with lithe, steeply inflected neck and powerful five- or six-foot wingspan presides over the double doors of the small eighteenth-century drawing room that serves as Stokes' studio. Buoyancy and flow inform her recent work. Both are essential to the strange hybrid trees – part pot, part woodwork, part a kind of performance art with a movable cast of perching birds, oscillating leaves and dangling fruit – that currently occupy the studio *(fig.1)*, exemplifying in three dimensions what Matisse meant when he said that when you draw a tree, the space between the leaves is as important as the leaf itself.[18]

Much the same principle underlay Stokes' exhaustive early ballet training. 'The dancer is painter, brush, canvas and paint in one,' Adrian Stokes wrote in *Tonight the Ballet*, a book that by Ann's account transfixed her when she read it in 1940.[19] For the next seven years ballet dominated her life. Forced to give up dancing on her marriage, she eventually resolved the bitterness of that renunciation through the unlikely medium of potting. Her work exemplifies the qualities – 'spin, balance and line' – she defines as common to the two arts.[20] 'The spread of the arabesque and the lift, as in a *pas de deux*, much like the final swoop of the Bluebird to her mate; this is what fascinates me in animals,' she wrote,[21] describing the apparently effortless elegance, confidence and clarity that constitute her ultimate goal as a potter. She comes close to it in bowls and dishes animated by the muscular flick of plaice or flounder, mirrors incorporating the wing-clap of swan or hoopoe. There are no parallels that I know of to Stokes' expressive earthenware. 'Clay ought to be grateful to her,' as she herself said of the great potter Lucie Rie. 'She is an extension of the clay itself.'[22]

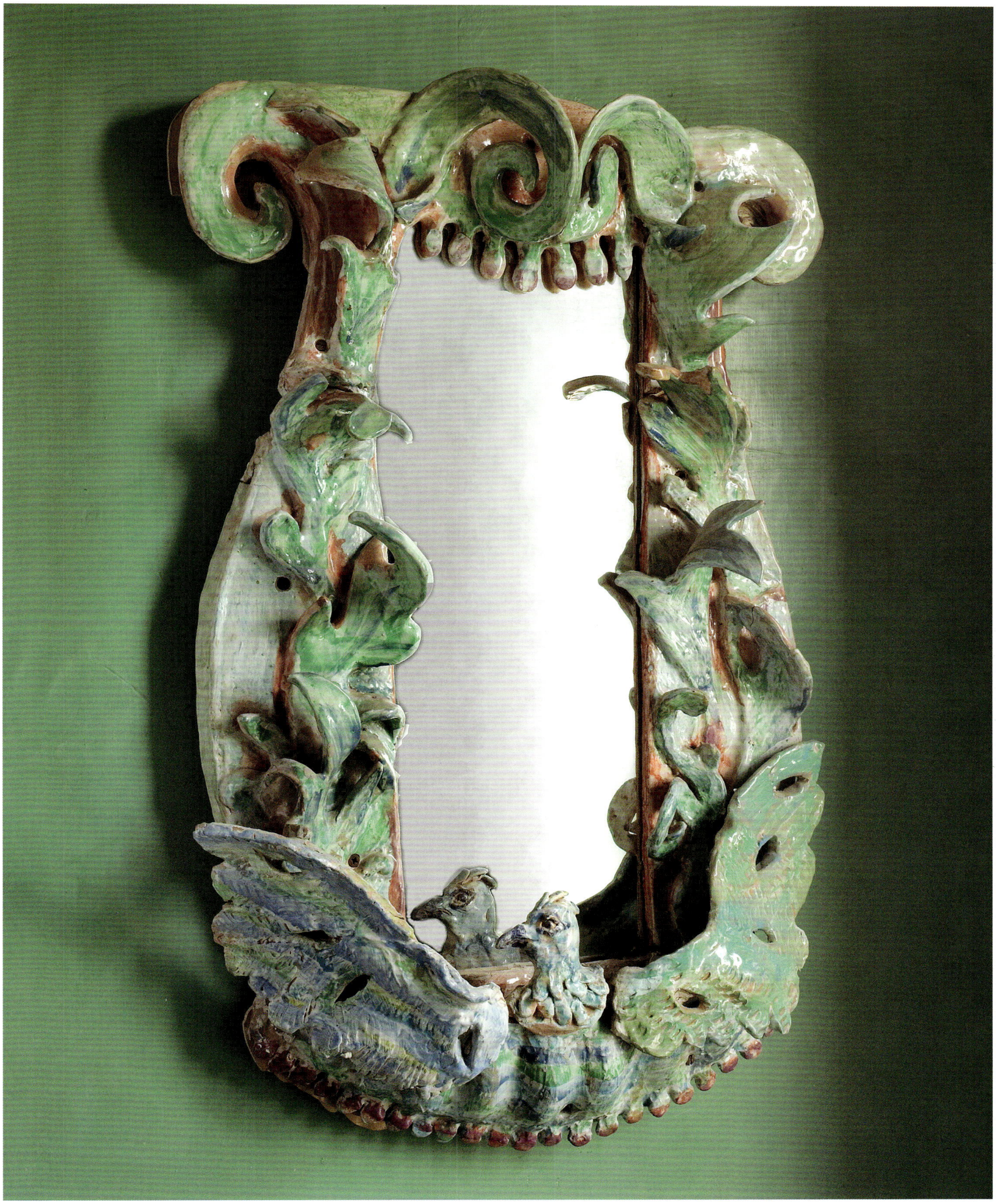

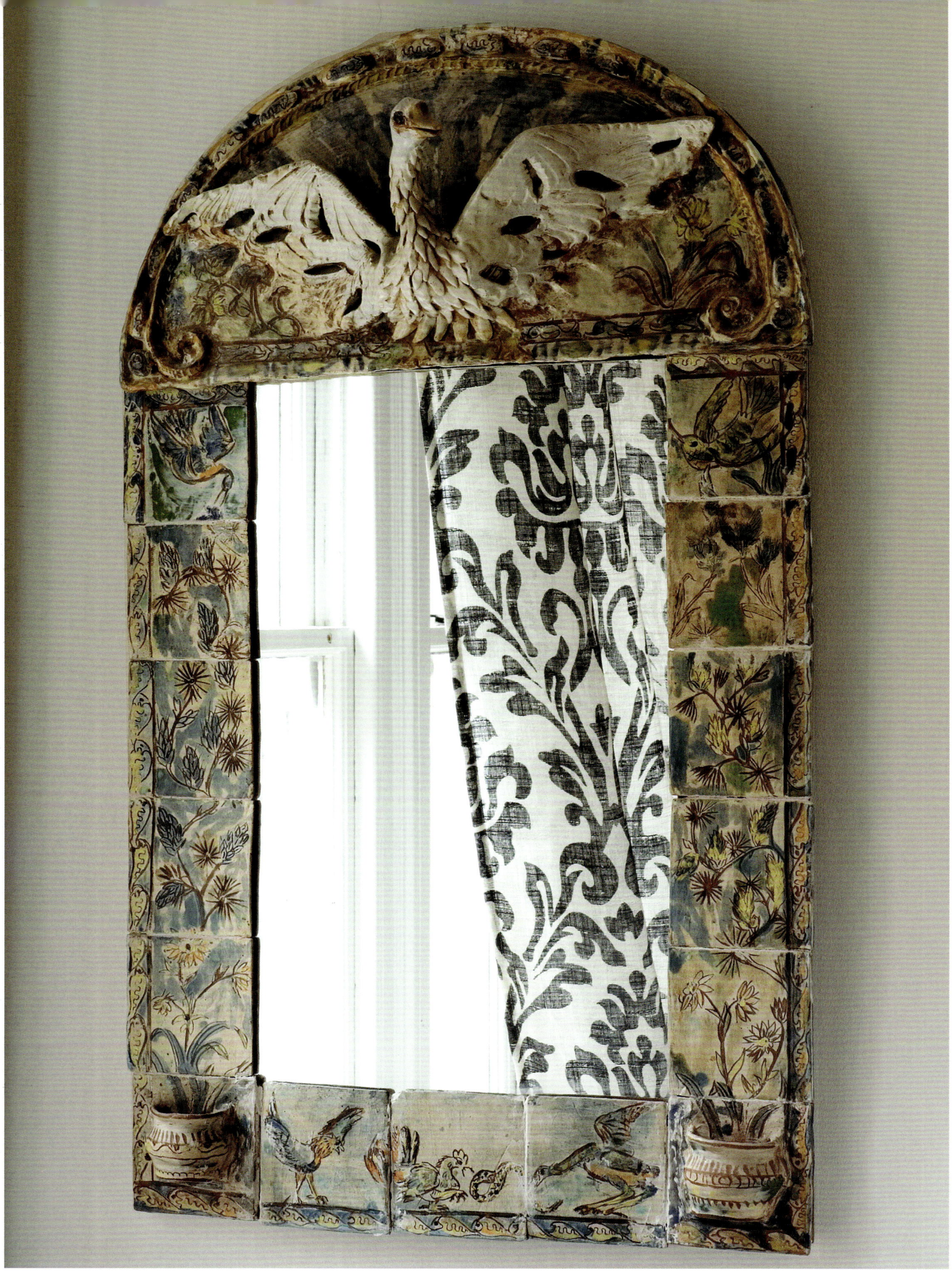

Notes

1. The first wave of young British artists to make a significant international impact after World War II – nearly all shown in the 1960s by Bryan Robertson at the Whitechapel Gallery in London, where I encountered them as a young writer – included Anthony Caro, Patrick Caulfield, David Hockney, John Hoyland, Bryan Kneale, William Pye, Bridget Riley, Michael Sandle and Gary Wragg.
2. Quoted in Richard Morphet's essay, p.61.
3. Ann Stokes interviewed by Linda Sandino, 2003, *Crafts Lives*, British Library Sound Archive.
4. Conversation with Ann Stokes, 11 July 2008.
5. See Richard Morphet's essay, p.44
6. *Crafts Magazine*, Nov/Dec 1985; for a more detailed exploration of this theme, see Tanya Harrod's essay, pp 78–82
7. Ann Stokes interviewed by Linda Sandino, 2003, op.cit.
8. In *Ann Stokes: A Retrospective*, exh. cat., Rebecca Hossack Gallery, London, 1998.
9. See Hilary Spurling, 'Debits and Credits: Henri Matisse, the Bussys and Bloomsbury', *The Burlington Magazine*, CXLVII, April 2005, p.239.
10. Ann Stokes interviewed by Linda Sandino, 2003, op.cit.
11. Adrian Stokes, *Inside Out*, 1947, in Lawrence Gowing (ed.), *The Critical Writings of Adrian Stokes, vol.ii, 1937–58*, London, 1978, p.159.
12. Adrian Stokes, *The Stones of Rimini*, 1935, in Lawrence Gowing (ed.), *The Critical Writings of Adrian Stokes, vol.i, 1930–37*, Thames & Hudson, London, 1978, p.235.
13. Ann Stokes interviewed by Linda Sandino, 2003, op.cit.
14. Adrian Stokes, 'Art Today', *The Spectator*, October 1933, in Lawrence Gowing (ed.), *The Critical Writings of Adrian Stokes, vol.i, 1930–37*, op.cit. p.306.
15. Adrian Stokes, *Inside Out*, 1947, op.cit. p.162.
16. In Lawrence Gowing (ed.), *The Critical Writings of Adrian Stokes, vol.i, 1930–37*, op.cit. p.254.
17. Adrian Stokes, *Inside Out*, 1947, op.cit. p.143.
18. See Dominique Szymusiak, *Matisse et l'arbre*, exh. cat., Musée Matisse, Le Cateau-Cambrésis, 2004, p.16.
19. Adrian Stokes, *Tonight the Ballet*, Faber & Faber, London, 1934, p.75; conversation with Ann Stokes, 9 August 2008.
20. See Richard Morphet's essay, p.40, and note 7.
21. See www.annstokes.com.
22. Ann Stokes interviewed by Linda Sandino, 2003, op.cit.

19 Mirror with a swan and cockerels fighting a snake, c.1992–3
Tiles, modelled bird, mirror glass on board
80 x 51 cm (31.5 x 20 in)
Collection: Jennifer Anderson
Photo: Stephen Brayne

TWO

Ann Stokes: Art and Life

Richard Morphet

20 Plate with Sweet Cicely as stencil, marked Σ 84
26 cm (10.2 in)
Collection: Dr Angela Hamilton
Photo: Stephen Brayne

ANN STOKES IS A DAUGHTER of the manse. Before she was born her father David Mellis had, like both her grandfathers, been a missionary in China. Her sister Margaret, the eldest of her parents' four children, was born there in 1914. By the time of Ann's birth in 1922 (following two brothers), the family had long been back in Scotland. Having been wounded on active service in the First World War, her father was now serving as a Scottish Presbyterian minister. Ann was born in Gullane, East Lothian; the family subsequently moving to Glenfarg, near Perth, while Ann was a child.

Life in the manse was lively and cultured. Reading, music and art were encouraged and in 1929 Margaret became a student at Edinburgh College of Art. Then in 1936, while Ann was still at school, Margaret met the writer Adrian Stokes. Ann's future would be radically affected by the unexpected consequences of this event. Adrian was twelve years older than Margaret and twenty years older than Ann, but during the next eleven years he would marry the two Mellis sisters in succession. Margaret later married the painter Francis Davison (1919–84), while Ann was Adrian's wife for a quarter of a century, until his death in 1972.

Adrian would have an enormous influence on Ann's life and art. The key impulses that would drive her future art were, however, evident before she ever heard of him. Nicknamed Tarzan by the family doctor, she spent much time climbing trees, in one of which she often slept. Having made many linocuts of animals, birds and trees when small, she began at the age of eight to move into the third dimension, using a fretsaw – as she has done ever since – and painting on the representational shapes she created. Then in 1935 a whole new world was revealed to her when she saw the film

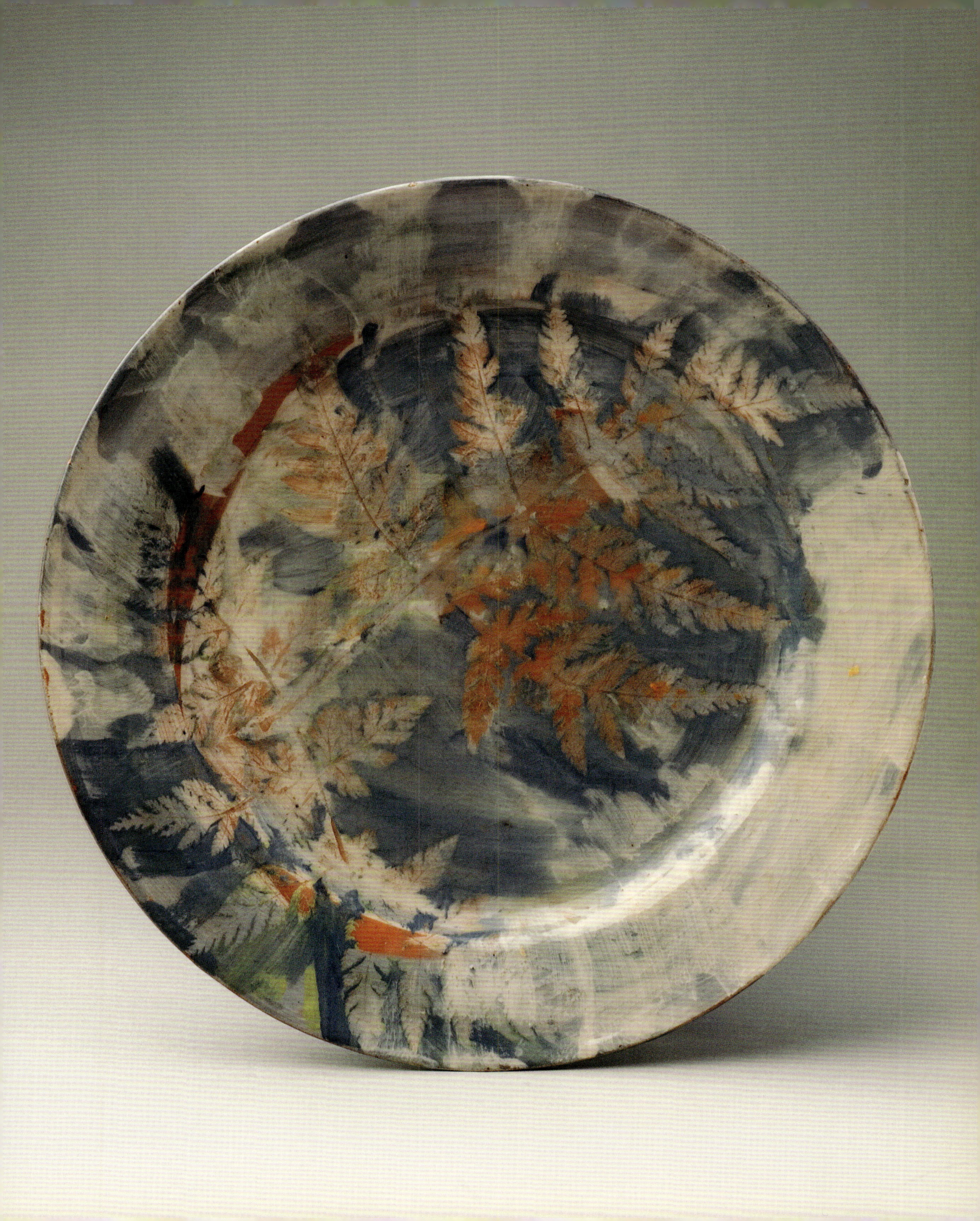

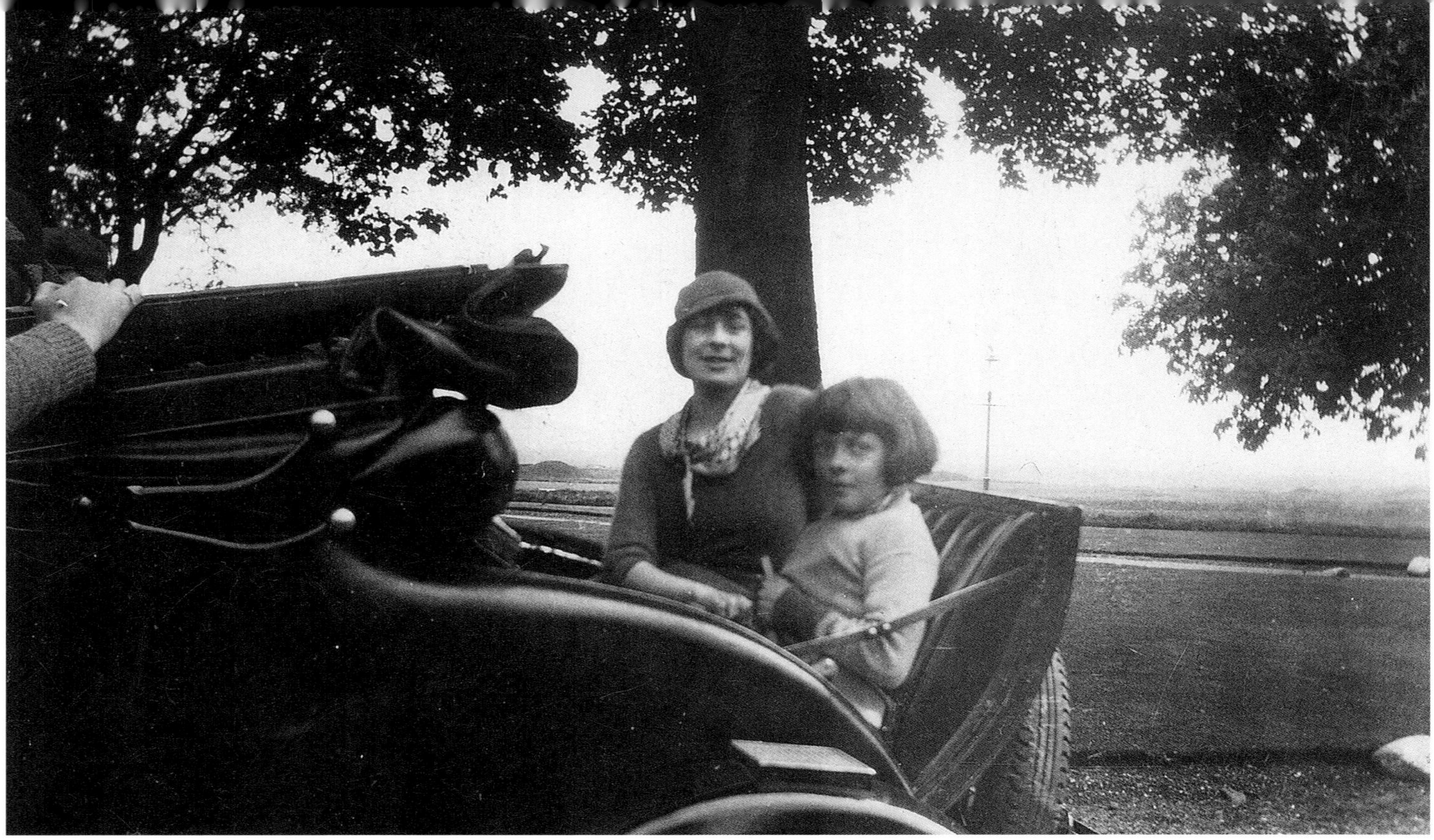

21 (left to right) Margaret Mellis and Ann Mellis aged nine, Gullane golf course, 1931
The artist's collection
Photographer unknown

Top Hat, starring Ginger Rogers and Fred Astaire. This made her 'long to dance, *any* kind of dance'.[1] Not only would Ann soon realise this wish in several years of ballet training, but the experience of dance would also lie at the inspirational heart of the work for which she later became best known – her art as a potter.

Ann first met Adrian when she was fourteen. He wrote chiefly on three subjects: architecture and sculpture (above all the low reliefs) of the Italian Renaissance; the art of his near-contemporaries Ben Nicholson, Henry Moore and Barbara Hepworth; and classical ballet. His insights on each of these topics informed the others. His writing was of extraordinary subtlety and originality, rich in visual and sensory observation, permeated by perceptions developed during the treatment he had been receiving, since 1930, from the Austrian-born psychoanalyst Melanie Klein (1882–1960). Around the time of his meeting with Margaret Mellis, Adrian, who had private means, started to paint. In 1937 he began to study at the Euston Road School, which was established in London in that year by the painters William Coldstream, Graham Bell, Victor Pasmore and Claude Rogers. In 1938 Margaret joined him, and they were married in July, living close to the school. Ann (still a schoolgirl in Scotland) did not visit Margaret and Adrian during this brief London period. Adrian was, however, a loved and compelling figure to the Mellis family and to Ann (however mysterious she found some of his interests and dislikes). At this time Adrian sent her one of his books. He was delighted when she told him that reading it had sent her to sleep, but that she loved its smell.

As war approached, Adrian bought Little Parc Owles, a large house at Carbis Bay, near St Ives, Cornwall, which had extensive grounds and a long, straight drive, said to be the only extended flat roadway in the vicinity, overlaid with fastidiously raked chips of shiny white granite. Backed by trees, the house stood on a slope high above the beach. Ann's first visit was with her parents, immediately before the outbreak of war in September 1939. She was greatly impressed, and found Margaret and Adrian's still life paintings 'almost indistinguishable'. Before moving to Carbis Bay, Adrian had already painted in the area, which was notable in avant-garde circles for the discovery by Ben Nicholson and Christopher Wood, in St Ives in 1928, of the untutored septuagenarian painter Alfred Wallis (1855–1942), some of whose works hung in the Stokes home.[2] In 1940, Adrian became a market gardener as part of the war effort. Margaret, who was expecting a baby in the autumn, asked Ann to join the household to help her in the run-up to the birth, and thereafter. Ann's school years had just ended and her father thought that living in a house with Adrian would be as good as going to university.[3] Ann arrived in Carbis Bay in the late summer of 1940. Her first stay lasted thirteen months and she later returned for another year.

Ann's nephew, Telfer Stokes, was born in October 1940, with Ann in support. By then Barbara Hepworth (who assisted with Ann immediately after the birth) and Ben Nicholson who, with their children, had lived with the Stokeses for some months in 1939, had moved to another house; and Naum Gabo and his wife were living in a bungalow, also nearby. The three households of artists were part of a close-knit, not always harmonious community, frequently augmented by visitors, including the art patron Margaret Gardiner and Desmond Bernal, the poet and art critic Herbert Read, the painter Julian Trevelyan and Barbara Hepworth's first husband, sculptor John Skeaping. At various times Ann vacated her bedroom for visitors and slept in a corridor. Among these were the poet Stephen Spender and his wife Natasha on their honeymoon, the writer and literary critic Cyril Connolly, and Graham Bell with Anne Olivier Popham (later Mrs Quentin Bell). The household ate off seconds from Bernard Leach's Pottery in St Ives.

In these years Ann saw Gabo's works when newly made and watched Ben Nicholson painting, but a recurring theme in her own and others' memories is of active outdoor life. Adrian was hard at work cultivating vegetables (both Margaret and Ann giving up part of their butter ration to bolster his health for this work). He played golf with Ben Nicholson, while croquet and tennis (at which Ann beat both Gabo and Nicholson) were played by all, as was poker by Adrian and Margaret, the Gabos, Ann, Skeaping and the artist and writer Sven Berlin. On the beach, while Gabo threw balls for his dog to catch, Adrian threw them for Ann to do the same.

Along the admired drive, Ann constructed jumps for herself. Adrian was so impressed by her strength and control that, supported by Gabo (whom he brought to watch), he urged her to train to be a dancer. Drawn to dance since 1935 and now also greatly struck by Adrian's book *Tonight the Ballet* (1934), Ann responded enthusiastically. Adrian arranged for her to become a student at the ballet classes given in the Palais de Danse at St Ives (later Barbara Hepworth's sculpture showroom) by Phyllis Bedells (1893–1985), another evacuee. Ann recalls that 'from then on I was lost to any other interest'.[4] Though injury obliged her to give up dancing in 1947, the taking up of professional dance was a turning point that provided the foundation for her entire output as a potter. Distinguishing ballet from dance in general, Adrian wrote that 'all other forms known to me fail to communicate this sense of completeness, of consummation, of all inner ferment externalised in the form of display'.[5] He described such dancing as 'an assault upon space, an assault of love, a similar assault to that of the carver upon his stone or that of the farmer as he ploughs the earth'.[6] For Ann, 'Pottery and ballet have spin, balance and line in common and birds and animals have their movement naturally which any acrobat, circus performer or dancer has to struggle so hard to get and which never ceases to fascinate me. The trees I make now have just the same qualities.'[7]

After Ann left Carbis Bay in the middle of the war, her time was divided for some four years between service in Britain and France as a Wren (in the Women's Royal Naval Service) and continuing her ballet training in London. This period ended when in 1947 she moved to Switzerland to marry Adrian and to live in Ascona. For a long time such a development had been inconceivable to her, for as Adrian's wife's sister she felt certain that she was one of the very few people it would be illegal for him to marry. The idea was also distressing owing to her belief in Margaret's marriage to Adrian and her feelings for her sister. The time between her learning of Adrian's wishes and the eventual resolution was the most stressful of her life. A factor in the final outcome was the importance attached by both sisters to Adrian having what he wanted. Adrian's remarriage was far from being opposed by their parents, their mother writing to Adrian that, 'We both think you & Ann suit each other to perfection in gaiety and doings and I know she will take good care of you and soothe you and keep you in perfect peace. If you aren't pleased with her I'm afraid we haven't any more daughters. My goodness 2 is plenty.'[8] The chief ground for Adrian and Margaret's divorce was incompatibility.[9] It had proved difficult for two artists (one of whom was also a writer and a worker in the war effort) to function in harmony. Perhaps ironically, part of the reason for Ann being asked to join the household was to make it easier for Margaret to work. Ann also found it easier than Margaret to tailor her life to Adrian's needs.

Having discovered that Switzerland was among the countries that permitted marriage to the sister of a living former wife, Adrian and Ann married in Italian Switzerland in 1947,[10] their son Philip being born there in February 1948. Adrian painted prolifically. When the three of them visited Margaret, Francis and Telfer at Cap d'Antibes in 1949, Ann saw at nearby Vallauris Picasso's ceramics, with which her own work would later have some affinity. In 1950 both families returned to England to live, Adrian and Ann first in Berkshire, where their daughter Ariadne was born in June 1951, and then in Surrey, where their home, Hurtwood House, commanded the view of a sweeping landscape. At Hurtwood, Ann made fret-sawed trees with dangling melon seeds, as well as children's toys, some of which she tried unsuccessfully to persuade Harrods to sell. In the 1960s she would

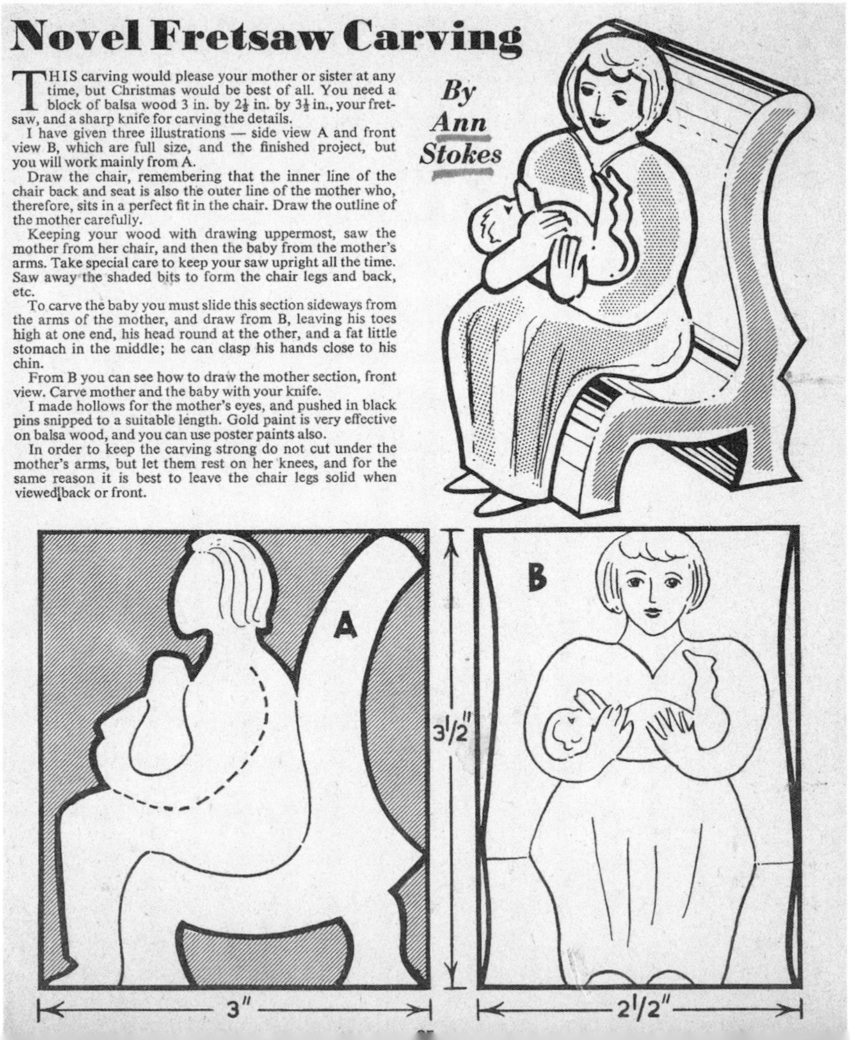

Novel Fretsaw Carving

By Ann Stokes

THIS carving would please your mother or sister at any time, but Christmas would be best of all. You need a block of balsa wood 3 in. by 2½ in. by 3½ in., your fretsaw, and a sharp knife for carving the details.

I have given three illustrations — side view A and front view B, which are full size, and the finished project, but you will work mainly from A.

Draw the chair, remembering that the inner line of the chair back and seat is also the outer line of the mother who, therefore, sits in a perfect fit in the chair. Draw the outline of the mother carefully.

Keeping your wood with drawing uppermost, saw the mother from her chair, and then the baby from the mother's arms. Take special care to keep your saw upright all the time. Saw away the shaded bits to form the chair legs and back, etc.

To carve the baby you must slide this section sideways from the arms of the mother, and draw from B, leaving his toes high at one end, his head round at the other, and a fat little stomach in the middle; he can clasp his hands close to his chin.

From B you can see how to draw the mother section, front view. Carve mother and the baby with your knife.

I made hollows for the mother's eyes, and pushed in black pins snipped to a suitable length. Gold paint is very effective on balsa wood, and you can use poster paints also.

In order to keep the carving strong do not cut under the mother's arms, but let them rest on her knees, and for the same reason it is best to leave the chair legs solid when viewed back or front.

22 *Ann Stokes, 'Novel Fretsaw Carving',* Hobbies Weekly: for all home craftsmen, *17 October 1962, vol.135, no.3488, p.35*

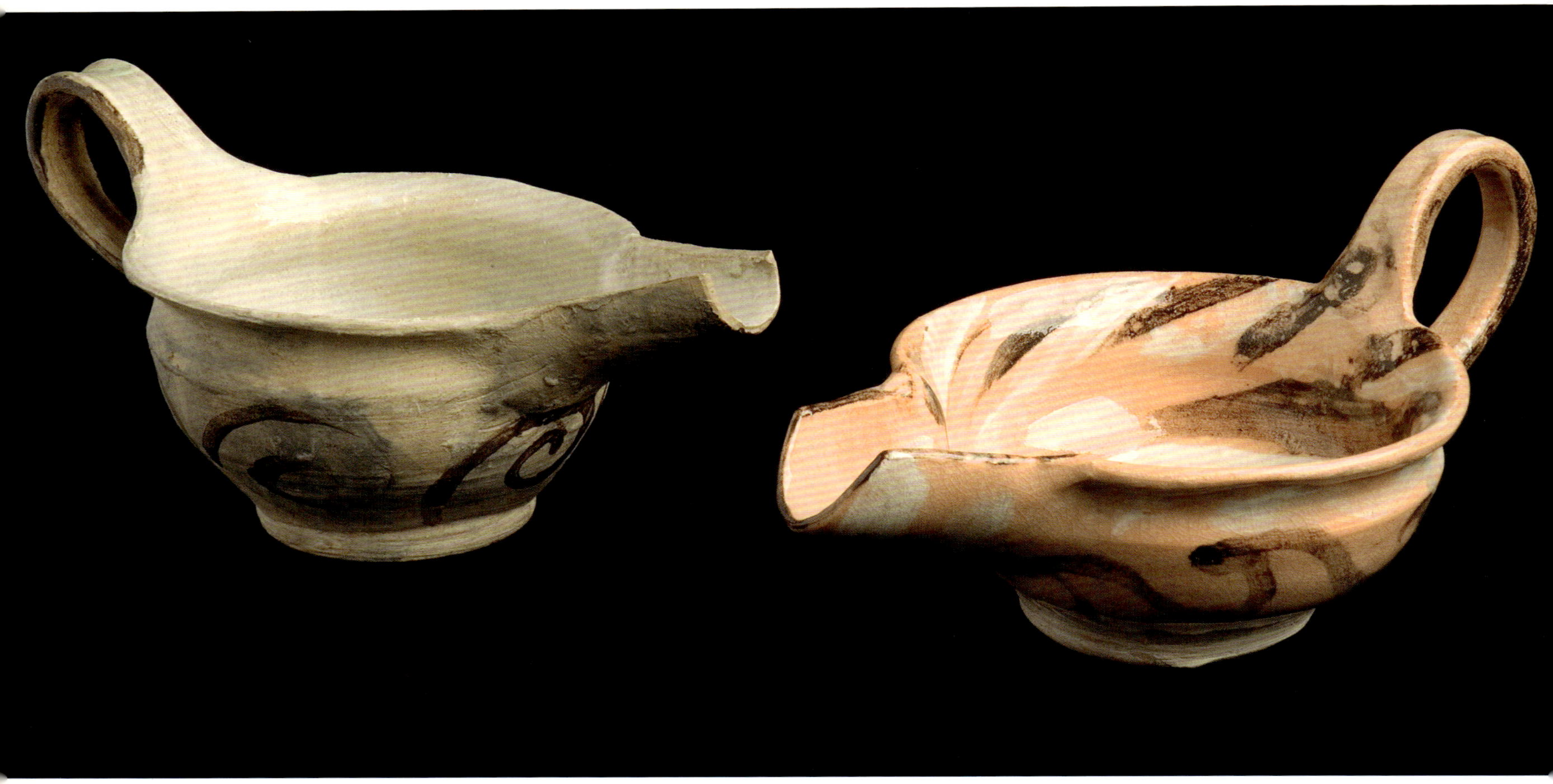

23 Two pouring cups with looped handles and cut spouts, unmarked, early 1970s
(left to right) 8 x 16.5 cm (3.1 x 6.5 in); 8 x 16 cm (3.1 x 6.3 in)
Collection: Jennifer Anderson
Photo: Stephen Brayne

contribute articles to *Hobbies Weekly* magazine, illustrated by her own drawings, explaining how to make fret-sawed toys *(fig.22)*. When, in September 1956, the family moved to Church Row, Hampstead (where Ann has lived ever since), her life changed and her circle expanded in ways even richer and more complex than when she became part of the community at Carbis Bay.

Before Ann put her hands on clay, a predisposition towards ceramics was a latent possibility. Her contact with Bernard Leach (1887–1979) and his Pottery was significant because, although Leach's approach was too pure and controlling for Ann, it gave her a feel of what a well-made pot was like. She admired Leach's *A Potter's Book* (published in the year she arrived in Carbis Bay) especially for the way 'he keeps all the romance of the thing, where other writers don't'. Ann's initiation in 1957 into her life's work as a potter is described in Tanya Harrod's essay, but to understand her work's context it is necessary to consider the dynamic of the relationship between Ann and Adrian. The close sympathy between them, both personally and aesthetically, explains something of Ann's inspiration as a potter, as do the dissimilarities.

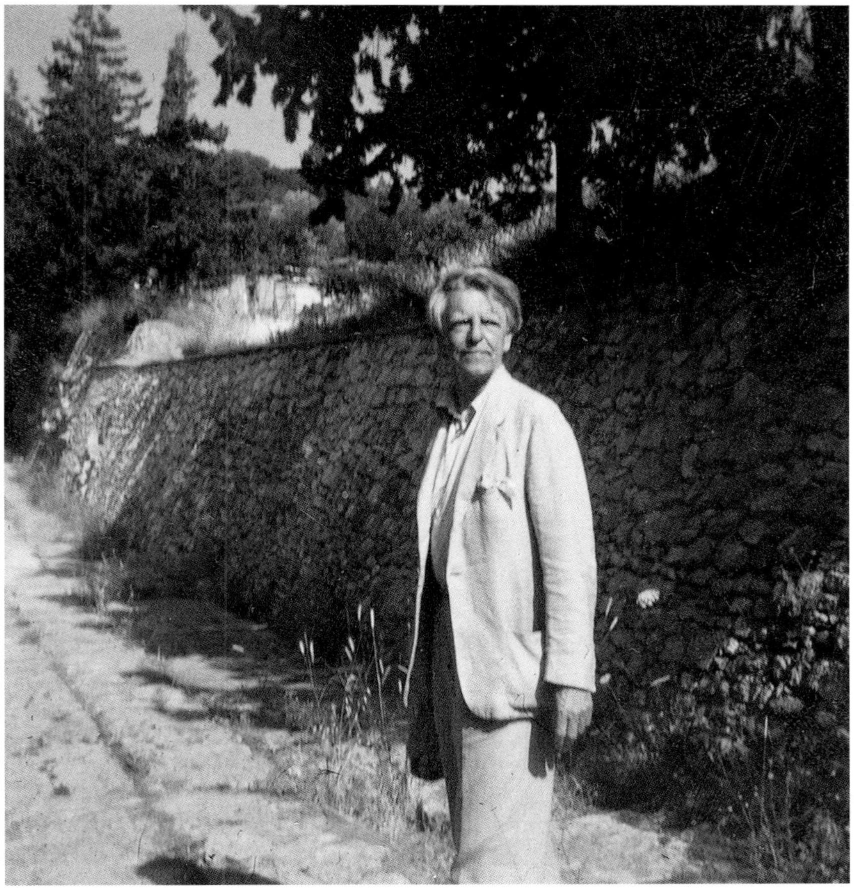

24 Adrian Stokes at the Sacred Way, Crete, 1969
The artist's collection
Photo: Ann Stokes

Influenced by W.W. Winkworth, a friend and expert on Chinese pottery, Adrian owned classic books on ceramics and gave Ann ones by W.B. Honey, chiefly on Chinese pottery and its technique. Adrian's deep interest in the Mediterranean and in the art of Antiquity led to her discovery of Cretan pottery, a major influence on her early work, not least in the protruding lips (or 'applied pourers') of her jugs *(fig.23)*. In the last three years of Adrian's life, he and Ann went on two cruises in the eastern Mediterranean, which included a visit to Crete. In an account written at the time, Ann records that in the museum at Heraklion she 'even saw some pots I did not know – what a boast – but some of the best in any group are so well illustrated in my 3 books that I felt at home.[11] It was violently exciting to see the 4crnd [cornered] alabaster beaker which I tried to reproduce so badly & the round one Day [Mary Day Lanier] loves so much.'[12]

As a painter, Adrian is perhaps best known for his still lifes, but it was his landscapes that spoke to Ann most intensely, for the chief motif was usually trees *(fig.25)*. One of her first acts when the family moved to Hampstead was to plant a Silver Poplar in the garden. More than fifty years

25 Adrian Stokes, Olive Trees, *1958*
Oil on canvas
76.2 x 63.5 cm (30 x 25 in)
Collection: Tate, London
Copyright and Photo: Tate, London (2008); and the Estate of Adrian Stokes

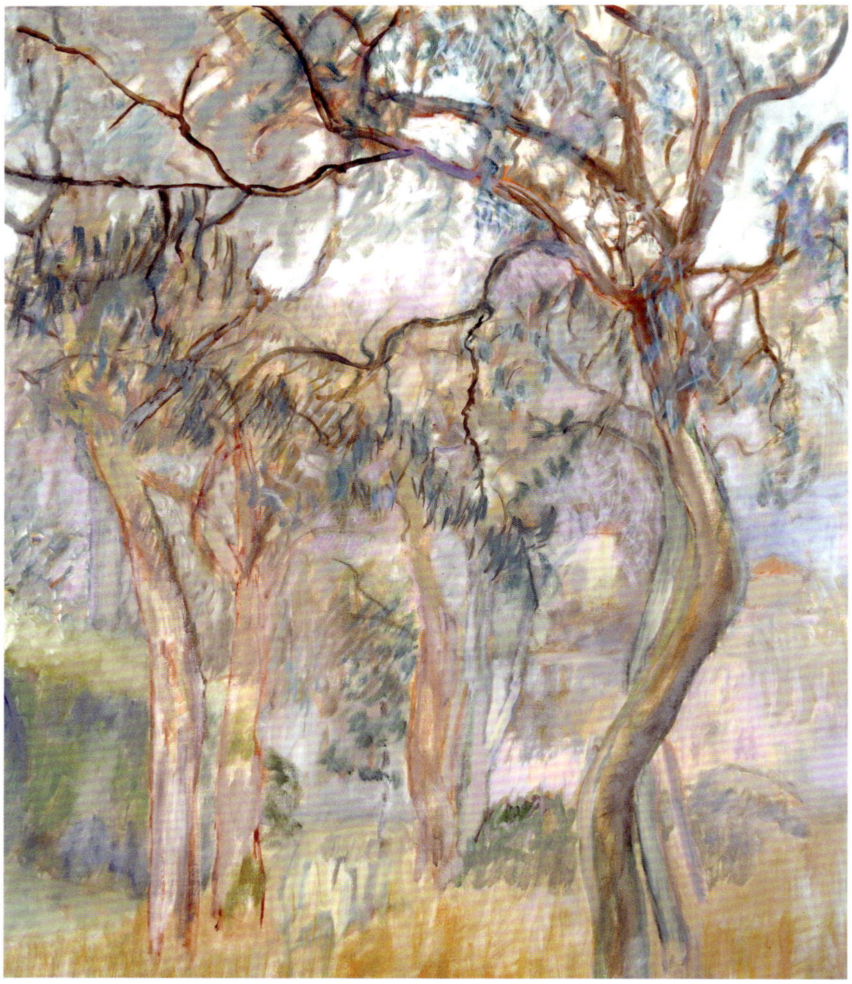

later it is enormous, but it inspires her work continually. As she observes of the rotating tree sculptures she is making now: 'I long to make their leaves shimmer as my Silver Poplar does in the garden ... It has line, balance and shimmer if not spin! It also houses squirrels, woodpeckers and other birds.'[13] At the age of seventy-six, Ann chose an earlier photograph of herself hanging upside down from a tree as one of the images in a promotional card from her gallery, with the caption (from a folk song): 'Si oiseau j'étais a toi je volerais.' *(fig.7)* She declares: 'I love trees from the inside and from the outside,' and recently wrote: 'Now I am making a dancing tree – i.e. the tree is budding into dancers like the Greek Daphne but just the opposite!'[14] On viewing an exhibition of Adrian's paintings at Marlborough Fine Art in London, the artist Sidney Nolan told him: 'I feel that if your paintings were touched they would have a charge in them like electricity. The kind of charge which trees must give out, if we could feel it. It is like walking into a room full of people.'[15] Ann recalls that, 'Adrian used to say I was like an oak tree.'[16]

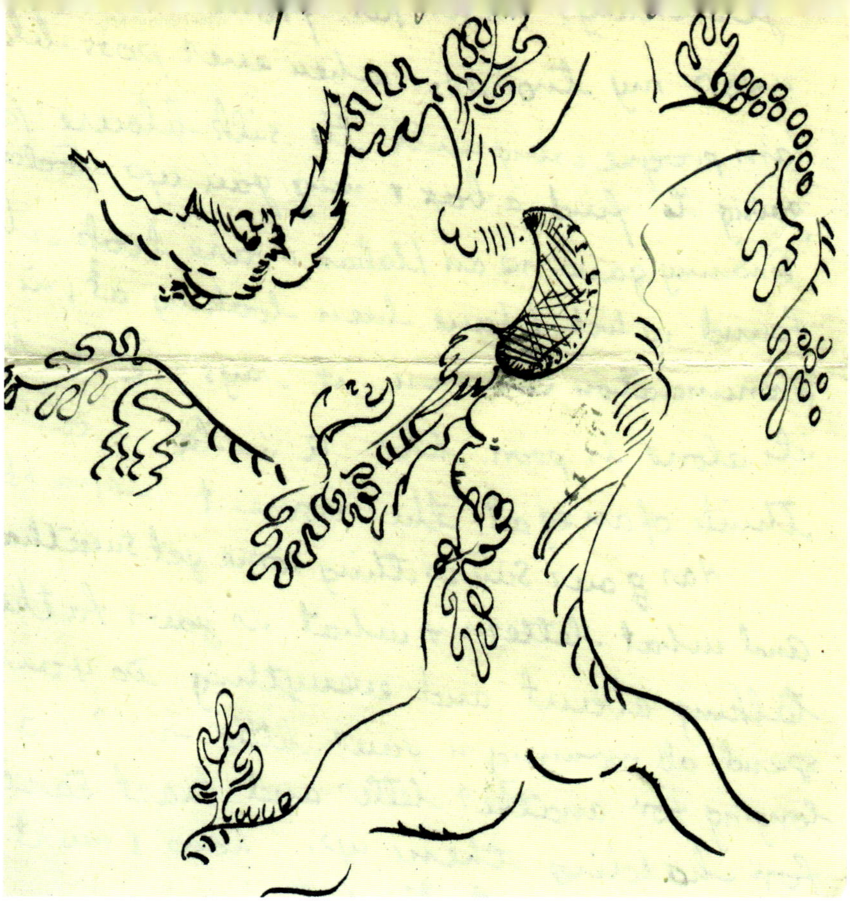

26 Drawing of a figure metamorphosed into a tree in a letter from Ann Stokes (then Mellis) to Adrian Stokes, undated
Collection: Tate, London
Copyright and Photo: Tate, London (2008); and the Estate of Adrian Stokes

A drawing in a letter she wrote to him is a self-portrait as an anthropomorphic oak tree in or on which Adrian, in the form of a bird, is about to alight *(fig.26)*.[17] Adrian also loved olive trees (and painting them).

A further direct link between Adrian's work and Ann's is the use of colour. Terracotta and black are among her very effective hues and ochre among his, but it is the green and blue in Adrian's paintings that mean most to her. She observes: 'I can't help getting back always to blue and green. Without them I'd be very lost.' This affinity is brought home in Ann's studio, where the surprisingly congruous backdrop to an orchard or jungle of her painted tree sculptures is tree-dominated landscape paintings by Adrian, closely hung and overwhelmingly green *(fig.1)*. For some time Ann experimented with a variety of framing styles for his pictures before securing his approval of the very thin, lightweight, unpainted curved-fronted battens that were adopted for all his work from the time of his Marlborough exhibition in 1965. Ann made and fitted these frames herself and Adrian valued the way their style facilitated the hanging of the works, in that first exhibition, in tightly packed blocks.

Ann was the model for a number of Adrian's paintings of the nude. She would sometimes set up the arrangements of objects for him to paint. In his last three months her assistance when he painted was crucial, as I will discuss later on. These last paintings were much looser in touch than before. Despite the continued concern they show with the form of the motif and despite the fact that painting them demanded great effort, their richness and radiance were in part a function of Adrian's being able, now, to relax. Ann recalls her relief when, in these later years, Adrian moderated, to some degree, his long-standing insistence on the pre-eminence of a 'carving' over a 'modelling' approach in the creation of art. According to Lawrence Gowing, Adrian's second marriage 'brought about a radical change in Stokes. He began to regard family life, affection and fidelity as positive, almost aesthetic virtues, and this immediately broadened his response to art ... He began to change his views on certain key artists: Michelangelo, Rembrandt, Hogarth, Turner, Matisse.'[18] Adrian's influence on Ann's work proved permanent. After his death, his absence had the paradoxical effect of boosting her output as a potter, because the process of creation enabled her in some degree to take her mind off her grief.

Despite the deep affinity between Adrian and Ann, the contrast between their personalities was pronounced. Adrian was anxious by nature, but the more anxious he became the less so (unlike Margaret) did Ann. While he wrestled over problems and was strongly engaged with psychoanalysis, Ann was direct, spontaneous and less questioning. They complemented one another, both in their personalities and in their art. Adrian needed implicitly to control those around him, yet his painting was subtle, unassertive and of a very refined kind. By contrast, Ann derived deep satisfaction from making things possible for Adrian, smoothing his existence, yet her work tended increasingly to boldness of image, colour or touch, open to the whole of creation and conveying her delight in movement.

Ann's jugs and cups do appear in some of Adrian's still lifes,[19] but less often than one might expect of vessels that were being made in the same house. In general Adrian's preference was to paint anonymous, commonplace, manufactured vessels. Once a given arrangement of objects had been decided upon, Adrian proceeded, touch by careful touch, in a method of working extraordinarily unlike Ann's. In the words of art critic Robert Melville: 'An almost convulsive diffidence, a positive fervour of undemonstrativeness, a resolute suppression of any mark resembling a flourish, a violently sustained serenity dictate the unruffled surfaces of his paintings. It's the high-strung calm before a storm, and the storm will never be allowed to break ... '[20] By contrast, Ann proceeded in a direct and workmanlike manner, loving 'flourish' and being intensely interested in description, even to the extent of seeking out photographs (to work from) of the frequently animate forms in nature that her work celebrates so assertively. The straightforwardness of her approach to realising her vision was in keeping with her reservations about analysis.

Stories abound of Ann's outgoing, celebratory temperament. Anne Crosby, a painter and close friend, notes how she has always been playful and that she dances wherever she is. Xanthe Sylvester recalls her father, the art critic and collector David Sylvester (1924–2001), returning one evening to the family home reeling, having just been with Ann at his nearby office/flat, in which works of art from various eras and cultures were displayed with fastidious sensitivity. Ann had taken an African mask and, putting it on, performed a wild dance on the spur of the moment. He was amazed by both the fun and the intensity of the dance she created, and by the fact that she could just *do* it. Ann loves the 'circus feel' of bullrings (though she has never witnessed a bullfight). At a historic performance of Bertram Mills Circus in London she rode the horse round the ring, watched by her children.[21]

For all the assertiveness of such acts, Ann's role with family and friends has been above all that of encourager and facilitator. She has helped both Adrian and her second husband Ian Angus, and has fitted the management of her considerable professional achievement seamlessly alongside their working lives. This is not to suggest that they, too, have not helped her immensely. Both have supported her work strongly. Adrian delighted in Ann's happiness in potting. He told her he had never seen her so excited as when she embarked on this work. A further cause of satisfaction was that it took place in their house, so that Ann remained close at hand. Anne Crosby has written thus of Ann's marriage to Adrian: 'Ann was alive in a completely different fashion to Adrian. Did his violent need of her grow from his perception that he would not be driven to compete with her? Invulnerable in her integrity, however dependent she might be, she would remain reassuringly a separate being, she would keep her spirit and leaven Adrian's.'[22]

While the sense of freedom that runs through Ann's work is a reflection of her nature, during Adrian's lifetime it was reassuring to know that she was not trespassing on his territory as an artist. From the start her work has eschewed technical and formal perfection. At first, this was in part a consequence of her having only a limited time each day to pot, but the very 'impurity' of her work became one of its positive features. As she observes: 'I bash the pots. I use the wheel to make it do something for me. If I make a bad shape, I think I can do something with it. This is why I moved away from Greek purity.'[23] As the last sentence implies, a greater proportion of Ann's early work emphasised the beauty of three-dimensional form in its own right than would later be the case. But while formal vitality is a consistent

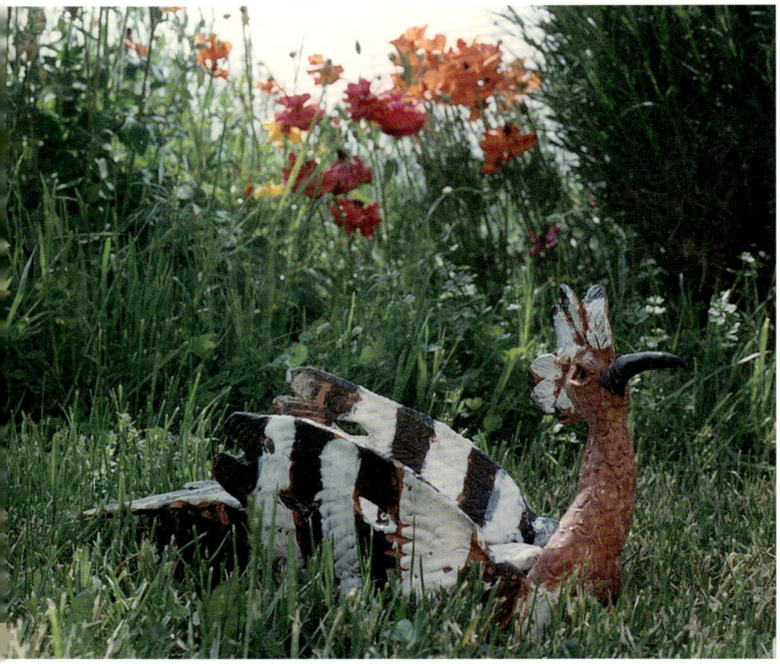

27 Hoopoe dish in the grass, c.*1981–2,*
Pergo, Italy
Photo: John Ross

concern, one of the striking differences between Ann's art and Adrian's is her interest in compelling stories and situations.

These would come to feature significantly in her output. When asked which works in London's National Gallery interested her most, Ann at once mentioned *The Procession of the Trojan Horse into Troy* (*c*.1760) by Giovanni Domenico Tiepolo. She loves the story, from Ancient Greece, and she finds the horse beautiful. She is fascinated by the fact that although the horse in the story was made of wood, Tiepolo has painted a real animal. This makes only a little less surprising Ann's extraordinary carved and painted fired relief *Odysseus Finds His Father (fig.11)*. Inspired by her memory of reading Homer's *Iliad* and *The Odyssey* while she had mumps, this presents an interior/exterior scene in which, prophetically, the central motif is a tree. Fruits hang prominently from its branches and it is growing in a ceramic bowl. The architecture and furniture are based on examples found in books and in the British Museum, and Ann succeeds in her aim of achieving a strong three-dimensional feeling. The key role played here by two figures makes it puzzling that Ann has represented the human figure so rarely. She counters that: 'I don't draw well enough,' and, 'As a dancer, I find the crucial thing is the body at its very best and do not think I can do it justice. The closest I have come is mermaids, though I did represent a ballet dancer on a plate.'[24] Human beings do, however, appear in disguise. Birds abound in her work, and Ann adds: 'Ballet dancers are birds,' and 'Adrian had such a beaky face. Someone said all my birds are him.'[25] *(fig.27)*

Ann's interest in things she sees, coupled with her evident skill in representing them, combines with her familiarity with painters to make it surprising that she has not been a painter herself. Her reply is that she has not done so because she wished above all to work in three dimensions. Yet a central aspect of her ceramic art is that it is not only painted but also frequently bears pictures. Indeed, she observes: 'Painting is what I pot *for*. It is to give myself something to put my leaves and animals on. Most potters do it for the pot itself.'[26]

Though Ann is self-taught as a painter, a merit of her work on flat surfaces (whether plates, tiles, plaques or the front of the supports of saucepan-lid racks) is its no-nonsense directness, allied to an infectious love for what she brings to life. Vigorous, spirited and full of movement, her touch often seems akin to the movement of the animals, birds, fish, water or weather that she depicts. An example is the smaller of two tiled pictures of an ancient naval vessel, *Greek Oared Warship in a Storm (fig.28)*. The viewer can really believe in the storm, the energy called for from the oarsmen and

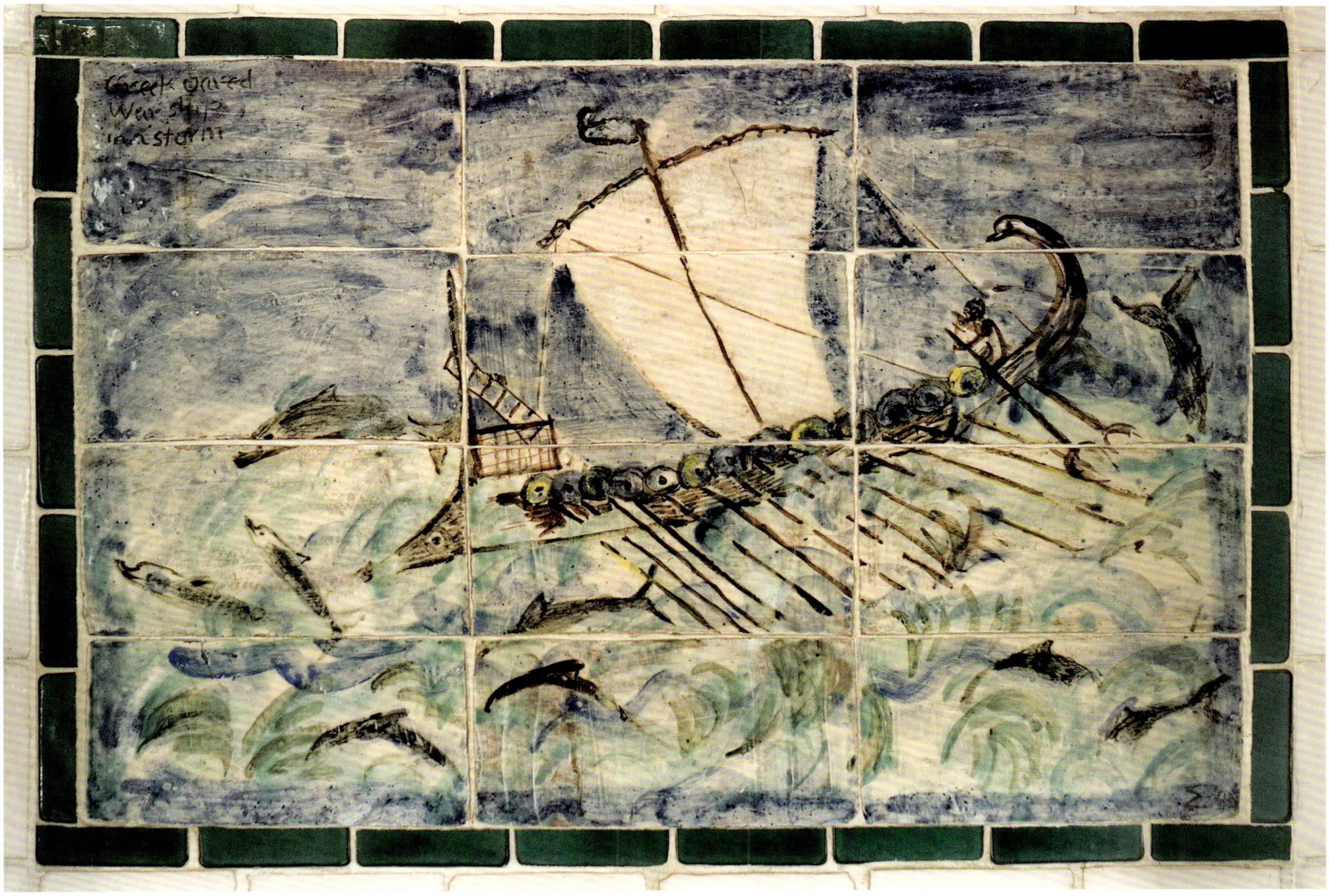

28 Greek Oared Warship in a Storm,
mid 1990s
Glazed tiles
49 x 74 cm (19.3 x 29.1 in)
Collection: Lord and Lady Ravensdale
Photo: Stephen Brayne

the reality of the sea creatures that surround the vessel. The larger version, with an elaborate decorative border, is less elemental but no less painterly, the presence of the boat in motion being brought to life amid a range of rich scumbles *(fig.29)*. On the lowest run of stairs in Ann's house the risers are animated by painted tiles in relief, representing doves in their setting. On close examination the sequence tells the story of the relationship between two doves. It is a most unusual strip cartoon *(fig.30)*.

Ann's sophistication as an artist can be traced directly to her spontaneity in childhood. Considering the intellectual concentration of the circle in which she has lived almost all her adult life, the retention of this quality is the more striking. The art of children appeals to her powerfully and this was very much the case when her children were young. They were among the first whose work was translated by Ann into her own ceramic art, often on the most unlikely supports, such as the occasional table on which she carefully transcribed the image of a painting by her son Philip *(fig.31)*. Tragically

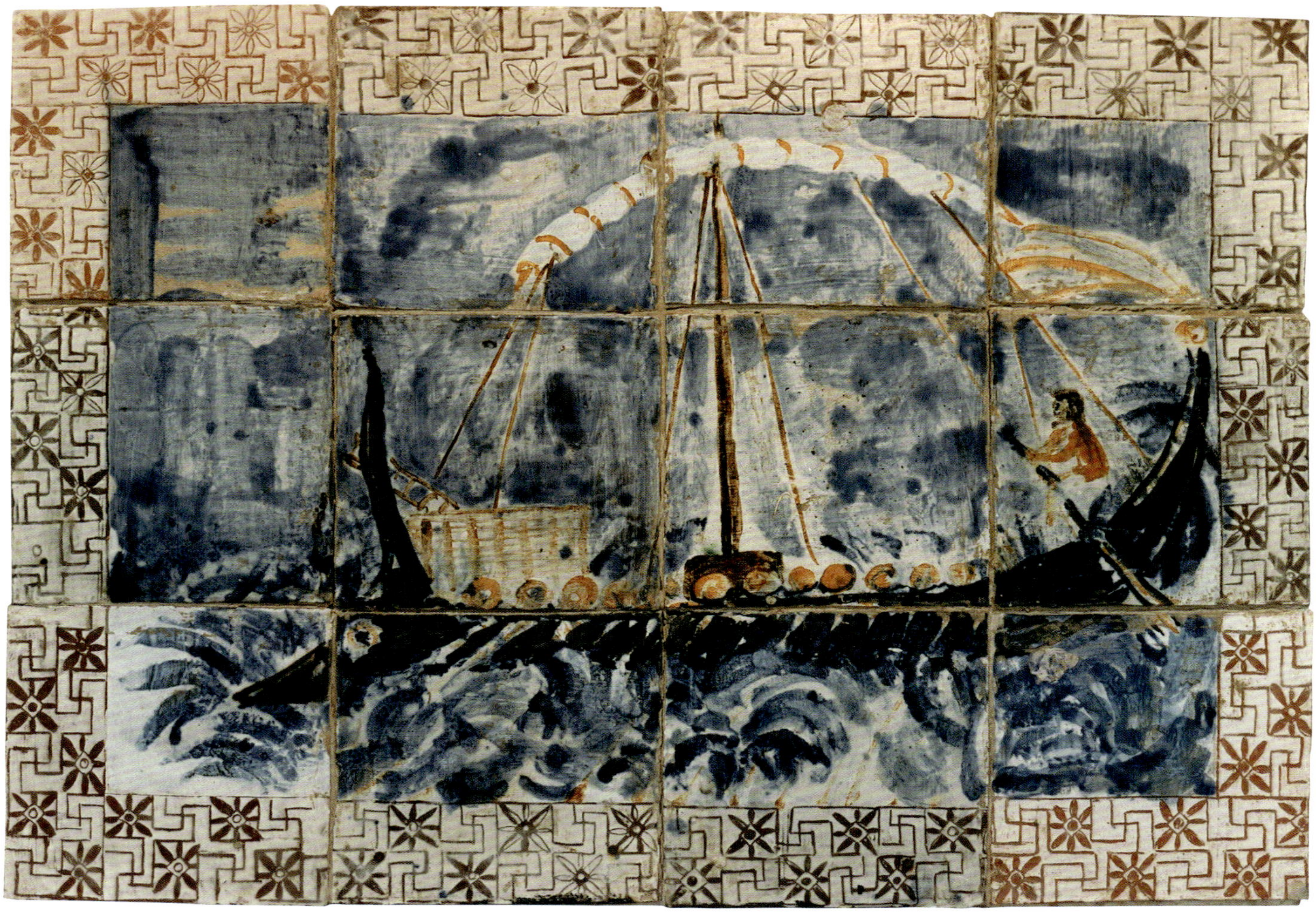

29 Greek Oared Warship in a Storm, 1998
Glazed tiles, with a border taken from a painted terracotta sarcophagus (500 BC), excavated at Clazomenae, near Smyrna, now in the British Museum, London
50 x 80 cm (19.7 x 31.5 in)
Collection: James Brett
Photo: Rebecca Hossack Gallery

for the whole family, Ann's younger child, Ariadne, was diagnosed with autism. Some years before Adrian's death, she entered care in the country, in her late teens. Grave though this was for Ann, it was an even more severe blow to Adrian as Ariadne had, at his wish, been psychoanalysed intensively from an early age; but the move was essential, not only for Ariadne, but also for Ann. Their friend Anne Crosby managed to persuade Adrian of this. As Ann explains: '[Anne] saved me ... It was really through her that I got some freedom and life changed. I saw my spirits rise up ... I didn't know I was depressed, but I must have been. It has been heaven since, every minute of it. Much to the annoyance of Julia Strachey, who said to me once: "Ann, is there *nothing* you don't like?"'[27]

Ann has never been psychoanalysed. In her oral history recording for National Life Stories, *Crafts Lives*, she makes clear how thankful she is that she has not, adding: 'I had too happy a nature to bother about such things.'[28] She did meet many analysts socially, partly through Adrian's

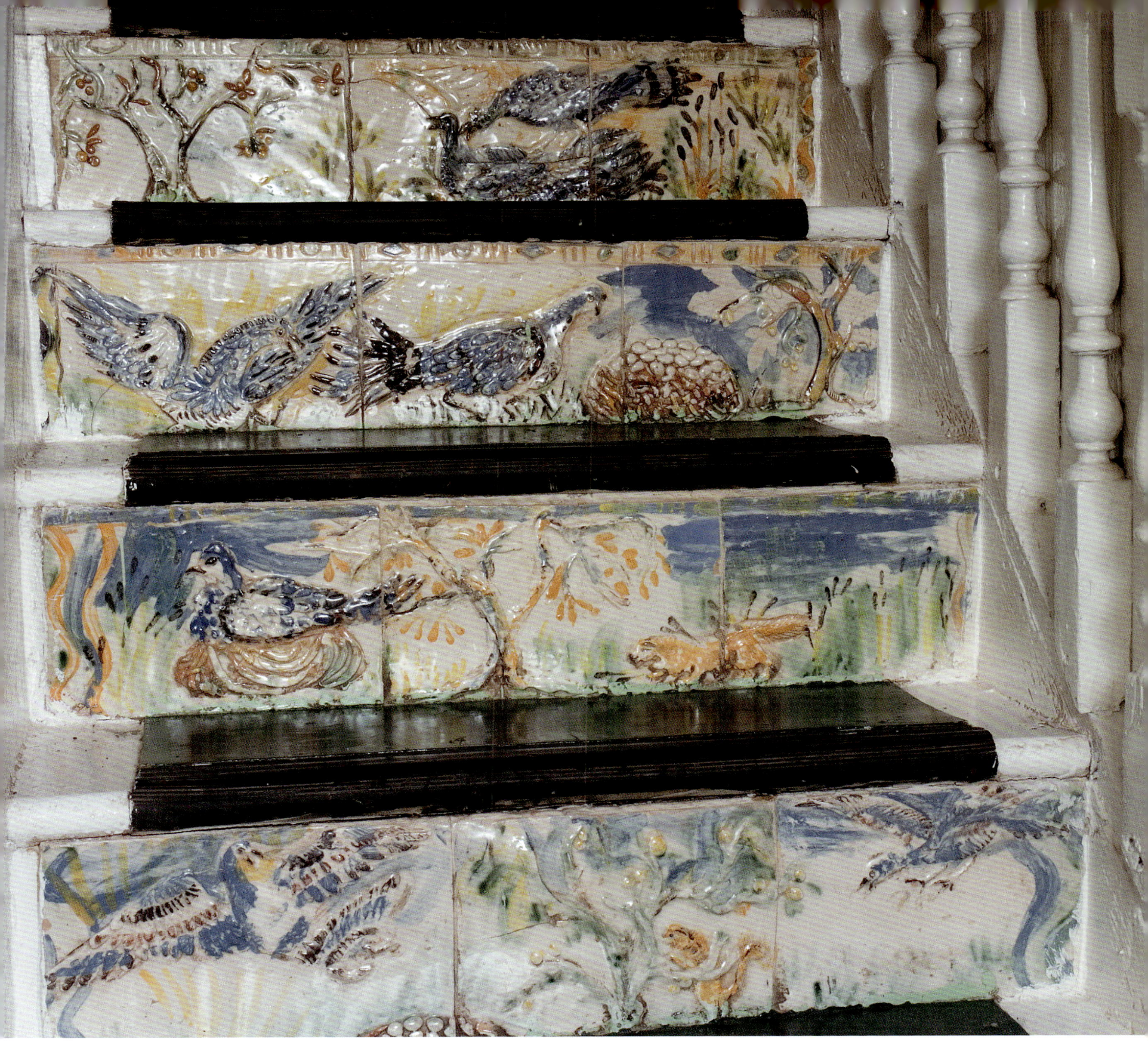

30 A Story of Two Doves, *late 1970s*
Relief tiles built into the staircase risers at
20 Church Row
Photo: Stephen Brayne

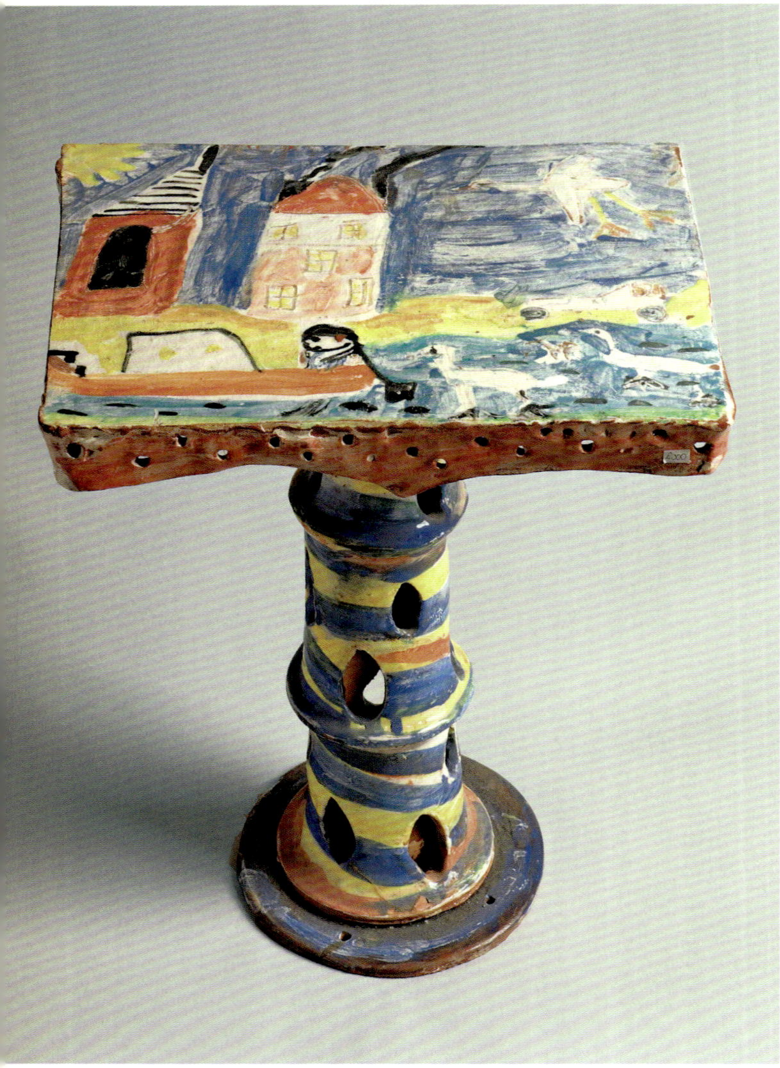

31 Occasional table decorated with a copy of a childhood painting by Philip Stokes, 1998
Slab-built top, thrown and pierced base
(height)46 x (table-top)27 x 34.5 cm
(18.1 x 10.6 x 13.9 in)
Collection: Philip Stokes
Photo: Stephen Brayne

membership of the Imago Group.[29] Among Adrian's friends, however, Ann's relations were closer with those who were active in the field of art. While Ann and Adrian were living at Hurtwood the two areas came together for them both, in acute form. Adrian was devoted both to the teaching of the psychoanalyst Melanie Klein and to the art of his friend William Coldstream (1908–87). In 1952 he commissioned Coldstream to paint Klein's portrait. There were a number of sittings, but while the work was still in progress Klein broke off the schedule and refused to sit further. In December 1952 she wrote to Adrian asking that the portrait (which he owned) be destroyed.[30] Adrian felt he had to concur, but asked Ann to destroy the picture for him. After agonising for days, he insisted on watching her do so. The debacle affords certain parallels with the destruction by Clementine Churchill, around the same time and also in the countryside south of London, of Graham Sutherland's commissioned portrait of her husband, Sir Winston, which had been presented to the sitter soon after its completion in 1954.[31]

The family's move to London in 1956 and Adrian's appointment in 1960 as a Trustee of the Tate Gallery greatly increased Ann's range of acquaintance in the art world.[32] It did so, too, through the annual pre-Christmas pottery sales she began to hold in the house in 1967, at first with her pupil and colleague Mary Day Lanier. Over the years Ann has shared her exhibition with changing artists, chiefly fellow potters but also painters, as well as with the jeweller Selima Guirey, daughter of Sylvia Guirey, a painter-friend. The hub, however, has always been the basement kitchen, where Ann's work is displayed and sold, and mulled wine dispensed. The setting is extraordinary, in that the space is barely adequate to accommodate the visitors, whose numbers have risen over the decades. Thus the relaxed party atmosphere is interfused with a subdued frenzy as buyers try to view the available pots (sometimes needing to distinguish them from the not-for-sale items in use by the family), to ascertain their prices (from labels stuck beneath each individual item) and then, holding their precious wares, to squeeze past other visitors in an effort to effect their purchases. The quest is complicated by the fact that owing to the limited space only some of the pots in a sale are displayed at any given moment or even, on a given day, necessarily at all (the sale usually taking place on two successive evenings). As pots are sold, Ann and her helpers mysteriously produce others from hidden sources. The whole experience therefore has something of the character of a lottery. A pot, once bought, has an added aura.

In late July 1972 Adrian suddenly fell ill with a brain tumour from which he would die less than five months later. Any form of writing now became

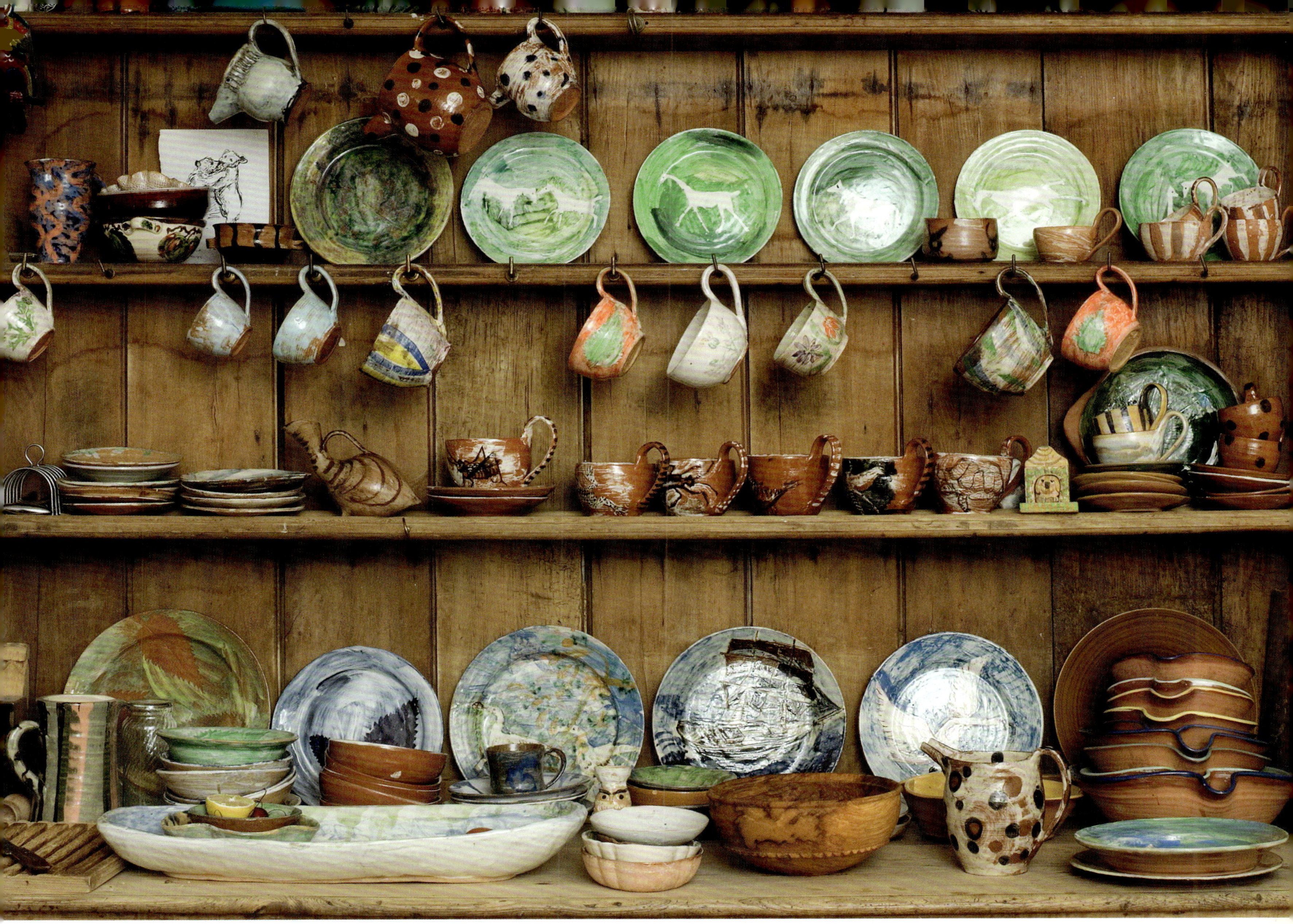

32 The dresser in the kitchen at Church Row, June 2008, showing four side plates, made in Spring 2008, depicting prehistoric White Horses
Photo: Stephen Brayne

extremely difficult. As if to compensate, his painting flowered in unexpected ways, yielding a final eleven canvases about which the philosopher Richard Wollheim (1923–2003) wrote: 'The hand and eye, so long the agents of the mind, turned incapacity into freedom, and the last paintings look like the earlier paintings burst into a final flame.'[33] Ann later recorded that, despite the gravity of the situation, from the end of September she and Adrian 'lived an enchanted 3 months and stretched time like a bit of elastic, and were aware of every second practically. I must have done 3 times as much in every 3 hours as I have normally done, and felt while shopping and waiting for the assistants to put the things in the bag that they were simply sleep-walking.'[34] The circumstances of their lives in those last months and of the creation of his last eleven paintings are recorded in vivid published accounts by Ann herself,[35] the novelist David Plante,[36] and Anne Crosby.[37] Some of the

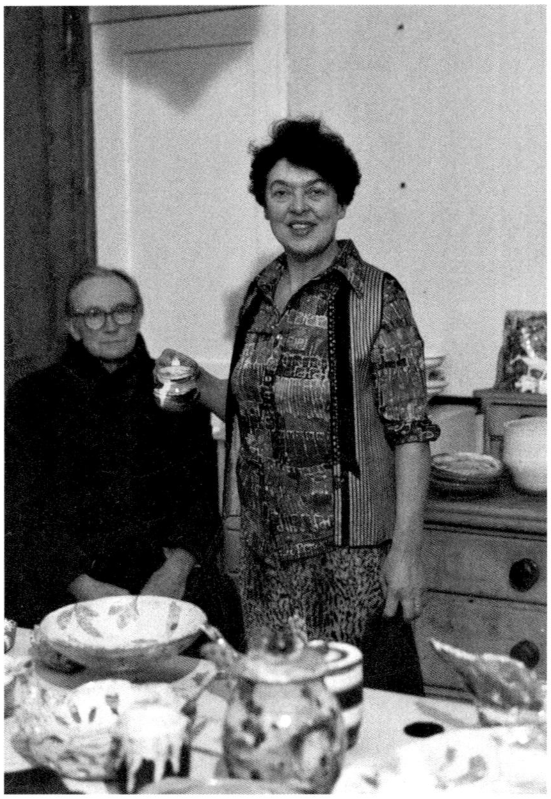

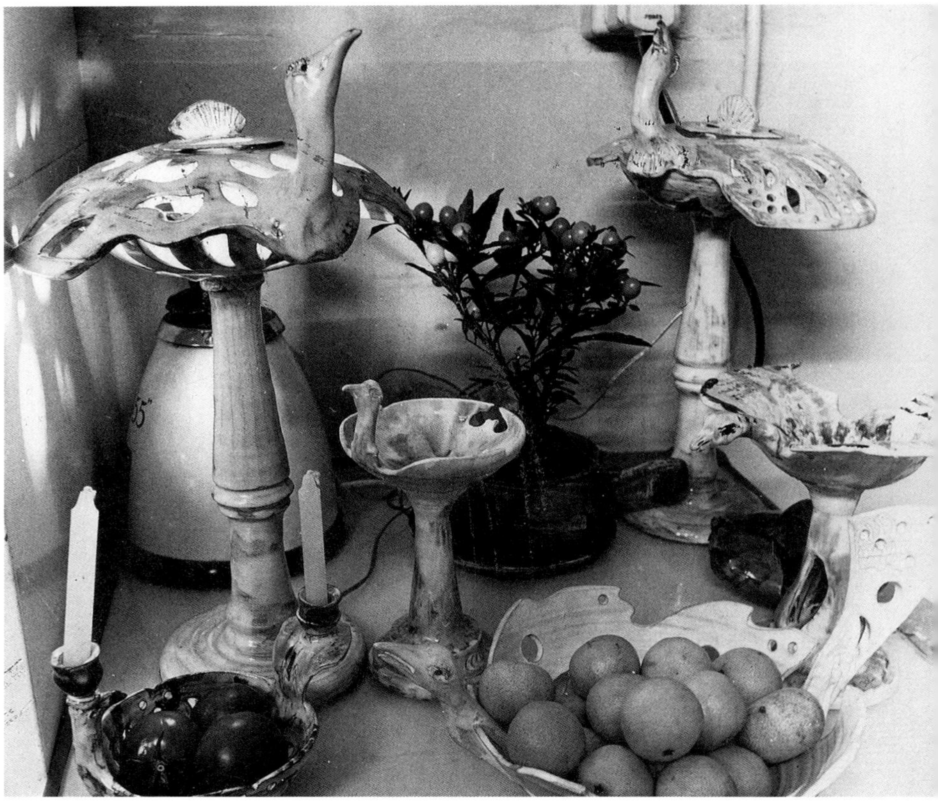

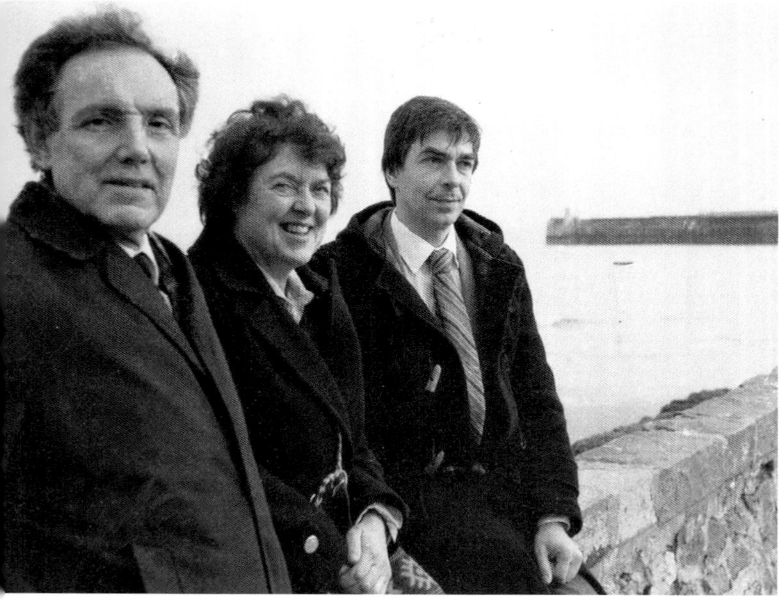

pictures were painted in Ann's pottery studio and, at the end, with assistance from Ann, at Adrian's direction. Adrian finished his last painting on 13th December 1972. By chance, Ann's pottery sale was in progress when, two days later, the final crisis began. Adrian died at home, later that evening.

Both Adrian's sons would work, directly or indirectly, in the visual arts. Telfer (Ann's nephew) has, for more than thirty years, been a notable exponent of Book Art, exhibiting in art museums in many countries. His works explore at once the structure of the book as an object, the artist's perception of the observed world (often concerned – with his own distinct vision – with Stokes/Mellis themes of light and nature) and the poetic use of language. Ann's son Philip occasioned Ann's entry into the world of pots,[38] and as an adult he has assisted her work in numerous ways. An electronics engineer, he began to explore his professional world when the Morse code Ann taught him (having learned it as a Wren) enabled him to explore radio communication. His electrical gifts, which eased some of the practical difficulties of Adrian's last illness, have been central to Ann's ability to make her sculpture kinetic and to emit sound and light.[39] He has administered her Christmas sales, transported her work annually from Italy back to England and helped spread awareness of her achievement (and Adrian's and Telfer's) through

far left:
33 Ann Stokes and Sir William Coldstream at the Christmas sale, 20 Church Row, 1979 or 1980
The artist's collection
Photographer unknown

left:
34 Christmas sale at Church Row, c.1968
The artist's collection
Photographer unknown

35 (left to right) Ian Angus, Ann Stokes Angus and Philip Stokes, Folkestone, 1980
Photo: Estate of Dennis Hawes

richly informative websites.[40]

In his last years Adrian had met the publisher Nikos Stangos who, with his partner David Plante, became close friends of Adrian and Ann. For several years David made pots with Ann. About this time he writes:

> Ann and I entered a Greek world, due mainly to Nikos and Adrian's love of Nikos, for my pots were based on Greek models, while she was reproducing Greek vases, cups, figures from the British Museum. She also did do huge pots, coiled. While we worked, we listened again and again to Greek music.[41] Adrian, up at the top of the house, would be painting, and come down for tea and examine the work Ann and I were up to our elbows in. This was Ann's Greek phase.[42] *(fig.37)*

David also observes:

> One of the changes that I felt in her after the death of Adrian was a pronounced extravagance of dress – sometimes like a Tartar, with wild colours dazzling in their incongruity – and an extravagance in ambitions: she asked if she should join a circus to be able to ride into the ring on the neck of an elephant. I think her pottery became more extravagant too.[43]

Freer to travel after 1972, Ann visited Italy with David Plante and on a sudden impulse she bought a flat that was for sale in Cortona. She had stayed in it only once when, in 1974, she met Ian Angus, who subsequently became Librarian at King's College, London University, before he and Ann married in 1976. The two had been introduced by Julia Strachey at her flat in Percy Street. Friends in common included Sonia Orwell,[44] with whom Ian had worked for years editing George Orwell's four-volume *Collected Essays, Journals and Letters* (1968). He also worked on the twenty-volume edition of Orwell's collected works, published in 1998. Ann has travelled abroad with Ian more than she ever did with Adrian. His passion for olives led to their exchanging the flat in Cortona for an early-nineteenth-century hunting lodge a short distance outside the town. Here, for half the year, Ian farms the estate's olives, while Ann works in the pottery they have built beside the house. Ann's second (and now longer) marriage has expanded her capacity to work, as Ian does the cooking and tends the garden. Their local friends in Italy are of many nationalities but one of the closest, Peter Bartlett (b.1953), is an English painter whose work speaks to Ann through the warmth of his

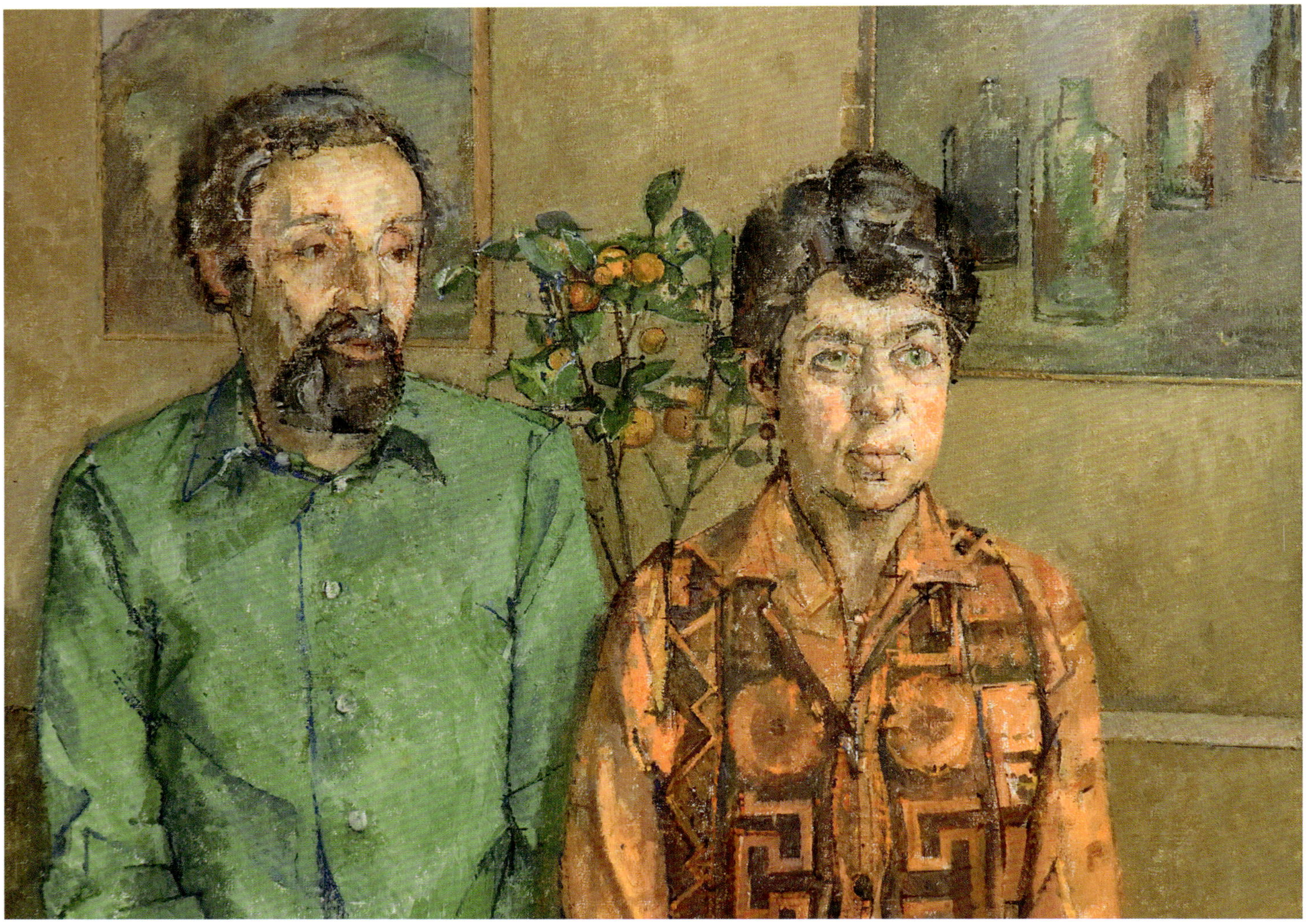

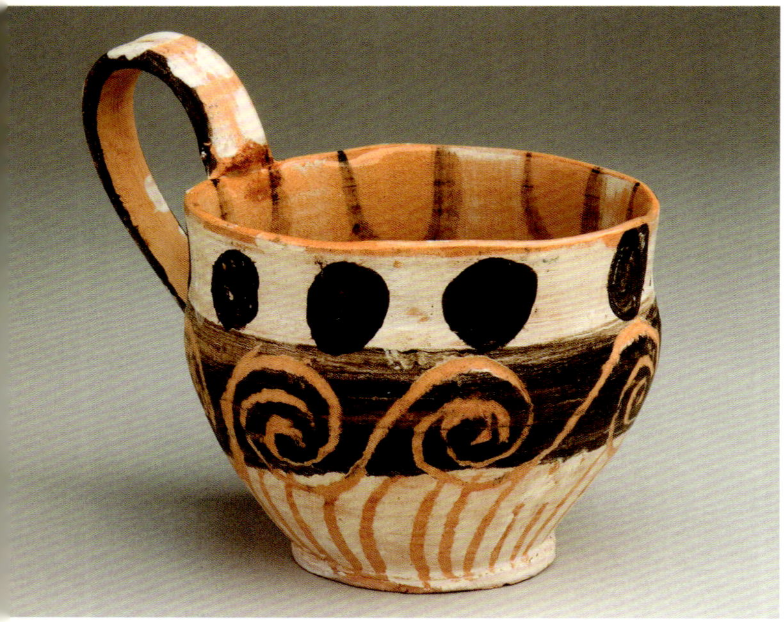

colours and his love of plant forms. For several years they have exhibited together in galleries in Cortona, Rome, Palermo and London, as well as at one of Ann's Christmas sales.

Soon after Adrian's death, William Coldstream began to spend much time in Ann's house in Hampstead, over the years using several of the rooms to paint in. Among his first works at Church Row was one of his most important nudes, *Seated Nude in Armchair (Willa Askew)* (1973–4), which is set in the drawing room.[45] Other works he painted in this room include *Orange Tree I* (1974–5),[46] and he painted other nudes and still lifes elsewhere in the house. Coldstream expressed amazement at Ann's happiness when potting. In 1979–80 he painted a double portrait of her and Ian seen side by side, with expressions of uncharacteristic solemnity, in front of a landscape and a still life by Adrian *(fig.36)*. The sitters learned only after Coldstream's death that he had wanted 'to get them to look like those Roman funereal

36 William Coldstream, Portrait of Ian and Ann Angus, *1979–80*
Oil on canvas
56.7 x 77 cm (22.3 x 30.3 in)
The artist's collection

37 Cup with Greek motifs, marked Σ1/78
9 x 12 cm (3.5 x 4.7 in)
Collection: David Plante
Photo: Stephen Brayne

reliefs, with staring eyes'.[47] All but one of the sittings were of them singly.[48]

Adrian had known the artist and writer Lawrence Gowing (1918–91), who succeeded Coldstream as Slade Professor in 1975, from their time at the Euston Road School. The two shared a predilection for painting green trees and exhibited simultaneously at Marlborough Fine Art in London in 1965 (Adrian writing the catalogue essay for Lawrence's exhibition). They maintained a continuous dialogue about art, not least of the Italian Renaissance. Gowing surprised Ann by suggesting that her work would sell well; only then did it occur to her that others might be interested in buying her wares.[49]

Another major writer on art and close friend of Adrian's was David Sylvester,[50] who ate off Ann's plates all the time. Indeed, in Ann's circle, one could (and can) go from house to house doing so. Sylvester was one of a number of friends who commissioned dinner services. His daughter Xanthe recalls how he always mixed English mustard by hand, using a mustard pot and spoons by Ann in glazed terracotta. No less enthusiastic, his wife Pamela has a candleholder, which is 'like things being born'. Ann states of Sylvester: 'Anything he said about pottery I regarded as gospel, so you could say he was a main influence.'[51] Ann bought from him a black Etruscan pot with unusually tall looped handles, raised gracefully on a small base, which became a kind of touchstone for her *(fig. 60)*. Displayed high over her bed in a niche, it commands the room. When Ann, David Sylvester and Lawrence Gowing's wife Jenny discovered they shared the same birthday (21st September), they all met annually for some years to celebrate, Ann bestowing pots as birthday gifts. Ann identifies Gowing, Sylvester and the painter and writer Andrew Forge as having been Adrian's closest friends. It was Forge who, soon after the move to Church Row, introduced Adrian and Ann to the painter Anne Buchanan (later the wife of the architect and designer Theo Crosby). She admired Ann's vitality, practicality and accessibility. As the mother, from 1964, of a disabled child,[52] she had a special sympathy for Ariadne and understood the strains that her care placed on both parents.

Richard Wollheim, another key advocate and analyst of Adrian's work, used to drive Ann once a week part of the way to the National Gallery, where she sought increased insight into pictures of importance to Adrian, notably Cézanne's late *Bathers* (which the Gallery bought in 1964). In 1962, Wollheim introduced Ann to Mary Day Lanier, a former sculpture student at the Slade, whom he would marry in 1969. In 1965, to Mary Day's surprise and initial scepticism, Ann suggested (at Wollheim's instigation) that she learn potting with her. She began doing so that December and rapidly progressed from simply decorating pots. She recalls:

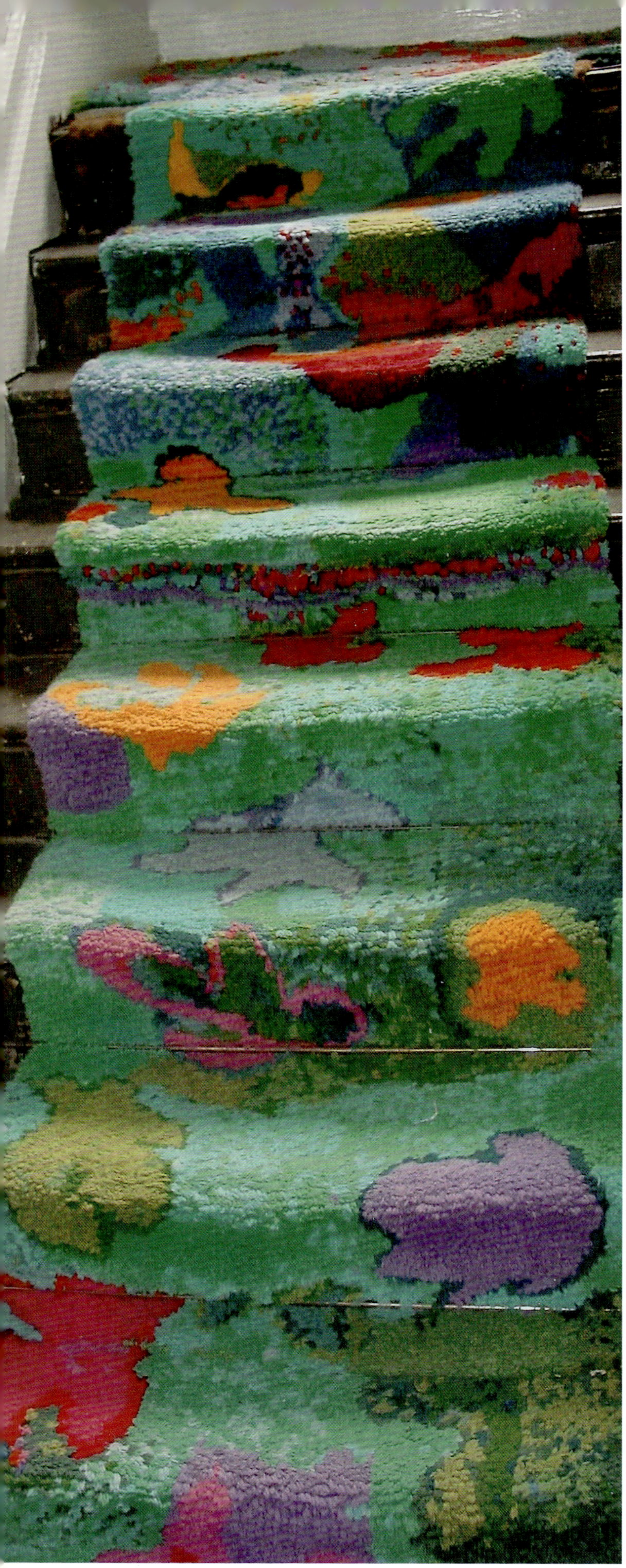

> I very soon got involved in the process of making the things, and the difficulties and pleasures of it all – and I never looked back. At first I went once a week; then soon I gave up doing anything else. Ann started me on throwing and turning, and I started working in her house every day. We had total, unending, unconditional, fun (at least on my side!) working and learning by experience together; I think she had only been learning it herself for a year or so![53] We seemed to have similar attitudes to everything – we went to museums together (still do) and reacted to things in the same way, learning all the time; we would draw, usually, but not always, different objects, wandering and drawing, separately together. There was (is) so much to talk about. We had both been professionally trained ballet dancers, adored horses and the same kinds of music (mostly), etc. ... As we developed, she became more and more of a painter, and I more and more of a thrower – I haven't decorated anything for decades! But very quickly we each made entirely our own things: the collaboration consisted of me using *her* house, *her* tools and *her* materials. But we shared space, which was much more than that – although going deep into ourselves to work, we were able to tune in and out with no effort, to suddenly talk about anything at all, if a talkable thought came up.[54]

A high point in Ann's experience of pots was when she and Mary Day visited the British Museum, having obtained permission personally to handle Cretan beaked jugs with 'breasts' and exceptional pourers. Ann's special love of Cretan pots combines with a sense of her own limitations as a thrower (compared with her gifted pupil) to explain her statement: 'I gave Day Greece and I kept Crete. I couldn't have both.'[55]

Some years before they first met Mary Day, Richard Wollheim had introduced Adrian and Ann to the historian James Joll and his partner, the painter and art historian John Golding. Ann describes John as 'one of my earliest fans and collectors'. His published appreciation of her work conveys its surprising diversity of mode and of inspiration,[56] as well as its freshness and spontaneity. Adrian identified as Ann's finest pot a monumental lidded bread-bin belonging to James and John. The powerfully ancient feel of its form is complemented by the grand, slow swirl of the spiral on its front face and by the 'ladder' of shallow crescents at the rear, which resembles a stack of bowls, yet is also like a tall container within the larger whole *(figs.58–9)*. Ann and John have collaborated, both in textiles and ceramics. John gave her some designs for birdbaths and for fountains *(fig.72)* and he also designed

38 Stair Carpet, 1976
Hooked wool, based on a design by John Golding
The artist's collection
Photo: Philip Stokes

two rugs and the imagery for two runs of carpet on the continuously eventful stairs at Church Row *(fig.38)*. For the rugs, Ann sought out high quality wool and made several of the dyes herself, before translating John's designs in adhesive coloured paper into the softer medium. She worked the stair carpet while watching television; where his design was in blue and white, Ann interpreted the flower-like shapes scattered throughout its length in a range of eye-catching rose-reds, creams, greens and yellows. Inspired, for John, by Matisse, these animate shapes float against a mottled blue ground and also, variously, recall Monet, Braque (whose birds are loved by Ann and John)[57],and even Andy Warhol.

Since 1956 many of Ann's friendships have been with other residents of Hampstead. Adrian used sometimes to paint from the same model with B.A.R. (Sam) Carter, who lived in the next street. Friends also included the painter Milein Cosman and her husband, the musicologist Hans Keller, and Nicolai Rubinstein and his wife, who lived opposite in Church Row. At the Warburg Institute, Rubinstein was a colleague of E.H. Gombrich, who discussed art with Adrian at length, to Ann's fascination. Gombrich's wife, Ilse, oversaw one of her pupils playing piano duets with Ann. Conscious of Ernst Gombrich's affection for rhinoceroses (and of his slight resemblance to the species), the Rubinsteins commissioned from Ann a ceramic rhino (Ann's first 'big' animal, though many larger would follow), which they presented to him. The author Nicholas Mosley, who at one time also lived opposite, became a copious collector of Ann's work. Adrian's exhibitions led to Ann's friendship with Elfriede Fischer, wife of Harry Fischer, co-founder of Marlborough Fine Art, who bought many pots, as later did Harry's son Wolfgang and his wife Jutta. Catherine Lampert (later an art historian and Director of the Whitechapel Art Gallery) met Ann when she was living in Redington Road, close to Church Row. A student for one year of history and philosophy at University College, and art history at the Slade School, she began attending Mohammed Abdulla's ceramics classes at Camden Arts Centre in October 1966. Her encounters there with Ann and with Mary Day Lanier led to friendship with them and the Stokes family, and to Catherine watching Ann working, and on a few occasions assisting her in the studio.

Also living nearby was the painter Derek Hill (1916–2000), whom Ann had known since he called on Adrian in Ascona, but got to know well only after Adrian's death. He was a frequent buyer of her pots, both to keep and to give,[58] and especially loved (in John Craxton's words) the undogmatic, constantly changing character of her art. Ann was one of a group that toured Turkey under Derek's leadership, and she and Ian were his guests at

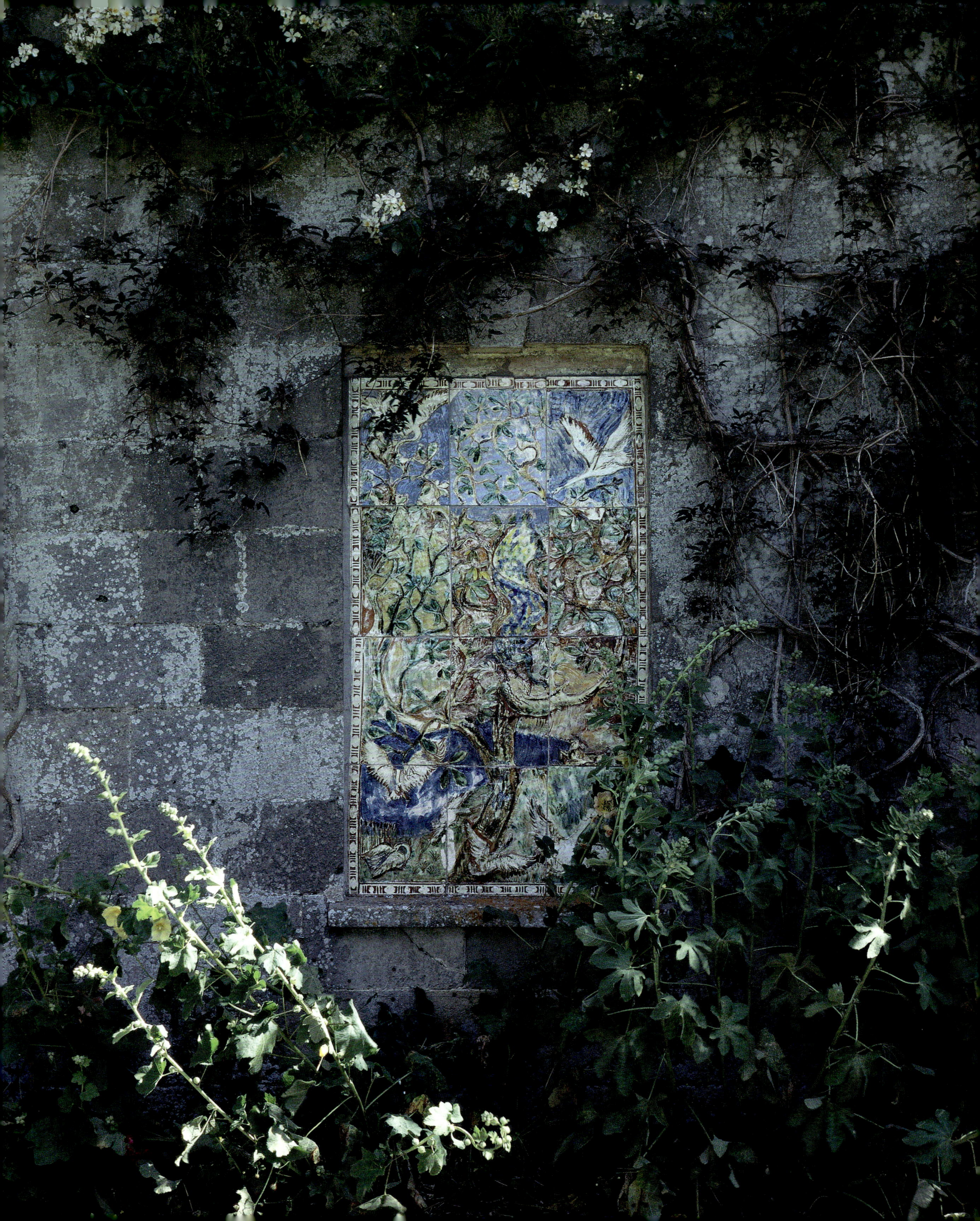

39 Tile panel, 1977, set in a blind window, Long Crichel, Wimborne, Dorset
Collection: Rose Jackson Campbell
Photo: Maisie Hill

40 Tile panel (detail), 1977, set in a blind window, Long Crichel, Wimborne, Dorset
Collection: Rose Jackson Campbell
Photo: Maisie Hill

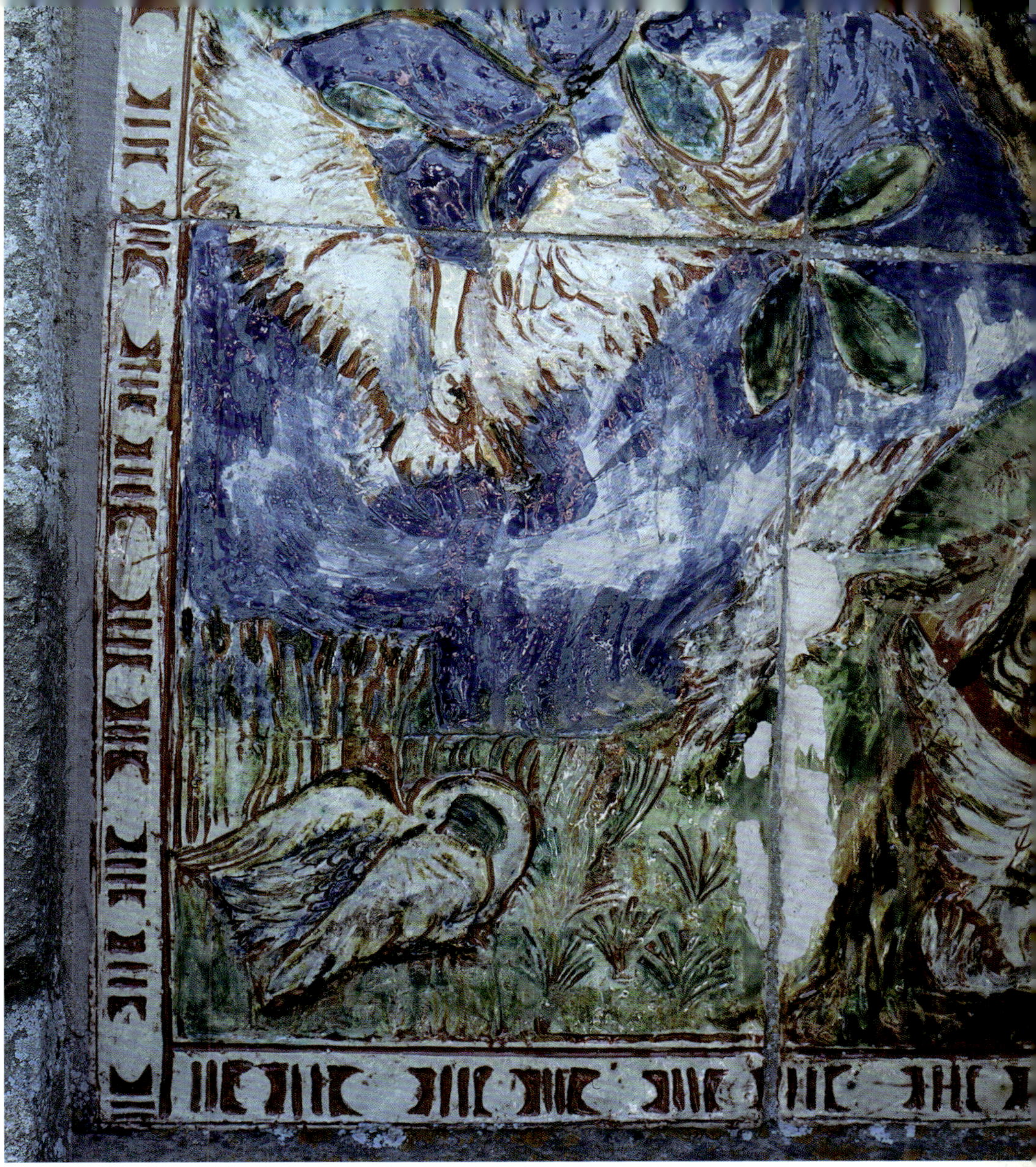

the house in Donegal that he presented to the Irish State. Through Derek, Ann was commissioned to create a ceramic panel representing birds and trees, to go over an external dummy window at Long Crichel House, near Wimborne, Dorset, where he stayed *(figs 39–40)*. The house's small community was originally established by Eardley Knollys, Eddy Sackville-West and Desmond Shawe-Taylor, and later continued by Raymond Mortimer, Dadie Rylands and Patrick Trevor-Roper. The panel's installation by Ann and Philip was witnessed by Michael Tippett.[59] It was with Derek that the Prince of Wales visited Ann and Ian, and Ann's pottery, in Italy in May 1991.

Another Hampstead friend is the painter John Craxton, whose family is famously musical and whose remarkable paintings include the Tate's *Pastoral for P.W.* (1948), 'a celebration of the power of music',[60] in which a young flautist (an emblematic self-portrait) enthrals goats. The landscape setting is one of Craxton's first overwhelmed responses to Greece. For

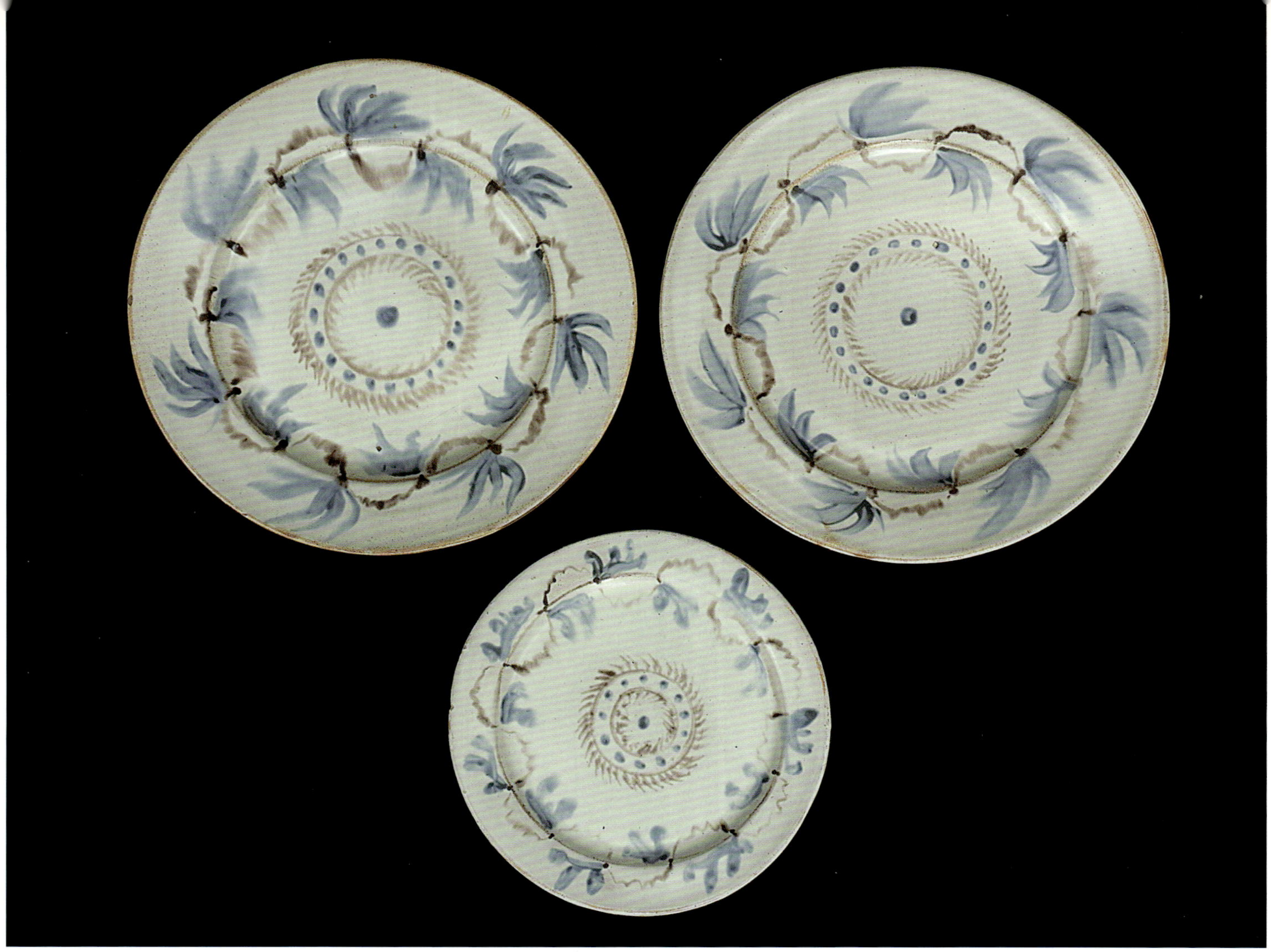

41 Dinner and side plates by Ann Stokes (throwing) and John Craxton (decoration), 1974, all marked Σ 7/74 (dinner plates above, left to right) 27.6 cm (10.9 in), 27.4 (10.8 in); (side plate below) 17.4 cm (6.9 in)
Collection: John Craxton
Photo: Stephen Brayne

many decades he has had a home in Crete where, in Derek Hill's words, he is 'indistinguishable from many of the citizens in the town of his adoption'.[61] When Nikos Stangos and David Plante introduced them, a shared love of Greece in general and of Crete and its pots in particular provided instant rapport with Ann, as did the preoccupation in both artists' work with animals, trees, birds and decorative elaboration. John recalls that when they met, many of Ann's works were strongly anthropomorphic and that a big influence on her was very early Cretan pots. Her spouts reminded Craxton of the special significance attached in ancient Cretan culture to the act of pouring and the arcs made by liquid as it was poured. Around 1974 Ann made many plates, bowls and dishes, which John decorated in his own distinct manner *(fig.41)*. Some of his designs were inspired by English delftware while, in general, the pottery John decorated displays a delicate yet animated touch, used to create all-over effects that are at once lively and controlled. None of it is representational, John observing: 'I don't want to eat off a picture, as with some of Picasso's plates. A plate should enhance the food and not work against it.' John inspired a concept for a fountain

Ann made for her garden, using shell shapes that protrude parallel to the ground.[62]

Not long after Ann embarked on her career as a potter, her work was discovered by John Fowler (1906–77), who in the last four decades of his life was an outstanding British decorator. For nearly two decades he bought Ann's pots, both for his own use and to give to friends. On the face of it, this is a surprising connection. Fowler is widely recognised as the creator of the 'English Country House' style of interior decoration. As Martin Wood has recounted:

> [the style] ... though it is based upon elements of the traditional look of English country houses ... owes its development primarily to the quite extraordinary talents of one man: John Fowler ... In collaboration with Nancy Lancaster, his style and tastes gradually came to dominate English interior decoration. John was, as Deborah, Duchess of Devonshire, observed, 'the Prince of Decorators, a scholar with a wonderful memory for whole rooms and the smallest of details, and the best appreciator of beautiful places and things I have ever known'.[63]

Asked where all the pots she made in the 1950s and 60s now are, Ann responds: 'It was nearly all done for John Fowler.'[64] His appreciative letters, written to Ann,[65] show that they covered a range of utensils for both practical and decorative use at The Hunting Lodge, near Odiham, Hampshire, his house of 1740 in the Gothick style (now the property of the National Trust) – including large terracotta pots to John Fowler's design, for use outdoors *(fig.42)*. While the style of his own home's interior design was recognisably consistent with that in his grand formal commissions, it was on a more modest scale (which, however, was itself enormously influential through published photographs). John Fowler's assistants Imogen Taylor and Donald Church and the head designer at Colefax and Fowler, George Oakes, all recall Fowler's love of Ann's work.[66] Ann states of him:

> He was a very nice person and I liked him very much. I used to go to his shop[67] ... and ask for [him] and the 'Sloane Rangers' used to look askance at my home-made trousers and bright coloured shirt etc. and wondered if I should be told 'No'; then John himself would call me to go upstairs to his room and I gave the girls a grin!'[68]

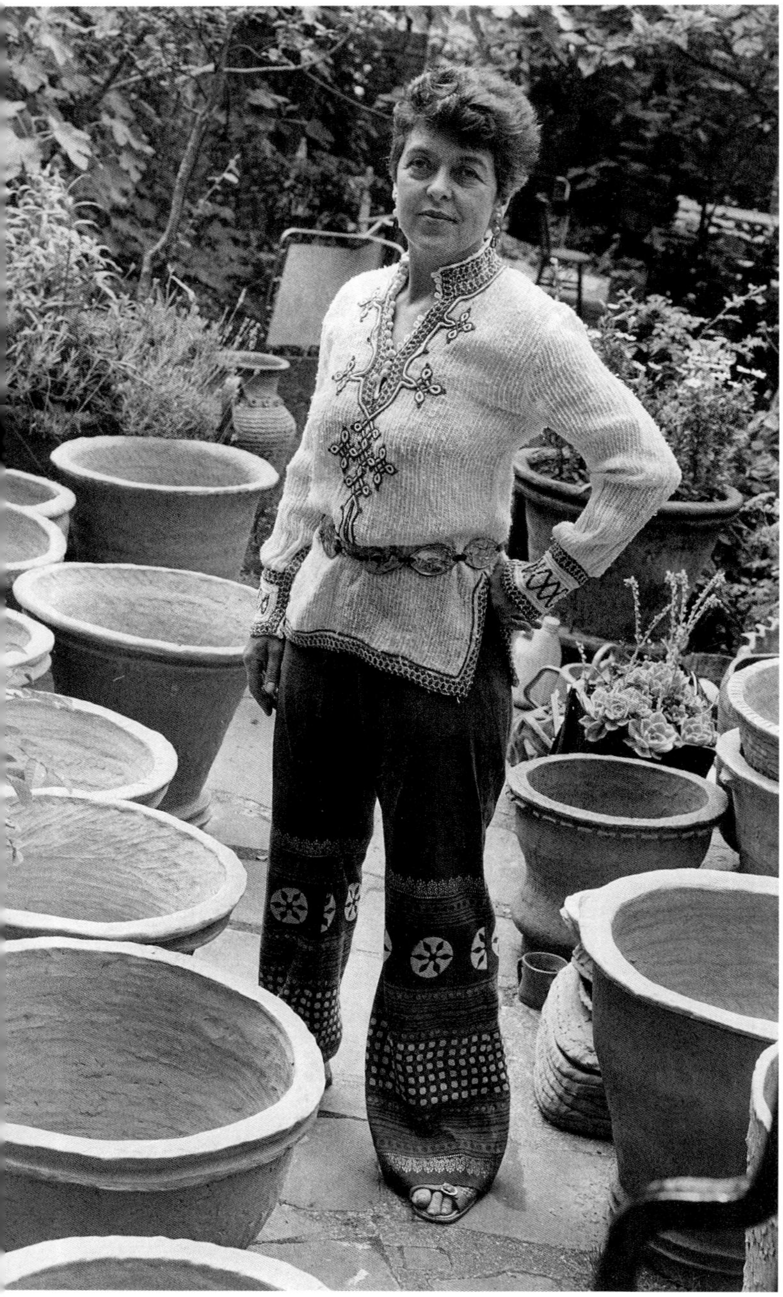

42 Ann Stokes with her coiled garden pots for John Fowler, 1976, taken for Angela Neustatter, 'Cheap Chic', The Guardian, *3 August 1976*
Photo: Kenneth Saunders

Ann's pots were also bought by Fowler's friend, the historian John Cornforth, with whom he collaborated on *English Decoration in the Eighteenth Century* (1974).[69]

In the 1970s Ann became friends with a succession of younger artists. In 1974 she briefly tutored the sculptor Barry Flanagan at Church Row. This was a meeting of two free spirits. Modern in their abruptness and in their open declaration of the artist's hand, yet also archaic in feel, the Flanagan pots that were the subject of his exhibition at the gallery Art & Project, Amsterdam, from November to December 1975, are not discordant with Ann's work, though obviously distinct. A further affinity lay in the two artists' interest in Etruscan ceramic art, which Flanagan drew in Cortona.[70] The two also share an interest in hares. When Ann met Flanagan she had already made them in ceramic, while the best-known aspect of his work of recent decades is his often massive hares in bronze. Two other artists, the weaver and ceramic sculptor Jos Tilson and her husband, the painter Joe Tilson, are neighbours in the Cortona area. For Jos Tilson:

> Weaving is/was another part of her life as it is in mine and I too work on clay in our various kitchens. So she is a great example of how women can integrate art into their more prosaic lives without it being a problem ... I always quote Gracia Deledda, who spent two hours a day writing, the rest being mother, wife and housewife, and then winning the Nobel prize!'[71]

The ceramic sculptor Stephenie Bergman,[72] who first met Ann in July 1976, worked in the Church Row studio for two years. She found Ann and Ian 'incredibly social, in a domestic way' and accompanied them to Paris to see the Grand Palais exhibitions *Cézanne, les dernières années* in 1978 and *Chardin* in 1979. Stephenie writes:

> I immediately warmed to the fact that everything was made to be used and not just to be looked at. There were some very funny things in the garden which were invented for holding canes for tomatoes (I think) and I immediately connected with those artless but specific objects ... because they used clay as a building material that no other material could replace. I also loved her sculptures. There was one I particularly loved of Ian in the bathtub under the stairs. Something to do with describing interior spaces. In general it was the natural explosion of ideas from looking at things – of being passionate about

animals etc. and turning these passions into subject matter for decoration or construction. I loved the inventiveness of the mirror frames, which were excuses for creating her fantasy worlds.

One would think that I would have started doing figurative things, but my work stayed stoically different. It was geometric and angular. However I did make things that were to be used and the function of an object became a path to invention. Ann always used to look at my work and say how neat it was. I think we both had lots of ideas and just did them and felt united in a passion for making things with clay.

I'd go round there once or twice a week ... We were both very supportive of each other's work. I would arrive and set myself up in one end of the studio and she'd work, often on the wheel at the other end. I knew exactly what I wanted to make. There were technical things I wanted to learn, but that's all. That's probably why we got on – there's nothing worse than having someone round who imitates you.[73]

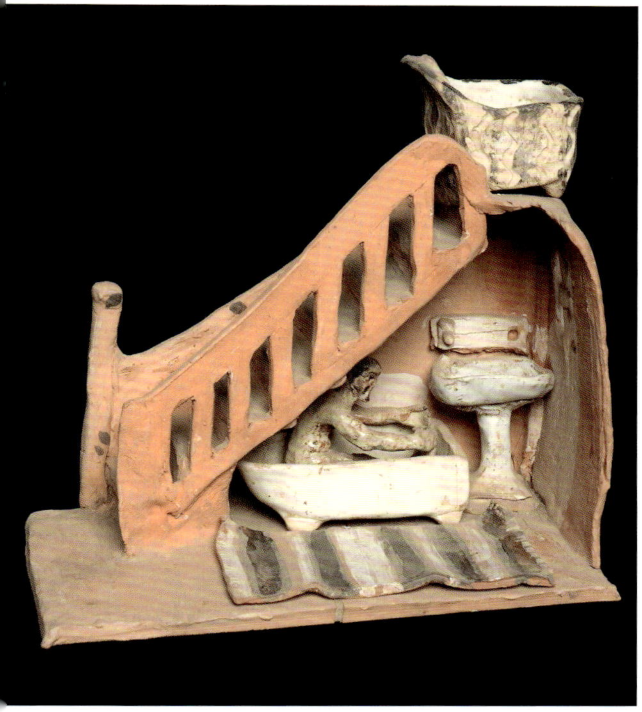

43 Ian in the Bath, *1977*
Modelled earthenware, plastic tubing
25 x 24.5 x 14.5 cm (9.8 x 9.6 x 5.7 in)
The artist's collection
Photo: Stephen Brayne

In an informative article on Stephenie's life and work,[74] Marie-France Boyer quotes her memory of the intellectual restriction of her thinking when a student, but 'When she met ... Ann Stokes ... she discovered three-dimensional work ... Working with Ann she learned about the freedom of using clay and, in addition, the rudiments of a life philosophy, consisting of work and imagination, independence of spirit and joie de vivre.'[75]

Ann met the art dealer Nigel Greenwood in 1966 when he sold her the first work of art she ever bought, at an exhibition of John Golding's work at the Axiom Gallery in London. Nigel became a devotee of Ann's work and her Christmas sales. In the Hayward Annual exhibition of 1985, *A Journey through Contemporary Art with Nigel Greenwood*, the display in the area given to Ann consisted of a large number of plates lent by Ann and collectors of her work. Other artists selected by Greenwood included Henry Moore, Francis Bacon, Fred Williams, Bridget Riley, Rita Donagh, Richard Long, Tony Cragg and Stephen Cox. In that context the inclusion of a potter and of work intended for domestic use was a striking and unusual mark of recognition. In his catalogue essay on Ann, Nigel wrote: 'If you ask her to make a fish tureen she will produce one which uncannily anticipates your choice of fish and writes the recipe. You can see the sparkle in Ann's eye willing you to approve of your mutual transaction.' He described how 'from year to year you have no idea where her capricious nature will guide you next ... There

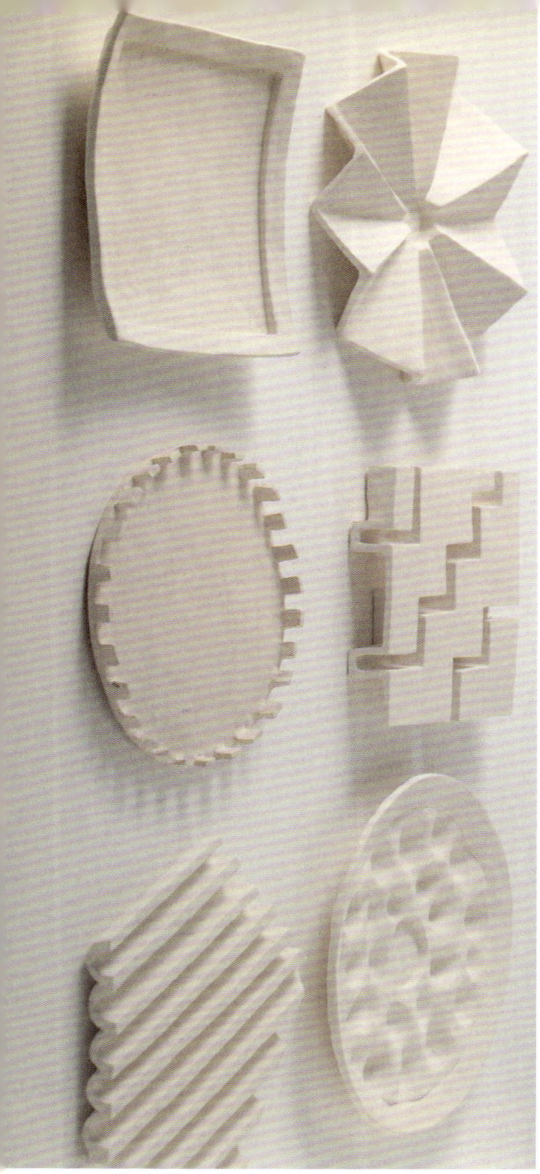

44 Stephenie Bergman, Forty Plates *(detail), 1990-2*
Unglazed earthenware
Collection: Stephenie Bergman
Photo: David Cripps

is a constant flow of ideas, one touching off another', and writing of the art world in general he noted that, 'In a profession where reputations are hard to win and fiercely guarded, [Ann's] openness and goodwill can sometimes be unnerving, or perhaps I should say disarming.'

In 1995 Ann acquired a dealer, Rebecca Hossack, whose London galleries include a library and study centre on Aboriginal artists and their work. Intuitively much closer to the Aboriginal art than to the British art the gallery represents, Ann admires the directness of Aboriginal mark making, the frequent subtlety of its designs and the importance attached to stories. The Aboriginal artist to whose work she feels closest is Jimmy Pike (1938–2002), whose drawing of a cat (which she watched him make at Rebecca's gallery) inspired her to transcribe the image onto two plates, 'as it was a very full-of-feeling cat'.[76] Ann delighted Jimmy by recreating in three dimensions one of the images he had made of Phar Lap, a thoroughbred gelding who is a national icon in his native New Zealand and in Australia.[77] She transmuted him into a ceramic rocking horse, ridden by a detachable ceramic cat based on one of Jimmy's drawings. For Ann, as a would-be bareback rider in the circus, this may also have been a form of wish-fulfilment. The special eyes Ann gave Phar Lap are inspired by Jimmy's drawings, but also remind one of Picasso.

Examples of Ann's Phar Lap rockers are displayed in Rebecca Hossack's remarkable house near her gallery, in the company of much Aboriginal art but also of ceramic work by Ann in many forms. This includes two of the three sequences of tiles painted by Ann for Rebecca, which address themes or tell particular stories. The natural world is at the heart of Ann's imagery and in Rebecca's house she pays tribute to Australian fauna with kitchen tiles depicting numbats teasing wombats. Another sequence of tiles in the house, for Rebecca's Cumbrian parents-in-law, depicts the flora of northwest England. But commissioning Ann can have unpredictable results and its beautiful centrepiece is an abundant fig tree. In Ann's 2007 exhibition,[78] a plantation of tree sculptures with hanging fruit, birds and birdsong was the setting for a life-size crocodile, an enormous peacock, a flock of smaller birds, each on its own shelf, and other singing birds in cages.

When Ann visited the prehistoric cave paintings at Lascaux in southwest France, she observed images that used the Earth's own materials to communicate the felt life of animals. They made her feel that she, too, was (in her own words) 'rather primitive'. She has repeatedly visited the Villa Giulia in Rome, to study its exceptional collection of Etruscan ceramic art. For over fifty years she has loved, alike, the detailed verisimilitude of Thomas

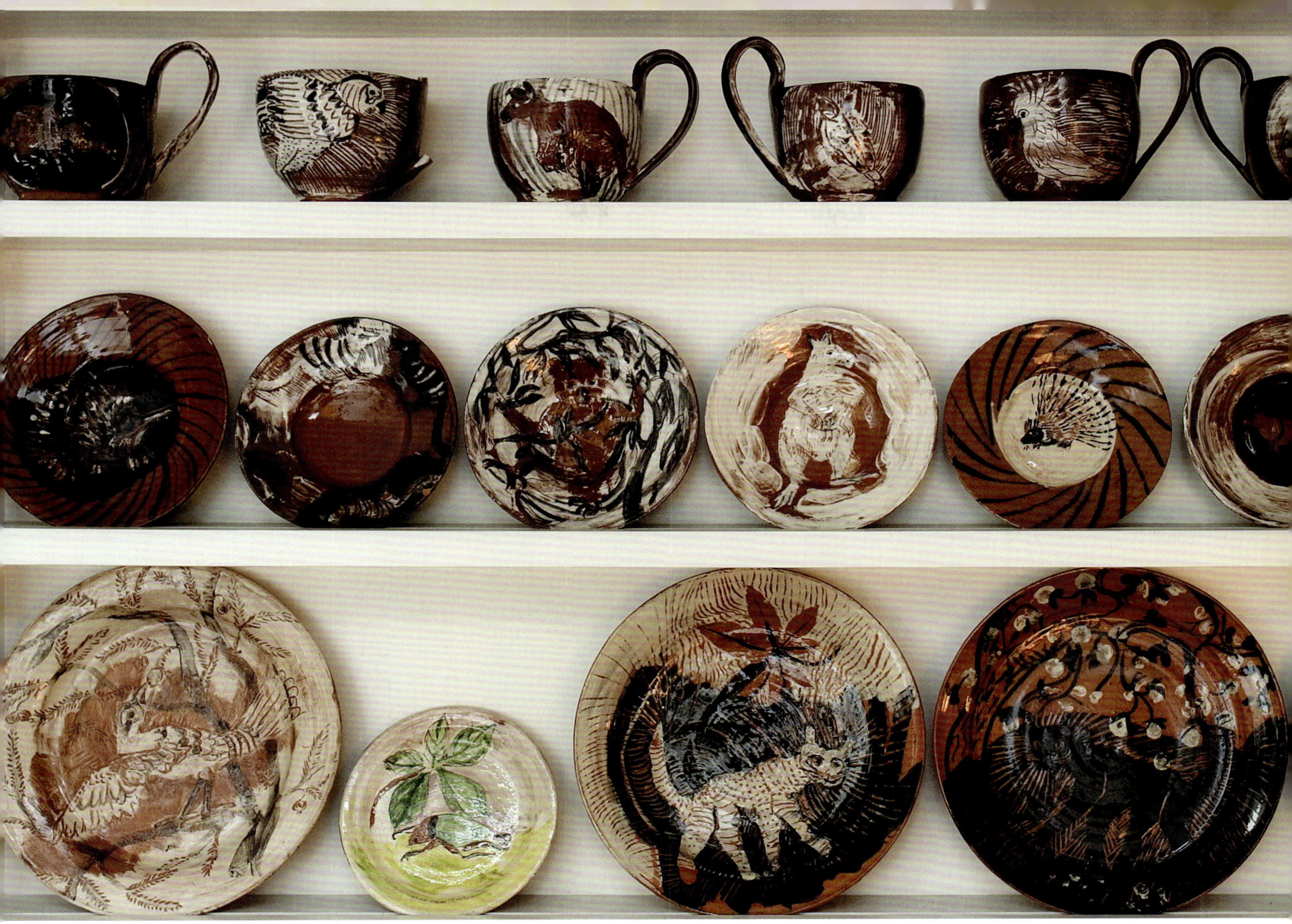

45 Dresser with plates and cups inspired by Australian fauna and the drawings of Jimmy Pike, 1999–2000
Collection: Rebecca Hossack
Photo: Stephen Brayne

Bewick's wood engravings and the painterly fluidity of the paintings of Monet. She speaks often, with delight, of the art of Bonnard, especially his landscapes. Her work also has affinities with that of six artists, all associated with St Ives, three of whom she knew well.

The work of Alfred Wallis was a lively presence in Adrian's English homes, from Carbis Bay onwards. *Schooner under the Moon* and *Voyage to Labrador* (both *c.*1935–6), which Adrian bought from the artist and presented to the Tate in 1958, embody Ann's love of boats and ships and relate to her own simplicity, directness and natural gift for fitting an image to its support. She considers that Wallis' work may have influenced her own. Ann did not know Winifred Nicholson, but admires the way her work exults in colour, light, space and the natural world. In the work of Ben Nicholson, which Ann watched being made, there is a natural grace, a correspondence between the poise and balance of hand and eye as he described a drawn arc and that of the ballet dancer, also using her body. In the St Ives years, when Ann was closest to Nicholson, she was training as a ballet dancer most days of the week. This, too, was when she was closest to Naum Gabo,[79] the balance and elegance of whose work she admired. 'Gabo told me "always look at nature before building anything" and he turned a cabbage leaf over and pointed out the construction.'[80] Ann's tree sculptures of the present day are made with this recommendation in mind. The art of Peter Lanyon, another St Ives friend, shares Ann's delight in graceful aerial flight and relation to the materials of the earth. Finally, the late gouaches of Roger Hilton, whom Ann barely knew however, struck a chord with her when she considered them in 2008. Direct, irreverent, radiantly coloured, celebratory, close aesthetically to Alfred Wallis, abounding in boats and populated by animals and birds, they have many points in common with her work, which she feels is tentative by comparison. Counterbalancing all these references to the art of St Ives, Ann volunteers a strong admiration for the work of Balthus and a love of the mystery of the story that each of his figure paintings tells.

A puzzle for admirers of Ann's work is her simultaneous closeness and distance from the Bloomsbury group and its ceramics. Ann had never heard of Roger Fry's Omega Workshops (1913–19) until she visited Charleston, the Sussex home of Vanessa Bell and Duncan Grant (two of the Omega's leading artists) in 1999, when she herself had a solo exhibition there. She had therefore been unaware till then of Omega ceramics, which ranged from distinctively substantial monochrome plates and vessels to plates and pots decorated (with unusual gestural freedom) with designs that were sometimes abstract and sometimes featured figures or boats.

From early in her career as a potter Ann did know of the ceramic art of Quentin Bell, son of Vanessa Bell and the art writer Clive Bell. In 1939 Quentin established his own pottery at Charleston and he, his mother and Duncan Grant decorated the ceramic forms he made. While all three continued the Bloomsbury aesthetic of pure decoration, Quentin also developed, on pots and in sculpture, a lively and often improbable figurative imagery. This drew strongly on the Antique as well as eighteenth- and nineteenth-century precedents, and introduced a narrative dimension that was variously mysterious or humorous, but always intriguing. Ann knew Quentin who, with his wife Olivier, visited the Stokeses at Hurtwood and sent Christmas cards. One of these, reproducing a tiered ceramic sculpture by Quentin, inspired Ann to embark on making fountains.

Apart from this link, neither Quentin nor Ann influenced the other, but each admired the other's work. Writing that 'Quentin was rather impressed by her things', Olivier Bell adds, however, that this was 'because they were quite different from his, he thought'.[81] Even when purely decorative, the work of each does, indeed, have its own distinct atmosphere and touch, though the contrast is especially marked in those of Quentin's sculptures that are eighteenth or nineteenth century in feel. Nevertheless, an affinity is undeniable, in terms of decorative exuberance and unorthodox spirit. This is perhaps most marked in both artists' abundant production of jugs, bowls and plates for the everyday use to which Ann attaches such importance, as did Quentin. Quentin also created beautiful ceramic light-shades peppered with small apertures through which electric light shines. Independently, Ann has used electric light inside penetrated ceramics, to striking effect.

While greatly influenced by older figures in their immediate circle, whose aesthetic was established prior to the beginning of their own work, Quentin and Ann also reacted against them. Quentin (with his strong narrative impulse) attached less importance than his parents to the idea of the primacy of formal values in art.[82] Ann reacted against the trenchancy with which Adrian – who was twenty years her senior – had preferred 'carving' to 'modelling' in art, in any genre. Her delight in the aesthetic she first experienced at Charleston in 1999 also showed independence; for Adrian, like his contemporaries Ben Nicholson and Barbara Hepworth, had marked reservations about Bloomsbury and its art.[83]

In much of the art that means most to Ann, discipline and control are important qualities. Examples include ancient Cretan pots, the constructions of Gabo and the work of Lucie Rie (1902–95), a controlled artist *par excellence*. Ann observes, revealingly: ' ... the potter I most admire is and was Lucie Rie.'[84] Despite their allegedly 'riotous' character, the decorations in the interiors at Charleston are also characterised by control. Though it is a key quality of Ann's own work, with her it goes hand in hand with a sense of the open and unconstrained. A distinction that can be felt between the mutually sympathetic work of Quentin Bell and of Ann is that he was an art historian, at home in studio and study alike, while she is a child of nature. The subjects of his ceramic sculptures include Ann-like circus scenes and ballet dancers,[85] but where one senses his delight in the colour and the theatricality of these motifs one feels that Ann in some sense *is* her remarkable trees, animals, darting fish and unhampered birds.

From an early age Ann knew by instinct what she liked. She slept in a tree, rode, sailed in the family sloop off the Scottish coast, loved animals and birds and creating their images in three dimensions, and yearned both

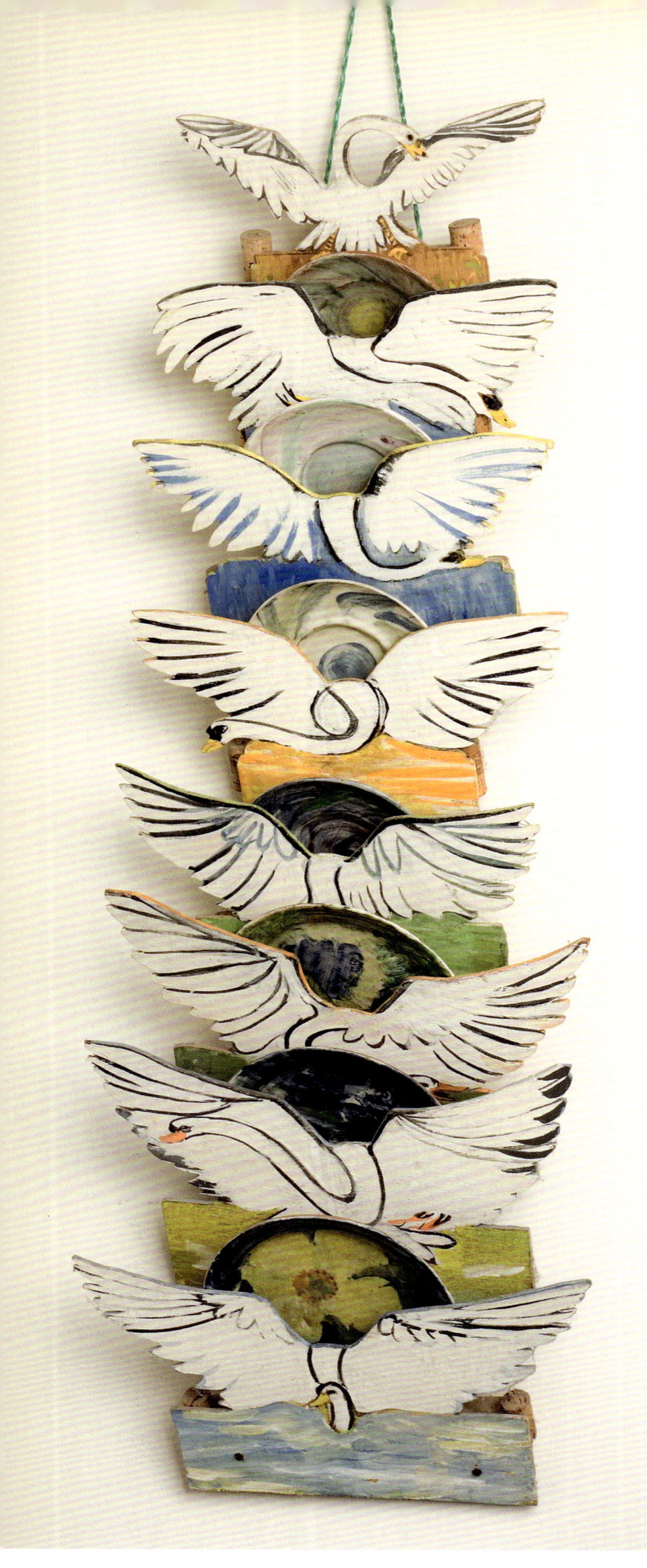

to have the experience of graceful movement and to convey it to others. In her mature work she carries through all these concerns. As Mary Day Wollheim puts it, Ann's pottery 'became ever more representational (for want of a better word), in different kinds of ways. She uses things she loves, clay, leaves, pictures of animals – and seems to convey more and more easily the soul, or breath, of the animal, or the leaf or the tree habitat ... She just seems naturally to live all the time with the things she loves.'[86]

46 Plate and saucepan-lid rack
Painted wood
98 x 30 cm (38.9 x 11.8 in)
Collection: Jennifer Anderson
Photo: Stephen Brayne

Notes

1. Ann Stokes, handwritten notes, September 2007.
2. Though Wallis did not die until 1942, and Adrian supported him and paid for his funeral and grave (with tiles by Bernard Leach), Ann did not meet him.
3. Ann Stokes interviewed by Linda Sandino, 2003, *Crafts Lives*, British Library Sound Archive, catalogue reference C960/13.
4. Handwritten notes, September 2007. Ann adds (email to the author, 4 May 2008): 'I always liked Leach's pots but thought potting was a dreadfully sedentary occupation; compared with dancing most other occupations are!!'
5. *Tonight the Ballet*, Faber & Faber, London, 1934, p.22.
6. ibid p.53.
7. Email to the author, 3 August 2007.
8. Margaret Mellis (Mrs David Mellis) to Adrian Stokes, 29 November 1946, Tate Archive, TGA 8816.245.
9. In a document in the Tate Archive (TGA 8816.251) Adrian adds that he was the 'guilty' party, any infidelity on Margaret's part having taken place only after he had left her.

On Margaret's subsequent career, see *Margaret Mellis: A Life in Colour*, exh.cat., Sainsbury Centre for Visual Arts, University of East Anglia, Norwich, July–August 2008 (84 pages) and the associated DVD (by forty and a half productions), of the same title and date.

The careers of the two sisters developed independently. Margaret's collages of the early 1940s, in coloured papers and found materials, had marked a sharp break with her paintings of the late 1930s. They had affinities both with the formal relations in Nicholson's painting and with the constructions of Gabo and of Cornish-born Peter Lanyon. Lanyon had painted from the motif in Cornwall with Adrian and studied briefly at the Euston Road School. He, too, had been influenced by Nicholson and Gabo and was to buy Little Parc Owles in the mid 1950s, living there until his death in 1964. In due course, Margaret resumed painting. Her succulent, partially abstracted images of boats, cliffs and still lifes, of the 1950s, led eventually to geometric abstraction, then finally to many years' use of driftwood to make striking, coloured constructions that are at once abstract and semi-representational. Gathered on the beach near her home in Suffolk, the planes and struts of wood she chose were almost always ready-painted. This use of found materials became concurrent with her still life drawings on the opened-up inner surfaces of envelopes, which provided unpredictable colour-printed grounds for her vigorous image making and engagement with the subject.

10. Curiously, Ann's paternal grandmother had succeeded her sister as her grandfather's wife (after his first wife died).
11. These must have included Leonard Cottrell, *The Anvil of Civilisation*, 1957 ('I don't know what this has to do with pottery, but *everything* has to do with pottery') and A.D. Lacy, *Greek Pottery in the Bronze Age*, Methuen, London, 1967 ('the only Age I like').
12. Diary of Greek cruise in 1970, Tate Archive, TGA 8816.246.
13. Email to the author, 3 August 2007.
14. Ann Stokes, handwritten notes, September 2007.

15. Handwritten on Marlborough Fine Art paper, undated (1965 or 1968), Tate Archive, TGA 8816.238.
16. Email to the author, 26 July 2008.
17. Undated letter, apparently from Scotland and written in anticipation of travel to Switzerland, Tate Archive, TGA 8816.245.
18. In 'Memories of Adrian Stokes – presented by Eric Rhode', *The Listener*, 13 December 1973, p.815.
19. As well as some objects by Bernard Leach.
20. In the catalogue of the Adrian Stokes exhibition, Marlborough Fine Art, London, January 1965.
21. 'It was the very last performance of the Bertram Mills Circus and the nearest thing to joining a circus that I managed to pull off. A friend of my uncle ... said they had seen an old Circus girl riding the horse standing up! My uncle guessed it was me!!' – email to the author, 4 May 2008.
22. Anne Buchanan Crosby, original English text, published in translation as 'Souvenir de Stokes', *Les Cahiers du Musée national d'art moderne*, Paris, Autumn 1988, pp 9–12. This provides a valuable context for Ann's early career.
23. Ann Stokes in conversation with the author, 17 September 2007.
24. This is not literally correct. See, for example, Ann's sculpture of Ian in the bath *(fig.43)*, and other such works.
25. Ann Stokes in a recent conversation with the author.
26. Ann Stokes in conversation with the author, 17 September 2007.
27. Ann Stokes interviewed by Linda Sandino, 2003, *Crafts Lives*, op.cit.
28. ibid.
29. A memorandum by J.O. Wisdom, apparently of 1973, regretting the group's dissolution, is in the Tate Archive (TGA 8816.244). This states that it was founded around 1957 by Adrian, Robert Still, Roger Money-Kyrle and himself and that, 'It was mainly composed of those interested in psychoanalysis who had either had a long analysis or were practitioners. Its concern [was] with applications of psychoanalysis to things of the intellect, society or culture generally ... It met once a month in private houses ... It had a constant membership of twenty ... '
30. An account of this problematic affair is given in Lyndsey Stonebridge, 'Portrait of an Analyst: Adrian Stokes and Melanie Klein', Stephen Bann (ed.), *The Coral Mind: Adrian Stokes's Engagement with Architecture, Art History, Criticism, and Psychoanalysis*, Pennsylvania State University Press, 2007, pp 105–21.
31. There are key differences too, however. Churchill's portrait was completed and preparatory works survive.
32. In Adrian's early years as a Tate Trustee, Coldstream was a fellow board member. When Adrian signed one of the Gallery's annual reports for the last time Colin Anderson, a Hampstead neighbour, had just retired as Chairman. Adrian had very close personal connections with a further four of his nine fellow trustees: Herbert Read, Barbara Hepworth and his devotees David Sylvester and Andrew Forge. Another trustee, Robert Sainsbury, who would soon become Chairman, had been a friend in Berkshire and was so in London. Lawrence Gowing (another devotee of Adrian's) had also been a fellow trustee, before becoming Deputy Director and Keeper of the British Collection during Adrian's latter years on the board. Tate issues would frequently be discussed over meals at Church Row. It was during supper at

Adrian and Ann's in 1964 that Lawrence received the telephone call telling him he had been unsuccessful in the competition to be Director of the Tate. The successful candidate, Norman Reid, had been an art student in Edinburgh with Margaret Mellis.

33. 'Adrian Stokes', *The Listener*, 28 December 1972, p.900.

34. Letter to Lawrence Gowing, 23 December 1972, Tate Archive, TGA 8816.246.

35. In *The Tate Gallery Illustrated Catalogue of Acquisitions 1982–84*, 1986, pp 330–6, which lists relevant additional published texts.

36. ibid.

37. 'Souvenir de Stokes', *Les Cahiers du Musée national d'art moderne*, op.cit. pp 9–12.

38. See Tanya Harrod, p.72

39. He designs, builds and installs the sound systems for individual works (including recordings of real birds and animals), designs and constructs the hidden templates upon which Ann's larger multi-part works are hung, installs electronic clock mechanisms and maintains and repairs the functions of Ann's potting apparatus.

40. See www.adrianstokes.com (with links to the website of Telfer's imprint *Weproductions*) and www.annstokes.com. Ann Stokes' second husband Ian Angus and nephew Telfer Stokes act together as literary trustees of the Adrian Stokes estate.

41. Ann learned to play the mandolin. Following the Greek Colonels' coup of April 1967 she made pots to be sold in aid of the wives of prisoners of the new regime. One was bought by the composer Mikis Theodorakis, whom she much admired.

42. Email to the author, 25 April 2008. In the home of Nikos Stangos and David Plante, the affinity between Ann's art and its ancient roots is reinforced strongly by the Mediterranean food served on abundant ceramics by her.

43. Email to the author, 2 April 2008.

44. Adrian had known Sonia since the Euston Road days. Ann first met her when she attended one of her earliest sales, at which Sonia bought work, and would later commission more.

45. Adrian had commissioned Coldstream's *Seated Nude (Miss Mond)* (1952–3), which the Tate bought from Ann in 1983. For some years, it was paired in Adrian and Ann's drawing room with Coldstream's equally monumental *Seated Nude (Monica Hoyer)* (1959–60), which Adrian bought in 1960. The sitter, whom Coldstream married in 1961, became a friend of Ann's. Ann taught pottery to their daughter Frankie.

46. Ann sold it to the Tate in 1991.

47. Reported by Bruce Laughton in his *William Coldstream*, Yale University Press, New Haven and London, 2004, p.291.

48. The models for a nearly contemporaneous picture, *Two Nudes (Double Nude)*, 1978–9 (not painted at Church Row) never posed together. The standing figure is Ann's niece and sometime lodger and pupil Charlotte Mellis, whose lively account of being painted by Coldstream is in Laughton, ibid pp 293–5.

49. Annabel Freyberg, 'Natural creativity takes wing', *The Independent*, 11 September 1998. After Adrian's death Lawrence Gowing edited and introduced *The Critical Writings of Adrian Stokes*, 3 vols., Thames & Hudson, London, 1978.

50. Sylvester bequeathed a major group of Adrian Stokes paintings to the Tate Gallery.

51. Email to the author, 2 March 2008.

52. Anne Crosby, *Matthew*, Philadelphia, 2006, is a moving and informative account of the short life of the Crosbys' son, who had Down's syndrome.

53. In fact, it had already been about eight years.

54. Email to the author, 20 April 2008.

55. Ann Stokes in conversation with the author, 17 September 2007.

56. In *Ann Stokes: A Retrospective*, exh.cat., Rebecca Hossack Gallery, London, September–October 1998.

57. On another occasion, John made large informal sketches of birds at Ann's request, derived partly from Braque's late birds and partly from drawings made, when a student, in a Mexican aviary.

58. He commissioned two plates from Ann to give to Queen Elizabeth the Queen Mother; she told him they reminded her of Monet.

59. Music is a continuous strand in these connections. It was a shared pleasure of Ann and Adrian (as well as being vital in dance); it was the professional field of Ilse Gombrich, Hans Keller, Sackville-West, Shawe-Taylor and, of course, Tippett; and instrumentalists performing are one of Milein Cosman's leading subjects, as well as being one of Derek Hill's.

60. John Craxton, quoted in the entry on this picture in *The Tate Gallery Illustrated Catalogue of Acquisitions 1982–84*, 1986, pp 134–6.

61. Quoted in Grey Gowrie, *Derek Hill: An Appreciation*, Quartet/Salem House, London & New York, 1987, p.133, beside a portrait of Craxton by Hill.

62. 'When Phil fixed up the water supply it was a moment of high excitement!' – email to the author, 4 May 2008. John Golding drew Ann a similar design for a shell fountain *(fig.72)*.

63. Martin Wood, *John Fowler: Prince of Decorators*, Frances Lincoln, London, 2007, p.240.

64. Letter to the author, 26 June 2008.

65. 'I was very flattered when he said my leaf plates were much better than the new Wedgwood ones!' – letter from Ann to the author, 26 June 2008.

66. 'He admired her original approach to design and colour.' – letter from Donald Church to the author, 17 June 2008. 'I was always seeing bits of pottery by Ann arriving for John.' – Imogen Taylor in conversation with the author, 24 June 2008.

67. Colefax and Fowler, 39 Brook Street, London W1.

68. Email to the author, 26 June 2008. After John Fowler's death Ann made very large ceramic lamp bases for Colefax and Fowler, as well as a set of large ashtrays for a hospital.

69. Barrie & Jenkins, London, 1974.

70. The British Council's catalogue for Flanagan's one-man exhibition at the British Pavilion, Venice Biennale, June–September 1982, pp 84–5, reproduces an installation photograph of the Art & Project exhibition, *Coil, Pinch and Squeeze Pots*, and drawings by Flanagan after examples of Etruscan art. Further examples of undated coil, pinch and squeeze pots are reproduced in larger size, p.70.

71. The Italian novelist Grazia Deledda (1871–1936) was awarded the Nobel Prize in Literature in 1926. Jos Tilson's reference to Ann weaving must be to her working carpets and rugs.

72. As explained in Stephenie Bergman's website, www.stepheniebergman.com: 'After working with sewn canvases she turned to clay as her medium ... She uses clay as a construction material, rolled out in slabs, cut into geometric shapes, re-assembled, fired and glazed ... Playing with a notion of function, she re-invents familiar objects. She gets ideas by making things for houses and gardens.'

73. Notes sent in reply to questions by the author, 4 March 2008.

74. 'Recess Positive', *The World of Interiors*, March 2006, pp 152–7.

75. Among many other artists who became friends of Ann's, R.B. Kitaj (an admirer of Adrian's writing) gave her his print *How to Read*, 1969, which reproduces the cover of Ezra Pound's publication of that title. Eduardo Paolozzi (whom she met through her student, the painter Marcia Blakenham) gave her a small sculpture. Mark Rothko visited Church Row. When Ann and Adrian were guests of John and Vera Russell to meet the Rothkos, Ann had no compunction in leaving the dinner table early, to tend her kiln.

76. Ann also made for Jimmy Pike a ceramic jigsaw based on one of his drawings of a cat.

77. As a boy, Jimmy had been given his English-language name after Phar Lap's jockey, Jim Pike.

78. Shared with the painter John Dewe Mathews, the bright hues of whose watercolours of birds, landscape and olive trees formed a sense of continuity with Ann's trees and ceramics.

79. It is interesting that both Ann's work and that of her sister Margaret Mellis should have been influenced significantly by that of Ben Nicholson, Gabo and Alfred Wallis. Though this was with very different results, the role of intuition is fundamental in both sisters' work.

80. Notes written by Ann for the author, 22 September 2007.

81. Letter to the author, 8 April 2008, dictated by Olivier Bell to her son Julian. In the same letter, Olivier explained that only when (well before her 1999 exhibition at Charleston) Ann exhibited at the nearby but unconnected Charleston Manor, did she and Quentin realise that Ann was a potter.

82. In 'Some Thoughts on Quentin Bell: A Man of Many Arts', *The Charleston Magazine*, issue 21, Spring/Summer 2000, pp 20–21, Quentin's son Julian recalls how his father ignored the demands of Modernism and drew cheerfully on the art of any past period. Ann's approach, too, could be so described.

83. These are exemplified amusingly in an anecdote of Lawrence Gowing's about an encounter at Adrian's easel at the Euston Road School in the late 1930s between Adrian and Vanessa Bell. It appears in a text published in the catalogue of Adrian's retrospective at the Serpentine Gallery, London, June–July 1982, pp 20–21.

84. Email to the author, 2 March 2008.

85. See Norbert Lynton, Noel Annan, Simon Watney and David Alan Mellor, *Quentin Bell: A Man of Many Arts*, The Charleston Trust, 1999.

86. Email to the author, 20 April 2008.

THREE

Smooth and Rough: The Ceramics in Context

Tanya Harrod

' … a productive confusion within the normal hierarchy of cultural prestige.'
Thomas Crow, *Modern Art in the Common Culture*, Yale University Press, 1996, p.33

Ann Stokes became a ceramicist in 1957 when she took her young son Philip to Saturday morning pottery lessons at the Well Walk Pottery in Hampstead, north London. This being Hampstead her tutor, Chris, was the son of David Magarshack, the Russian biographer and translator of Dostoyevsky. On one of these visits Philip, then aged nine, was perturbed to find fragments of glass in his lump of clay and he decided pottery was not for him. Ann Stokes, on the other hand, had experienced that odd *coup de foudre* familiar from biographies of studio potters. She fell in love with the material and with the possibilities of clay. Initially, it was not easy for her to pursue her new interest. Her husband, Adrian Stokes, was twenty years older and a figure of great, if maverick distinction in the art world. And hers was, in many ways, an old-fashioned marriage in which she had practical responsibility for the household and for the care of their two children.

Here we need to digress briefly into areas covered more fully in Richard Morphet's essay. Born Ann Mellis in 1922, her background was cultivated, Scottish and musical (there was a small family orchestra) and the house was filled with oriental rugs brought back by her father from the Middle East, while her mother embroidered with silks acquired during the years she and her husband had spent as missionaries in China. Her sister Margaret Mellis went to Edinburgh College of Art, won travelling scholarships and during 1935–7 held a fellowship at Edinburgh. In 1936, in Paris, Margaret met Adrian Stokes, already an admired writer on aesthetics (wealthy enough to

47 Horned owl, c.2000
Modelled
(height) 26 cm (10.2 in)
Collection: Hilary and John Spurling
Photo: Stephen Brayne

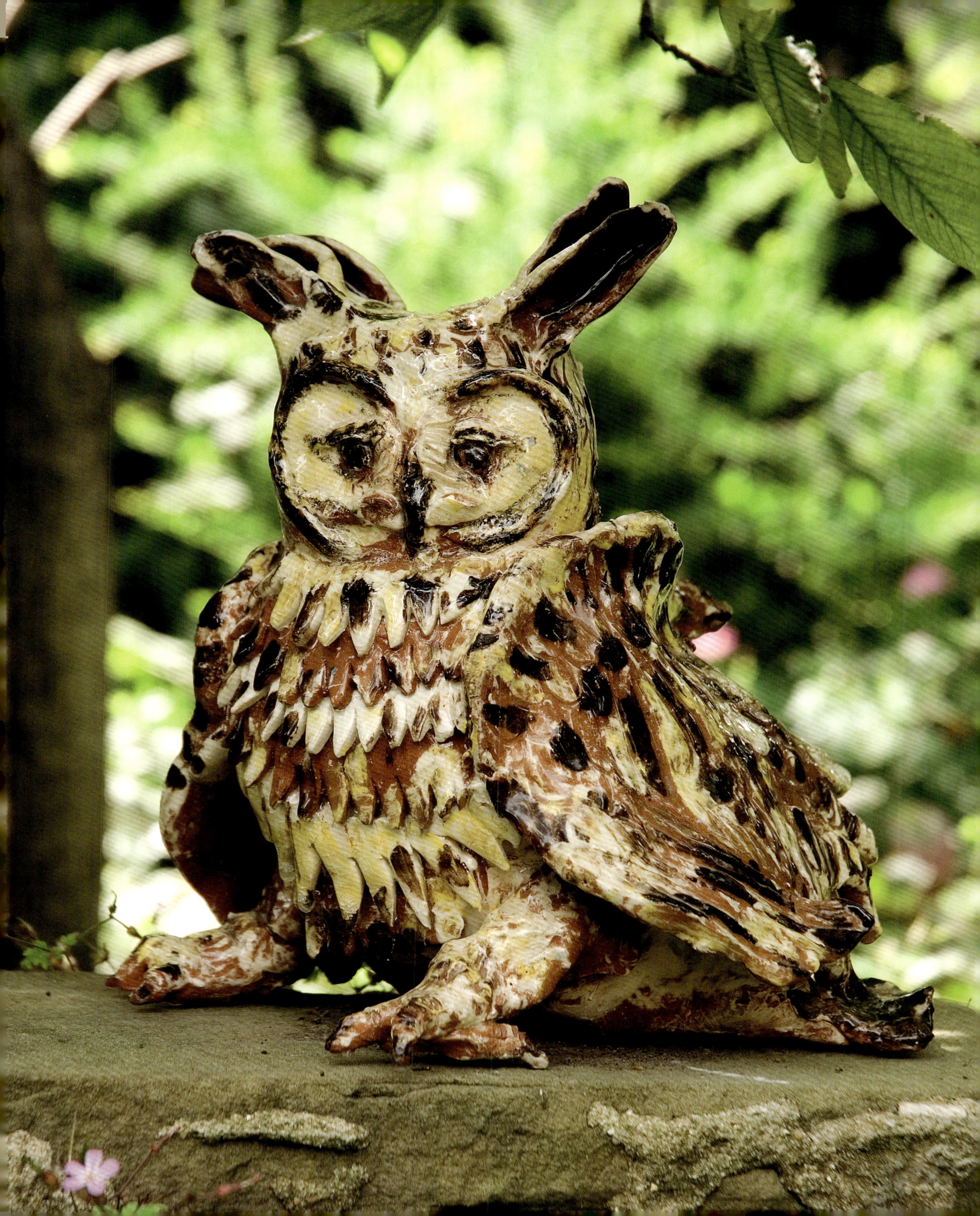

think as he pleased, like Ruskin before him), who had just taken up painting. This encounter led Margaret to move to London and join the independent studio of painting and drawing set up by the artists Graham Bell, William Coldstream, Victor Pasmore and Claude Rogers that came to be known as the Euston Road School. Margaret Mellis married Adrian Stokes in 1938.

Thus Ann's sister was involved with a circle of slightly older British avant-garde painters. (As a woman, Margaret's commitment to her art proved problematic, possibly undermining her marriage to Adrian Stokes.) Ann, meanwhile, had left her Scottish boarding school aged seventeen in 1940. Her immediate role was as helpmeet and, briefly, nanny before and after the birth of Margaret and Adrian's son Telfer. The household was just outside St Ives, at Carbis Bay, and there she was to encounter a remarkable cluster of artists (including Ben Nicholson, Barbara Hepworth and Naum Gabo). Strongly encouraged by Adrian, she cherished the hope that she might become a dancer. She had wanted to dance ever since she saw the film *Top Hat* aged thirteen and became still more eager after reading Stokes' vivid and highly original short book *Tonight the Ballet* (1934). But despite promise as a classical ballerina, an injured knee put paid to that ambition. She was to marry Adrian Stokes in 1947. Thus we have two sisters, the elder committed, professional and highly qualified, the younger appearing to settle for a life of domesticity, putting her husband's work before her own. That these sisters married the same man makes the dyadic tension more pointed and haunting.

But this is not to say that during those years Ann Stokes was not a creative person in her own right – like many an angel in the house she was always busy making. If we say that she was making 'things' rather than 'art' we would be merely endorsing a commonplace perception. At the age of eight Ann had been given a fretsaw by her brothers and when in 1951 she and her husband moved to Hurtwood House near Guildford in Surrey, she had a room of her own in which she made clothes as well as toys and trees out of balsa and plywood. While her sister would have been scanning the journals for exhibition reviews, Ann became a regular reader of *Hobbies Weekly*, a pamphlet-like publication aimed at fretsaw enthusiasts and the 'Home Craftsman'. She seems to have consciously chosen housework over heroics.[1] Meanwhile, predictably, she was the model in her husband's paintings, becoming the subject matter of art rather than its producer. But to see her situation as stereotypically marginalised and secondary hardly assists in opening up her private world – and in any case it is not an interpretation she would favour or recognise. Quietly, she set out to create her own creative context with the home as its staging ground, a place of 'sweet ordering, arrangement and decision'.[2]

What survives from those years – balsa wood toys, articles and covers contributed to *Hobbies Weekly (fig.22)* and some furniture, including the prototype for a long line of saucepan-lid or plate racks in the form of a descending array of boldly painted cut-out horses, birds or bats *(fig.46)* – suggests an aesthetic that comes close to popular or traditional art as defined by figures like Enid Marx or Barbara Jones. Enid Marx saw in the Staffordshire flat-backs, ships' figureheads, barge decorations and fair-ground horses which she collected, 'forthrightness, gaiety, delight in bright colours and a sense of well-balanced design'.[3] Ann Stokes' painted wood-work certainly could hold its own in that kind of company. She had already, in the 1950s, begun her work of productive confusion – between high and low or popular art, between professional and amateur, between culture and nature, and public and private.[4] These are binaries that have helped sustain and define the art world and currently, of course, many artists challenge them by knowingly invoking domesticity and DIY – we only have to think of the work of Tracey Emin, Mike Kelley and Grayson Perry. But to see Ann Stokes as a strategist in this vein would be a misunderstanding and would mask a much stranger progression.

Ann Stokes was certainly not the first to take up pottery on a part-time basis in her mid thirties. Usually the results are conservative in nature. Making ceramics is so technically demanding that most beginners settle for some quiet bowls and vases, clothed with glazes that fit the clay body. Indeed the technology can take over, glaze recipes proliferate, throwing skills are honed and stylistic nods are made in the direction of acknowledged leaders in the creative ceramic field – from Bernard Leach to Lucie Rie to Edmund de Waal. But when Ann Stokes turned to clay something very different occurred. For her, skill was only a means to an end and although she admired in particular the work of Lucie Rie, Stokes has always displayed a marked lack of deference towards (or maybe a lack of interest in) the world of studio pottery. Instead, as a potter she continued to make 'things'. The manipulative qualities of clay have allowed an extraordinary world of fancy and complexity to flourish, all created very much on her own terms.

This did not happen immediately and some cups and a teapot with a well-fitted locking lid and a heavy spout attest to her early activities at the Well Walk Pottery. At first she worked entirely at Well Walk, but determined to practise throwing, she made her own wheel cannibalising a car wheel for the heavy flywheel. She ordered the wheel head and some clay from a pottery supplier, blushing with excitement as she posted the letter.[5] Only in 1962 did she acquire an electric kiln. In effect she served a self-imposed apprenticeship in which she took lessons first with Chris Magarshack and subsequently with Mohammed Abdulla at Camden Arts Centre, where she concentrated on hand building. Despite the fact that visitors were struck by the intensity of her domestic responsibilities, during those first years she experimented adventurously not simply with tableware but also with tile panels and mirrors and then with fountains and birdbaths. Adrian, meanwhile, was surprised at the passion with which she pursued her new interest. She recalls making a bird on a column. And Adrian's response – 'Fancy you having that sort of feeling!'[6] She was suddenly an artist, the area occupied with such seriousness by Adrian and his friends. In ceramic terms she was outside the mainstream. As she began to create her own ceramic world, tellingly she did not exhibit with fellow potters (aside from her own pupils and workshop companions). She sold her first plates to the philosopher Richard Wollheim, a regular visitor to the house. From 1967 onwards she held an annual 'Christmas sale' at her house in Hampstead to which were invited a network of friends (and friends of friends). Her choice of the word 'sale', as opposed to 'exhibition', says something about Ann Stokes' deliberate modesty *(fig.48)*.

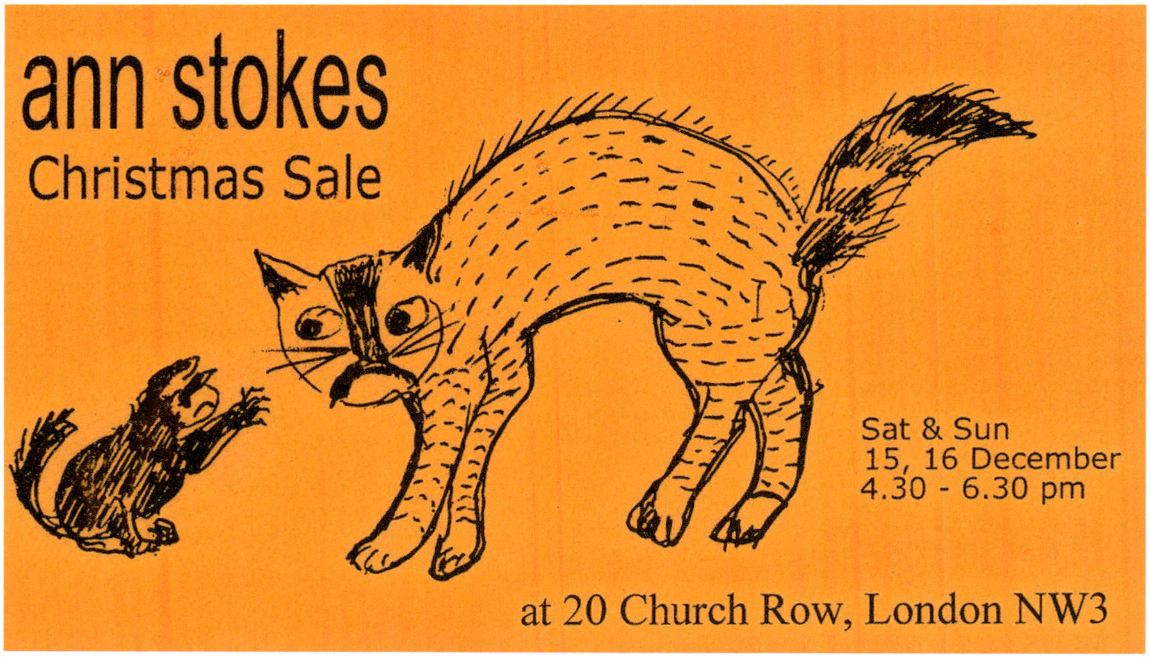

48 Invitation to Christmas sale 2001, drawn by Ann Stokes, designed by Philip Stokes
The artist's collection

Carving and Modelling

'Man, in his male aspect, is the cultivator or carver of woman who, in her female aspect, moulds her products as does the earth.'
Adrian Stokes, *Stones of Rimini*, Faber & Faber, London, 1934, p.110

Ann Stokes' sudden interest in clay as an artistic medium in 1957 might cause readers of Adrian Stokes' pre-war writings to smile – particularly as he occasionally bestowed a gender upon modelling, designating it a female pursuit. His 1934 masterpiece *Stones of Rimini* contained many passages that interrogated the difference between the adamantine qualities of stone and the plasticity of clay, between carving and modelling. At that point in his career Stokes saw carving as a superior form of artistic expression – in which the 'sculptor is led to woo the marble'[7] – while modelling was seen as a lesser activity because it was freer and lacked restraint. There was a moral aspect to this line of argument, familiar from John Ruskin's writings on truthfulness in sculpture. But such ideas also go back to the Renaissance paragone debates in which Michelangelo defined sculpture as a process of cutting away rather than one of building-up or modelling. (Although, strangely, Adrian Stokes saw Michelangelo as a modeller at heart.) Modelling gave an artist especial agency, allowing for possibilities that were described somewhat negatively by Stokes as 'wilful'.[8] He noted that clay could produce a simple 'pure' form when thrown on a wheel, most triumphantly in early Chinese pottery. But it also could serve as a record of every touch of an artist's hand. Adrian Stokes cited Rodin, but the clay models made by many sculptors share this tactile quality.

In an earlier article on Ben Nicholson written in 1933, Stokes had compared carving to farming. Both, he argued, stood for the collaboration between man and nature. Modelling, on the other hand, was analogous to manufacturing, in which materials were transmuted according to the manufacturer's will.[9] The reader is left with little doubt as to which – farming or manufacturing – was the most worthwhile and fulfilling activity. By identifying Nicholson as a carver, Stokes suggests that painters too can be judged in terms of carving or modelling.

As Richard Wollheim has pointed out, Stokes never intended to convert 'the history of art into an enormous game with the good carvers against the bad modellers'.[10] And Stokes was, in any case, to modify his prejudice against modelling. In his post-war writing he identified modelling and carving with two over-arching psychic relationships that had been defined by his analyst Melanie Klein as central to the development of an individual. The artistic interaction between Ann Stokes as a potter and Adrian Stokes as an aesthetician and a painter is not particularly clear or obvious. But allowing modelling an importance equal to carving seems connected to the happiness that Adrian Stokes found in his second marriage.[11] And although Adrian's inter-war writing might appear antithetic to Ann's pottery activities, his descriptions of the limitless (and 'wilful') possibilities of modelling chimes rather appositely with the kinds of objects that Ann Stokes went on to make as a studio potter. In any case, Adrian Stokes was far from indifferent to the applied arts. In his 1933 review of Ben Nicholson's work he was careful to praise the 'debonair' quality of Nicholson's designs for rugs and fabrics. In general, Stokes saw the decorative as undervalued in our culture. But he also believed that the applied arts, particularly ceramics, were less a reflection of an individual artist's identity than, say, painting. In the case of a 'Korean dish or the Song bowl' he argued that 'only a cultural identity, by and large, is likely to survive'.[12]. This was really a reprise of Herbert Read's assertion that pottery was an expression of national identity because it was 'so fundamental, so bound up with the elementary needs of civilisation'.[13] Paradoxically, the ceramics made by his wife Ann Stokes did not follow this model, being strikingly individualistic and difficult to position – both aesthetically and culturally.

The World of Studio Pottery

' ... it does seem that ideas on pottery have fallen into a very narrow groove, which reflects a "pure aesthetic" attitude.'

Philip Rawson, *Ceramics*, Oxford University Prees, London, 1971, p.1

Earthenware is Stokes' ceramic medium, to be decorated with brightly coloured slips, oxides and stains applied to biscuit-fired clay, subsequently glazed and re-fired in an electric kiln. So far, so straightforward. But when she set out as a potter this approach was strikingly out of step with studio pottery's conventions and standards. Stokes certainly works 'in studio' – but is she a studio potter?

Studio pottery, which emerged as a new genre in art in the early twentieth century, took as its principal models early Chinese Tang and Song dynasty ceramics (dating from the seventh to the thirteenth centuries) and Korean Yi or Choson dynasty ceramics (1392–1910), of the kind so admired by Adrian Stokes and most of his art-loving contemporaries. Medieval

English and some archaic Mediterranean pottery were also influential. Thus, by endorsing a limited range of ceramic models, early studio pottery embraced Modernist renunciation. This taste in ceramics was part of a wider canon, taking in other media and artistic genres such as pre-Columbian sculpture, Giotto's frescoes at Padua and Romanesque architecture, which had been set out by the formalist critics Clive Bell and Roger Fry in the first decades of the twentieth century.[14] It was reiterated in a purely ceramic context in Bernard Leach's opening chapter 'Towards a Standard' in his *A Potter's Book* of 1940. Although Leach made handsome slipware chargers and Michael Cardew demonstrated even greater commitment to slipware at Winchcombe Pottery in Gloucestershire from 1926 until the outbreak of the Second World War, the emphasis on early Chinese ceramics meant that most of the innovative studio pottery of the early twentieth century was carried out in stoneware and porcelain. The pure forms of this inter-war stoneware drew frequent comparisons with abstract sculpture, bestowing status on the genre. As Herbert Read put it: 'Pottery is plastic art in its most abstract essence.'[15] When in 1943 *The Times* art critic Charles Marriott argued that there were no British artists comparable to Brancusi (aside, he noted, from Barbara Hepworth) but 'pottery is, precisely, abstract sculpture' and here British artists were proving themselves 'second to none', he was reiterating a generally accepted notion.[16]

After the Second World War ceramics became one of the pleasures of peace. But although the numbers of men and women involved in the craft increased rapidly, studio ceramics continued to explore an aesthetic based on abstract or pure form. As the number of practitioners expanded, however, ceramics became less a part of the art world (as it had marginally been in the inter-war period) and came to resemble a separate little republic, with its own rules and principles, inward-looking and almost sect-like, demanding a high level of understanding and sensibility from its consumers. The world of studio pottery had its own magazines (*Ceramic Review* and *Pottery Quarterly*) and membership organisation (the Craftsmen Potters Association), and from the early 1970s celebratory gatherings took place in the form of so-called Potters' Camps – held in white-tented summer meadows where the craft was performed and technical information eagerly exchanged.

Stoneware continued to dominate. The great potter Lucie Rie, who had arrived from Vienna as an émigré before the Second World War, felt obliged to abandon her finely wrought earthenware, finding that in England there was no context for such work and that stoneware was seen as superior and more intellectually challenging. As David Canter, the founder of *Cranks*

49 Exhibition at the Studio Club, Swallow Street, London, 1953, showing figures by Margaret Hine and dishes, cactus holder and cat by Nicholas Vergette
Copyright: Pottery Quarterly *and Murray Fieldhouse*

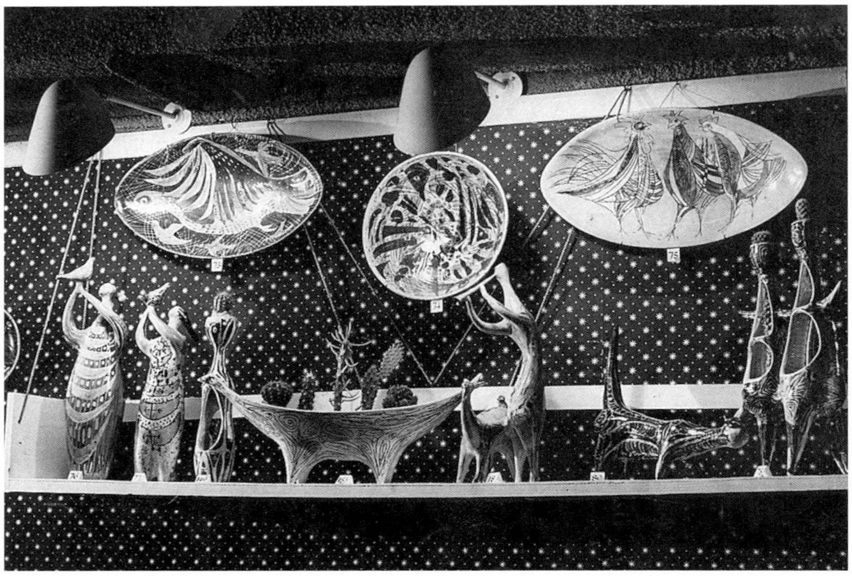

restaurant in London and great patron of studio pottery, explained, 'anything worth aesthetic enjoyment needs to be worked at', and he went on to compare the contemplation of stoneware to the demands made by a Bach fugue.[17]

If Ann Stokes' approach seems remote from most post-war studio pottery, a tentative comparison can be made with the brightly coloured tin-glaze ceramics made by William Newland, his wife Margaret Hine, James Tower and Nicholas Vergette in London in the 1950s *(fig.49)*. This little grouping had been inspired by Picasso's post-war foray into ceramics, but unlike Picasso they all became hands-on potters, making and decorating prancing bulls, figurative groups of fishermen and harlequins and women releasing doves, and handsome, large thrown dishes decorated with doves or with classical scenes such as Newland's *Europa and the Bull*. They formed an aesthetic in opposition to the neo-Orientalists, and Leach in particular predictably responded to their work with hostility, labelling them the 'Picassiettes'. They all had links, through William Newland, with Dora Billington, who taught ceramics at the Central School of Arts and Crafts in London. Even before the Second World War Billington had been bored by stoneware, greatly preferring the 'spirited experiments' made in tin glaze by Duncan Grant and Vanessa Bell.[18] After the war she continued to argue for a 'New Look' in ceramics, one that relinquished stoneware. In her view most studio potters were simply 'mechanically improving their technique and refining their aesthetic formula',[19] and had nothing new to say. Billington was excited by the work of Newland and his circle but their

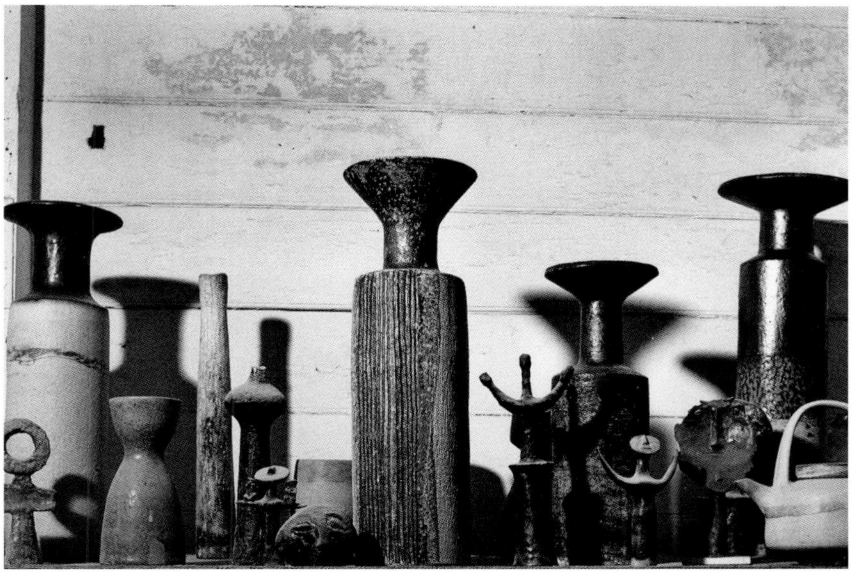

50 Ruth Duckworth's studio in Kew, 1962, showing stoneware and porcelain vessels and sculptures
Photo: John Donat Photography

little movement was to fizzle out. Vergette emigrated to the United States in 1958, and Newland and Hine taught and went on to concentrate on architectural commissions. Tower abandoned ceramics for sculpture, resuming only in the 1970s. In any case the 'Picassiettes' were very much products of a certain post-war moment.[20] It is easy to date their work. This is not the case with Ann Stokes, who throughout her career has been surprisingly immune to changing visual fashions. But some of Newland and Hine's coffee bars and their later restaurant interiors (like the Indian restaurant *Muntaz* on the edge of Regent's Park) anticipate Stokes' narrative qualities and her playful-serious borrowings from other cultures.

Michael Casson's *Pottery in Britain Today*, published in 1967, just when Ann Stokes first started selling, sets out the studio pottery orthodoxies of a slightly later period. The Picassiettes do not feature. Stoneware continues to dominate, which means that the absence of colour illustrations in Casson's book is hardly a drawback. The work is not colourful – with a few exceptions, such as Lucie Rie's uranium glazes and Alan Caiger-Smith's lustre ware. Whole areas of ceramic inspiration remained excluded. European ceramics from the sixteenth century onwards and most Middle Eastern ceramics were beyond the pale. Nonetheless, as Casson's book reveals, ceramics went deeper into sculptural abstraction in the 1960s and 1970s, a tendency that went hand in hand with a profound understanding of the ceramic medium. Casson illustrated a great range of stoneware mugs and other production wares that fitted in with fashions in informal dining. But he also included figures like Ian Auld, Gordon Baldwin, Hans Coper, Ruth Duckworth, Ewen

Henderson and Gillian Lowndes *(fig.50)*. Their ceramics had, as Hans Coper put it, 'ambiguous reference to purpose and function',[21] and were mostly thrown and assembled or hand-built, with sculptural ambitions that explored all the possibilities of the abstract vessel. But ceramics' synchronicity with sculpture, which characterised the inter-war period, did not survive the Second World War. By the mid 1960s the austere beauties of Gordon Baldwin, Ruth Duckworth or Gillian Lowndes' work had no visual links with 'New Generation' sculpture that was experimenting with materials like Plexiglass, resins and fibreglass, and cut and welded steel painted in bright colours. Parallel to the art world, therefore, there existed an intense ceramics universe. To appreciate its logic and expressiveness demanded an immersive commitment. It had nothing in common with Ann Stokes' aesthetic, the roots of which will emerge as we progress through her rich and varied output.

Some Tableware

'A most important aspect of all ceramic surface design is the way in which it may (or may not) pick up and relate to the plastic qualities of the pot to which it is applied.'
Philip Rawson, *Ceramics*, Oxford University Press, London, 1971, p.151

Ann Stokes' ceramic taxonomy is complex. However, first must come the great array of dinner and side plates, each an individual work of art. The fact that Stokes makes her own plates is for her of crucial importance. Simply to paint a plate made by someone else, as so many artists have done, is in her view doomed to failure. This purism, perhaps unexpectedly, leads her to dismiss Picasso's substantial contribution to ceramics together with John Piper's ceramic forays: 'Hopeless. It just doesn't cohere.'[22] Plates were Ann's first ambition and she soon put away 'our factory plates and forced us all to eat off mine'.[23]

But her approach is idiosyncratic. Plates are conventionally decorated in a way that honours their ceramic form, discrete areas being created by banding, with additional pattern or graphic representation adapted to that logic. A co-operative venture with the artist John Craxton in 1973–5, in which Ann made the plates and Craxton painted them, follows this time-honoured approach. Craxton's banding is playfully embellished with leaves, dots and feathering *(fig.41)*. The results are attractive, and familiar – recalling Delft colouring and Luneville and other French faience tableware. Aside from her collaboration with John Craxton, Stokes' only other nod in the direction of

51 Nigel Greenwood's dining table with Ann Stokes' plates, illustrated in his article 'Avant Guardian', World of Interiors, *May 2004*
Photo: Eric Morin, © The World of Interiors

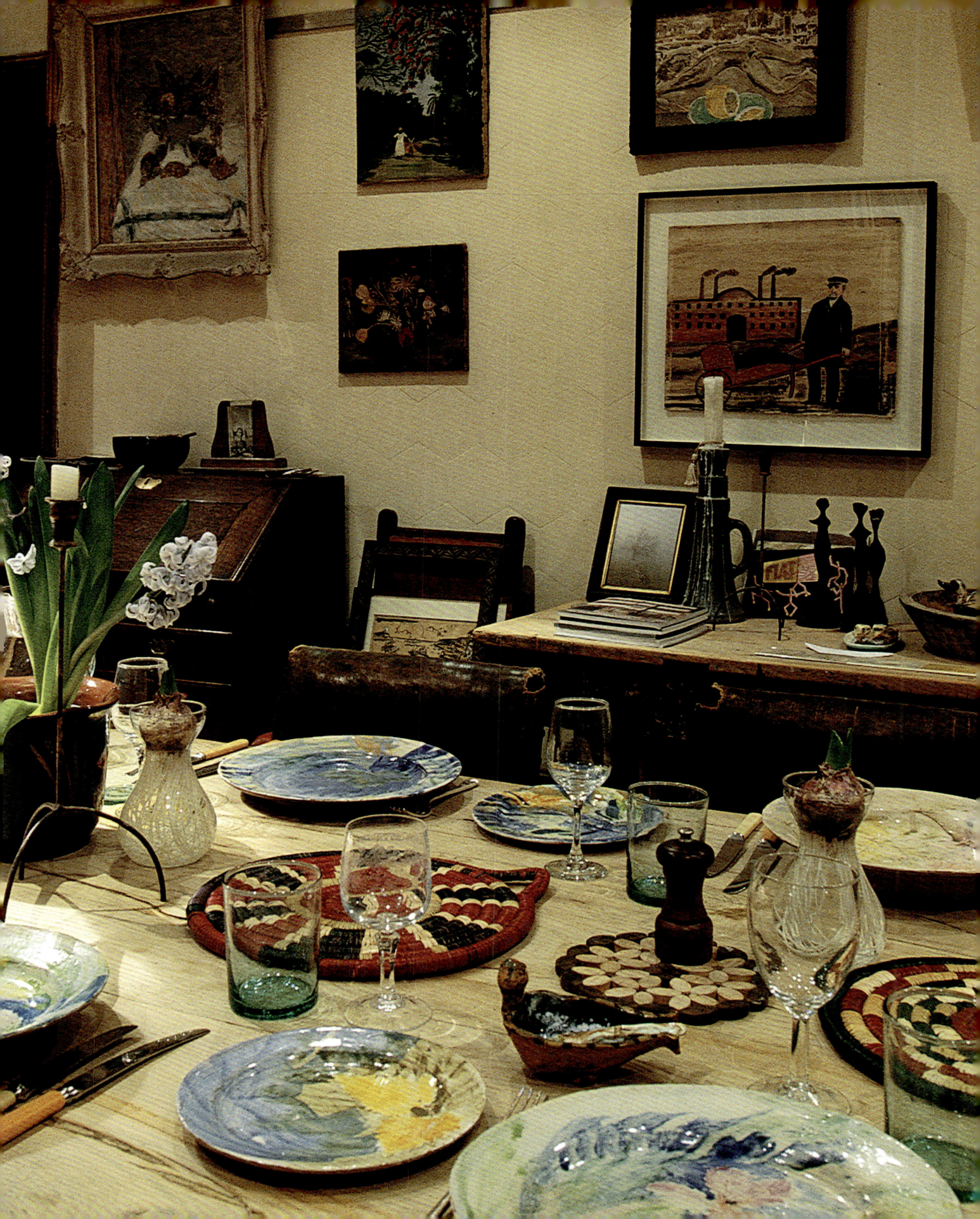

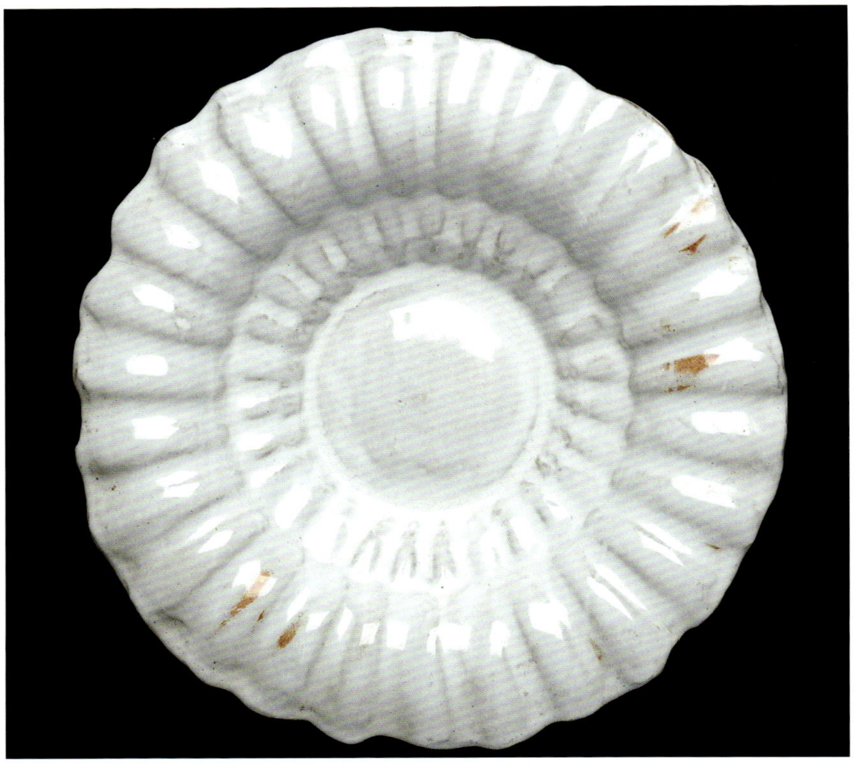

52 Gadrooned dish, marked Σ 9/72
Press moulded, mould taken from a Renaissance dish
31.5 cm (12.4 in)
Collection: Jennifer Anderson
Photo: Stephen Brayne

historicism has been a series of white tin-glaze plates and large platters – the forms of the latter made from moulds taken from historic gadrooned dishes *(fig.52)*. Otherwise she has never followed flatware decorative conventions.

Stokes favours an unorthodox, all-over approach based on loose brush-work sometimes articulated with an overlay pattern of vegetal branches, or enlivened by a vivid, casually placed sketch of a bird, a frog, or a flower, using a cut outline as a stencil or as the basis for *sgraffito*. In 1969, quite early in her professional career, she made a series of dinner plates painted with rolling passages of sombre brown, blue and white brushstrokes and pools of colour.[24] Not many artists, presented with a plate, would dare to be quite so free and so detached from the drive to frame and fill in *(fig.53)*. But then her effects are often fugitive by ceramic standards. She frequently employs a natural stencil in the form of an actual leaf simply placed on the biscuit-fired clay or pressed on the slipped surface so that its veins make an impression *(fig.54)*. She then paints around it, creating what she describes as 'a leaf fossil'.[25] The immediacy of the procedure recalls the Arts and Crafts silversmith and architect Henry Wilson's recipe for modelling a jewel in the form of a nightingale: 'First go and watch one singing ... head thrown back and his throat throbbing in an ecstasy of song.'[26] As so often in Ann

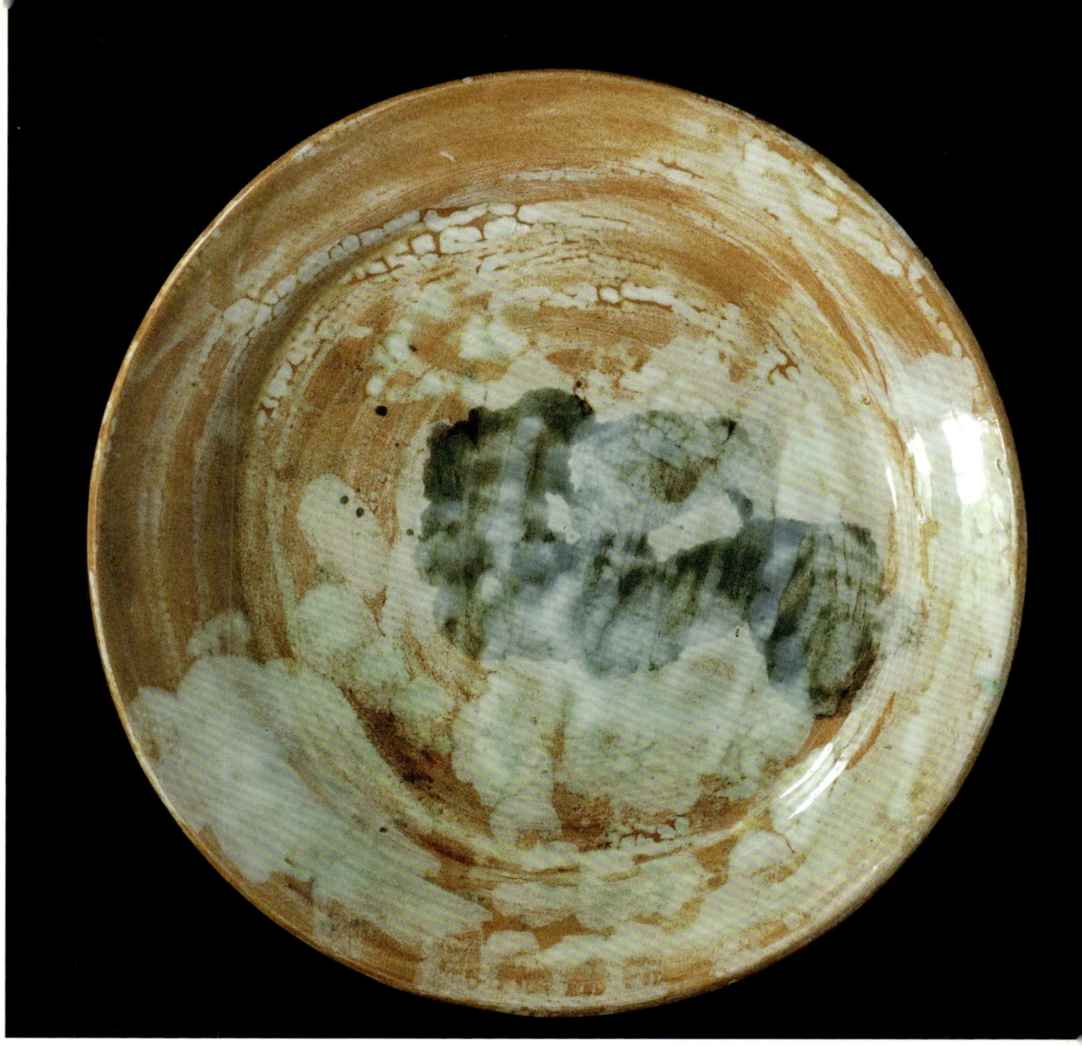

53 Dinner plate, marked Σ 7/69
27 cm (10.6 in)
Collection: Sarah Whitfield
Photo: Stephen Brayne

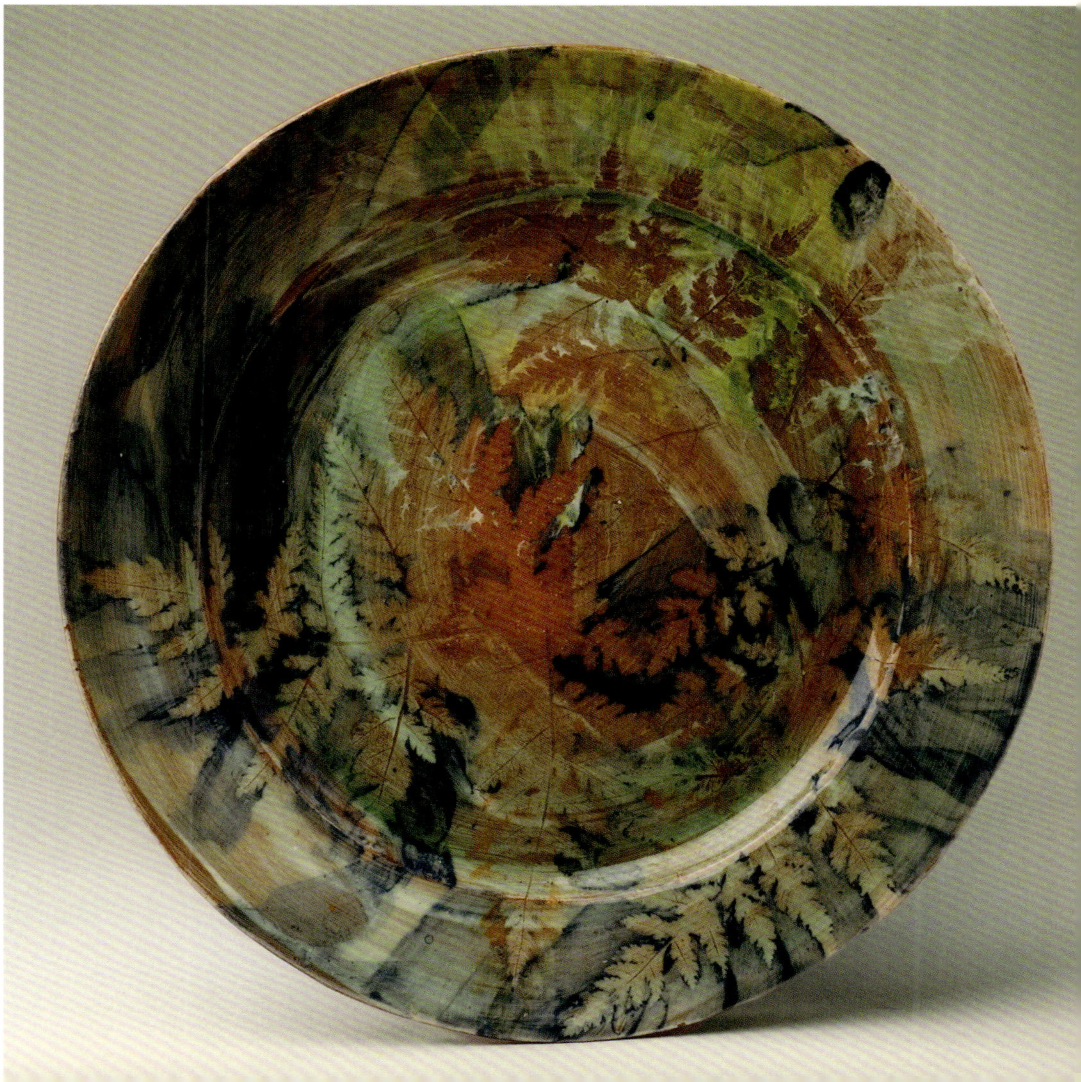

54 Dinner plate stencilled with Sweet Cicely, marked Σ 85
25.5 cm (10 in)
Collection: Angela Hamilton
Photo: Stephen Brayne

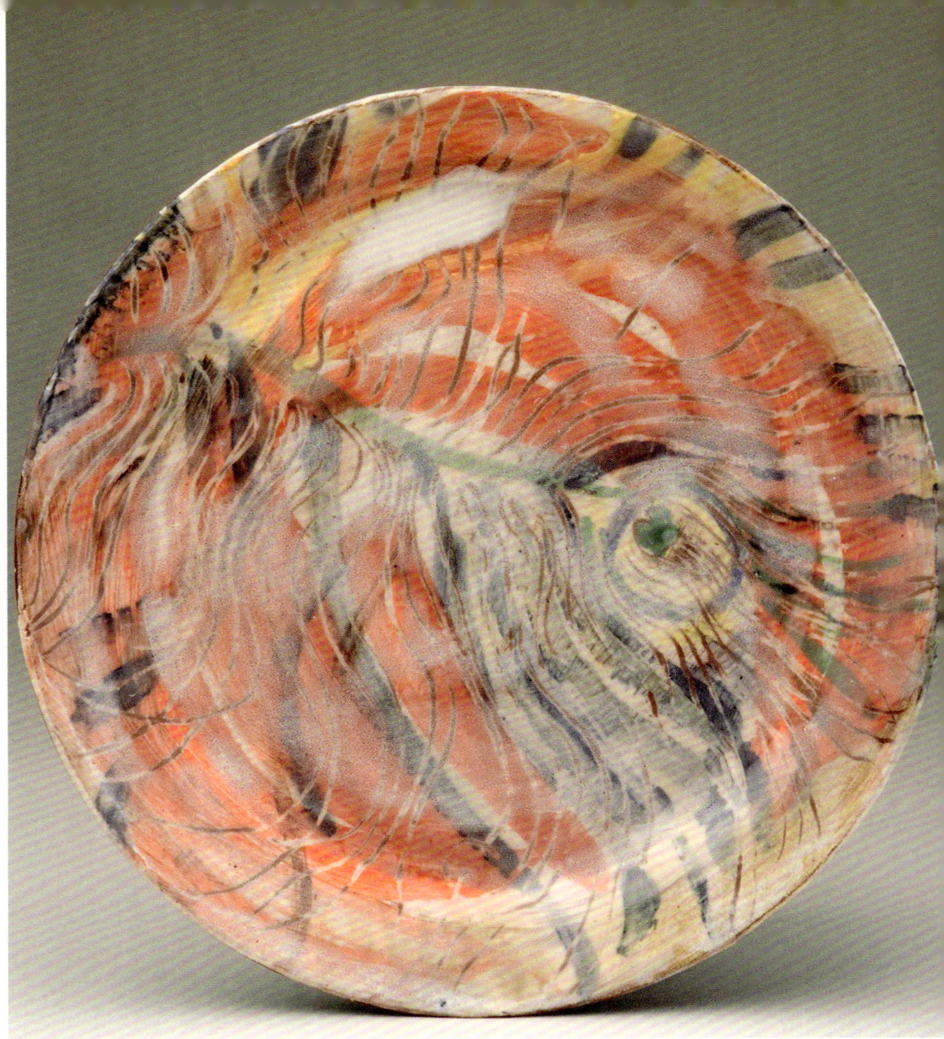

55 Side plate with peacock feather, marked Σ 6/91
17 cm (6.7 in)
Collection: Angela Hamilton
Photo: Stephen Brayne

Stokes' work, innocence and ambition collide – her leaf plates manage both to recall Victorian flower-pressing activities *and* those of Man Ray's rayographs of the 1920s, which were made by placing ferns directly on light-sensitive paper.

Remarkably varied in mood, ranging from metaphorical springs and summers bright with flowers to golden autumns and sere winters, Stokes' plates form an important backdrop to the rest of her work. Motifs are explored and abandoned and re-presented a few years later in an exploratory continuum. As the dealer Nigel Greenwood put it: 'One year she is all blue and yellow glazes, vivid and summery. Another year found objects like leaves are pressed into service, and her own role is more reticent ... a patch of white will metamorphose into a swan gliding though a summer evening.'[27]

He was to include some twenty of her plates when he curated the 1985 Hayward Annual in London – the first and last time a modern potter has been shown in the Hayward Gallery. As Greenwood suggests, Stokes is adventurous with colour but, in particular, soft blues and green recur and here a connection can be made with Adrian Stokes' paintings. It is not simply a matter of colour. There is a delicacy, even tentativeness about some

56 Dinner and side plates with daisy motif, all marked Σ 87
Collection: Lord and Lady Ravensdale
Photo: Stephen Brayne

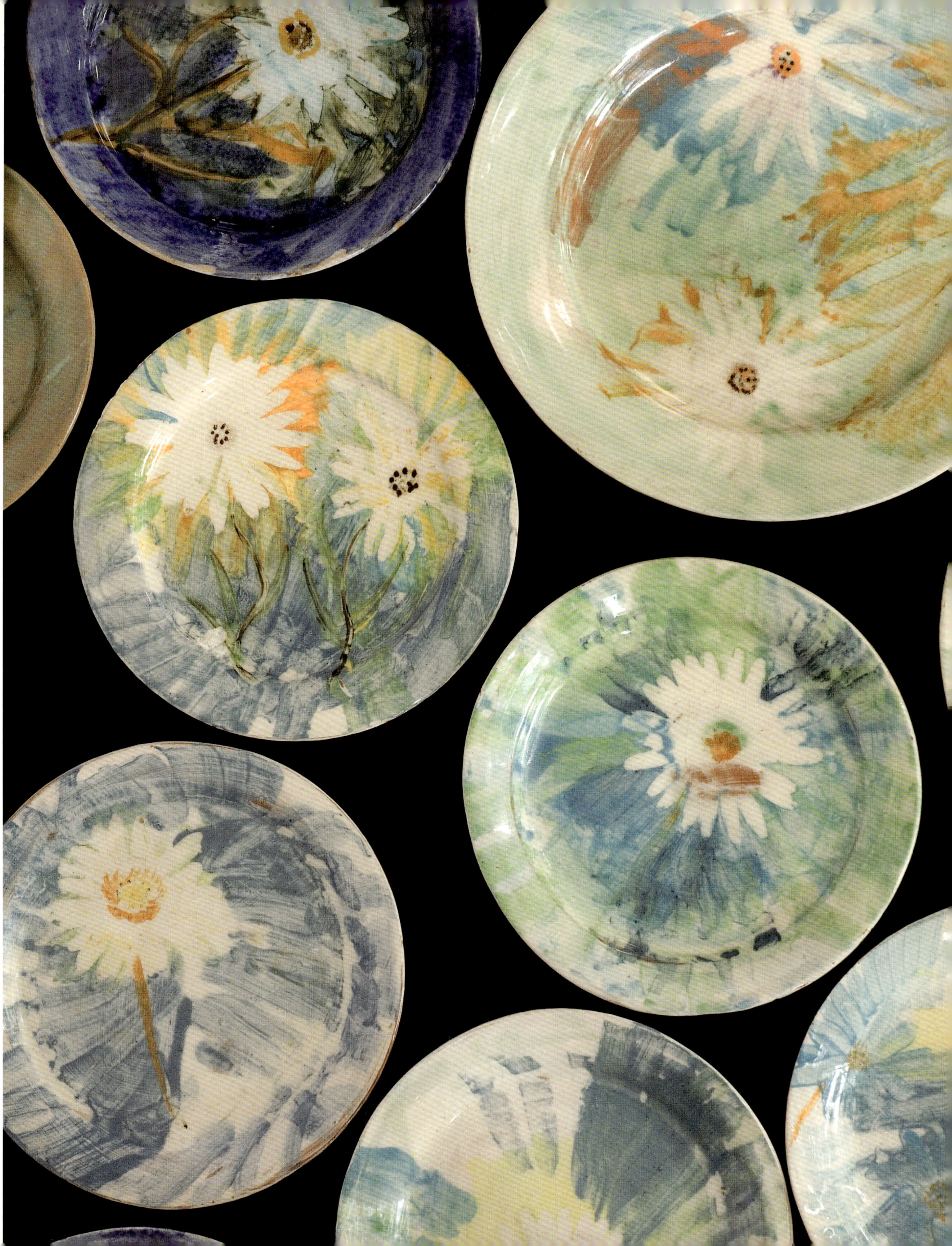

of her brushwork that recalls his shimmering diaphanous effects. A group of his paintings, closely hung, cover one wall of her studio *(fig.1)*.

Helpfully, Stokes invariably scratches the month and the year of facture on the base of plates and vessels together with her potter's mark, a *sigma* that stands both for Mellis and for Stokes, and which also signals her love of early Greek culture. There is plenty of graphic narrative on her plates, especially on dinner services made to order or made with a particular user in mind – for instance, a dinner service of sprightly sailing boats, with an Alfred Wallis air, made in 2006 for the writer Nicholas Mosley's son. But many of her decorative schemes are abstract or semi-abstract, the plate camouflaged with brushstrokes, devoid of that sense of order which we so powerfully associate with the decorative arts.

Some comparisons can be drawn between her all-over style and the forays into ceramics by the followers of Gauguin known as the Nabis in the 1890s. Both Edouard Vuillard and József Rippl-Rónai were similarly untrammelled by ceramic conventions and several of Stokes' plates appear consciously to follow Vuillard's use of tentative passages of wandering parallel lines, in Stokes' case, scratched through a white slip *(fig.10)*. The handsome tin-glaze ceramics decorated around 1906–9 by Henri Matisse, André Derain, Jean Puy, Kees van Dongen and Maurice de Vlaminck seem less relevant. On the whole these artists either treat the plate surface as a tondo or create the usual banding lines to frame pattern and image.[28] Interestingly, a selection of these Fauve ceramics was included in 1910 in Roger Fry's *Manet and the Post-Impressionists*, better known as the First Post-Impressionist Show, and may have inspired Fry's own forays into ceramics. The knotty question of the relationship between Ann Stokes' work and that of the Bloomsbury group is discussed in Richard Morphet's essay.[29]

Stokes' plates sit alongside cups, jugs, serving dishes and cooking pots that have more in common with normative ceramic decoration, sometimes being roughly fluted or painted with bold stripes or whorls of colour *(fig.57)*. Stokes' hollow wares are, unlike her plates, rich in ceramic echoes. She does not make direct copies – although in 1969–70 she replicated a massive *pithos* owned by the painter Andrew Forge's wife Sheila. But archaic Mediterranean pottery has been a constant underlying influence, both as regards shape and decoration. Stokes pays frequent visits to the Cycladic, Minoan and Mycenaean, Cypriot and early Egyptian rooms in the British Museum.

Thus Ann's ceramic sources were (and to an extent still are) mostly located around 2000–200 BC – her jugs have open cut spouts, her cup

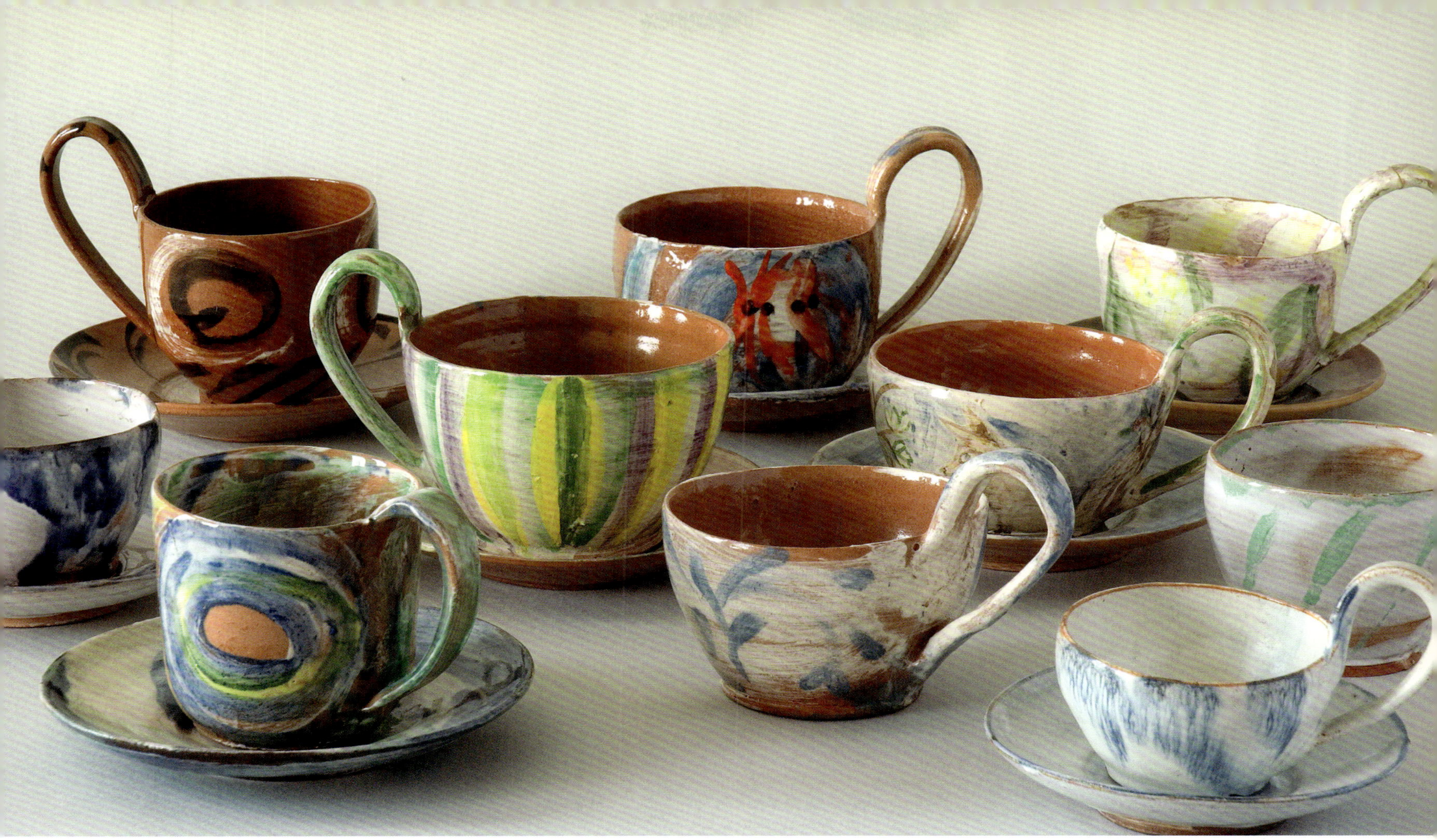

57 *Tea and coffee cups, all individually marked, 1979–2004*
Collection: Phoebe Greenwood
Photo: Stephen Brayne

handles loop upwards like the large Etruscan black-ware drinking-cup or *kantharos* sold to her by David Sylvester in the 1970s *(fig.60)*. These influences are so powerful that they perhaps explain why teapots appear to be relatively alien forms to her (although she does make them). A number of her early pieces honour this love of the archaic through an absence of an exterior glaze. A handsome white-slipped bread-bin made around 1968, owned by the painter and art historian John Golding, is simply decorated with a whorl-like mark in grey slip and exposed clay. (The reverse side of the piece carries an equally powerful ribbed sequence of lines in slip, *figs 58–9*). Stokes' bold spiral motif echoes the decoration on a two-handled, hole-mouthed Minoan jar in the British Museum. But it also recalls the decoration of a fourteenth-century English pitcher made at Cheam in Surrey, now in the Victoria and Albert Museum, described by W.B. Honey, whose books Ann possesses, as instinctive brushwork 'of undeniable grandeur'.[30]

Golding has been a collaborative presence since the late 1960s, supplying drawings for birdbaths *(fig.72)* and a fountain, designs for a hooked rug stair-carpet *(fig.38)* and two impressive abstract rugs, as well as lending an oval-lobed French serving plate *(fig.62)*, from which Stokes took at least two

58 Bread bin (i), late 1960s
(height) 33 cm (13 in)
Collection: John Golding
Photo: Stephen Brayne

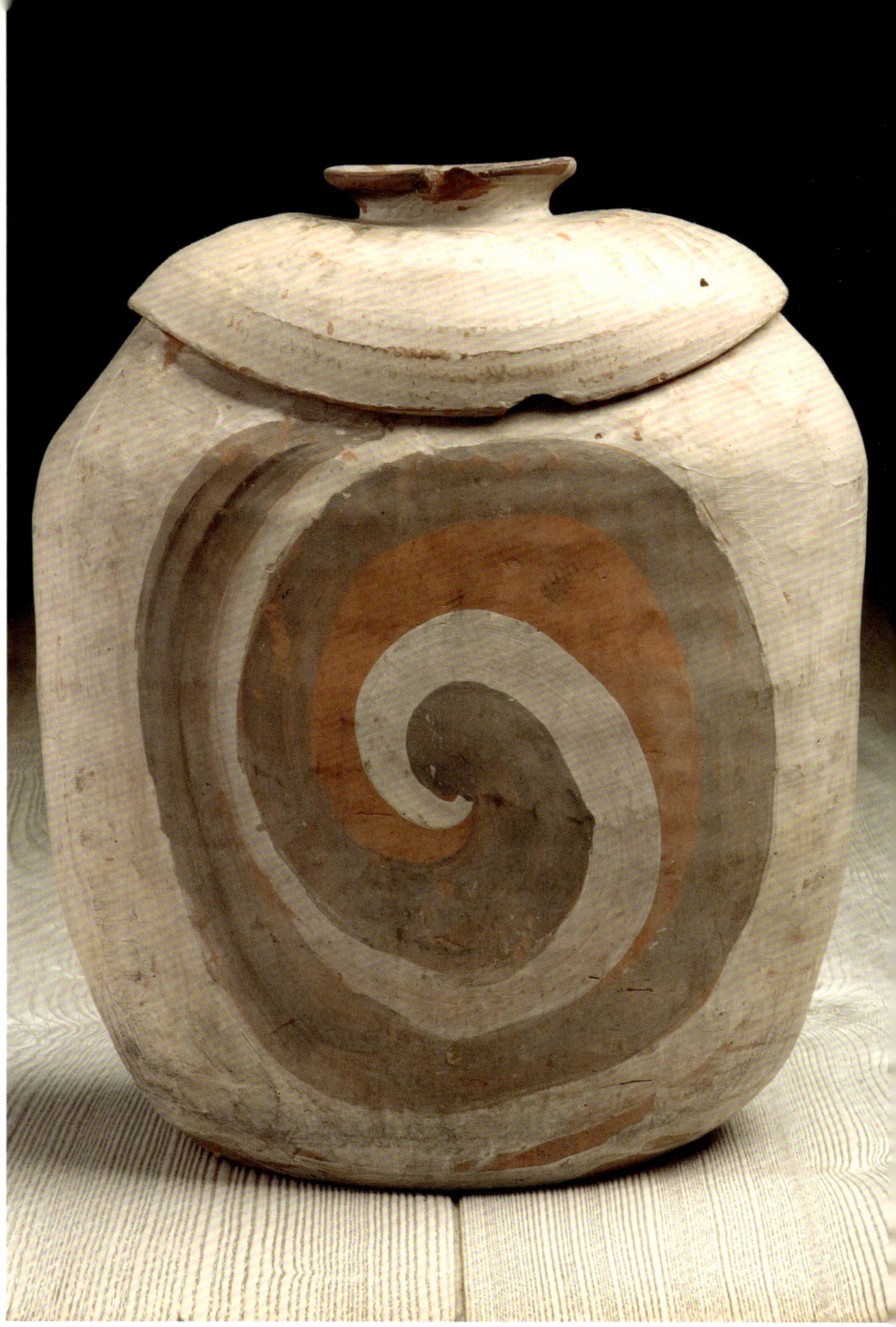

plaster moulds which she put into production to carry every kind of decoration, from sprawling vegetation to peacocks, to sharply delineated cheetahs in a wilderness of bold marks and splashes of colour. Golding's taste as regards her own work has always been greatly valued by Stokes. But she is cautious about influences and while enjoying collaborations she invariably goes her own way. Her white tin-glaze plates were much admired *(fig.52)*, and both Golding and the art critic and collector David Sylvester (a magus in the field of taste) encouraged Stokes' forays into blue and white. Sylvester owned a blue and white dinner service, and admired one of her blue and

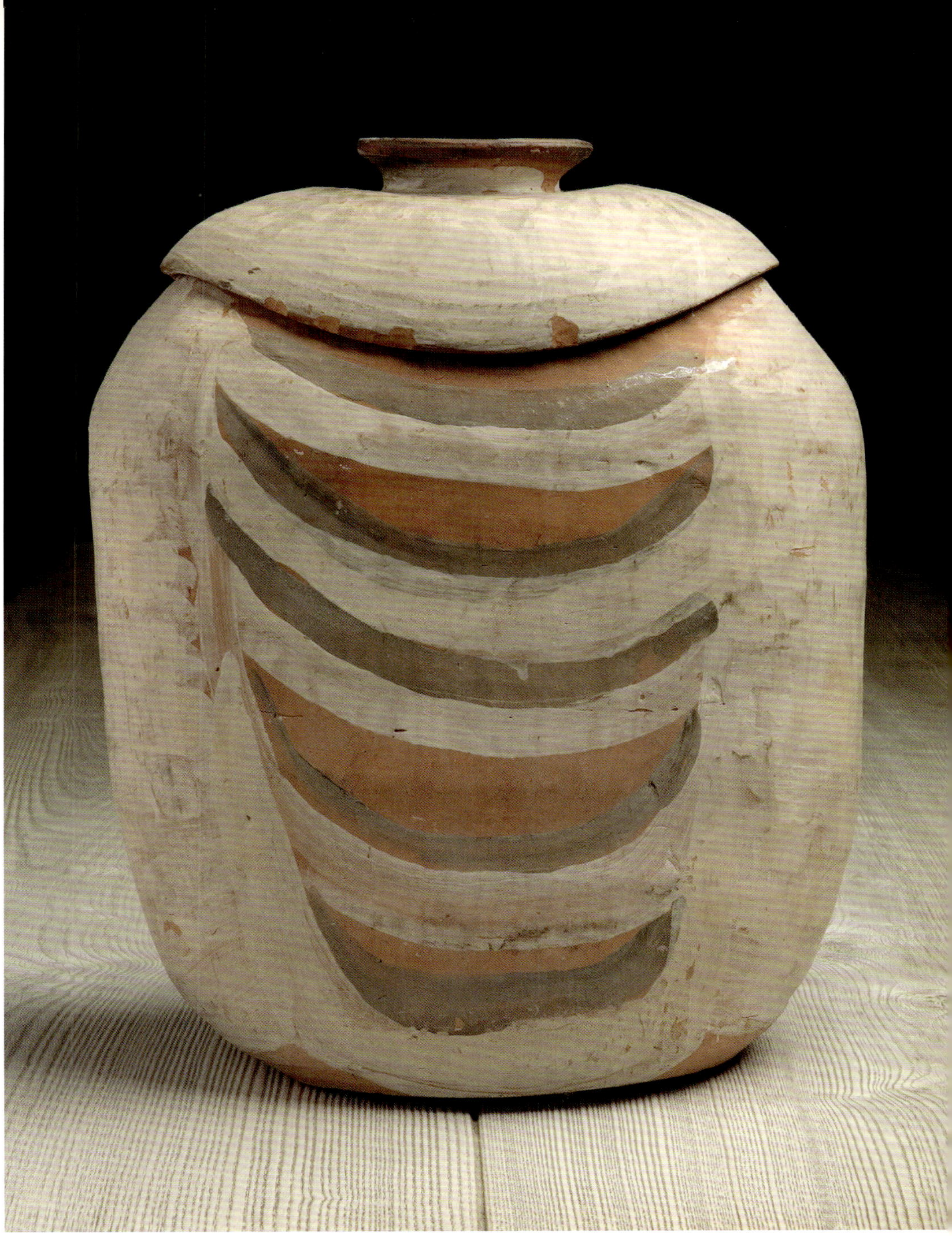

59 Bread bin (ii), late 1960s
(height) 33 cm (13 in)
Collection: John Golding
Photo: Stephen Brayne

white small tables very much, while Golding possesses a number of her blue and white dishes *(fig. 61)*. Blue (in the form of cobalt) is the commonest and oldest non-clay glaze colour in the history of ceramics and has a multitude of ceramic associations – from Chinese Yuan dynasty porcelains to Iznik earthenwares from Turkey, to the banalities of Willow Pattern and Cornishware.[31] In short, 'blue and white' stands for ceramic safety and Stokes has wisely limited her use of this beguiling combination, just as she has resisted the demand for pure white tin-glaze.

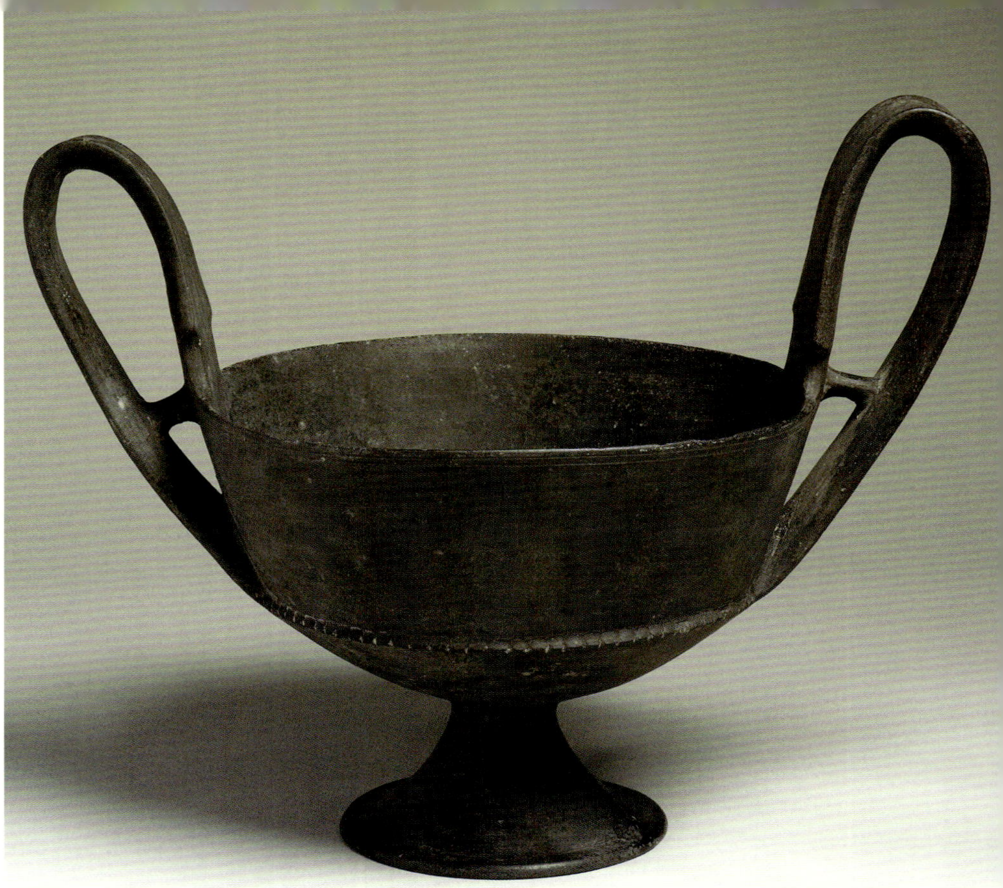

60 Etruscan drinking cup or kantharos with loop-shaped handles, c.730 BC
Reduction fired black earthenware
29.8 x 39 cm (11.7 x 15.4 in)
The artist's collection
Photo: Stephen Brayne

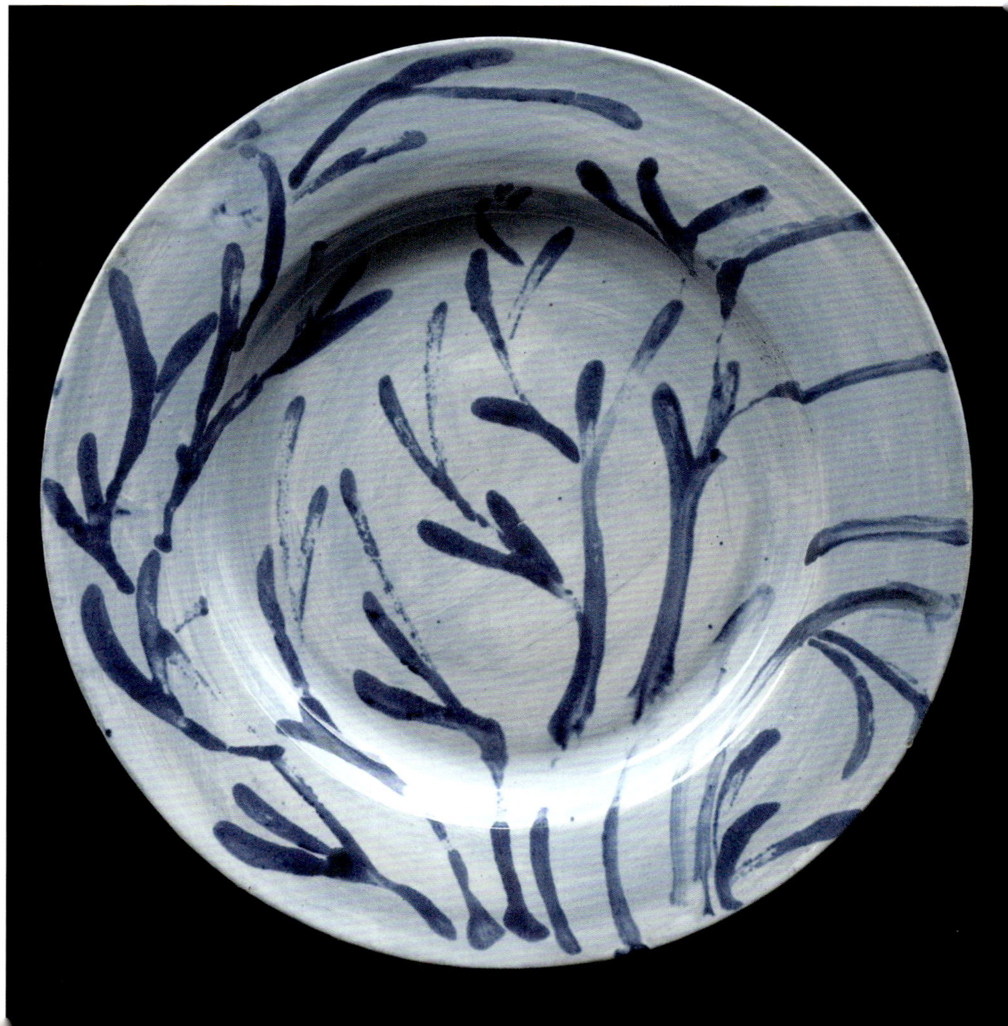

61 Dinner Plate, marked Σ 1/74
25.5 cm (10 in)
Collection: John Golding
Photo: Stephen Brayne

opposite:
62 Lobed serving plate, marked Σ 10/95
Press moulded, mould taken from a French plate owned by John Golding
(length) 42 x (width) 33.5 cm (16.5 x 13.2 in)
Collection: Lord and Lady Ravensdale
Photo: Stephen Brayne

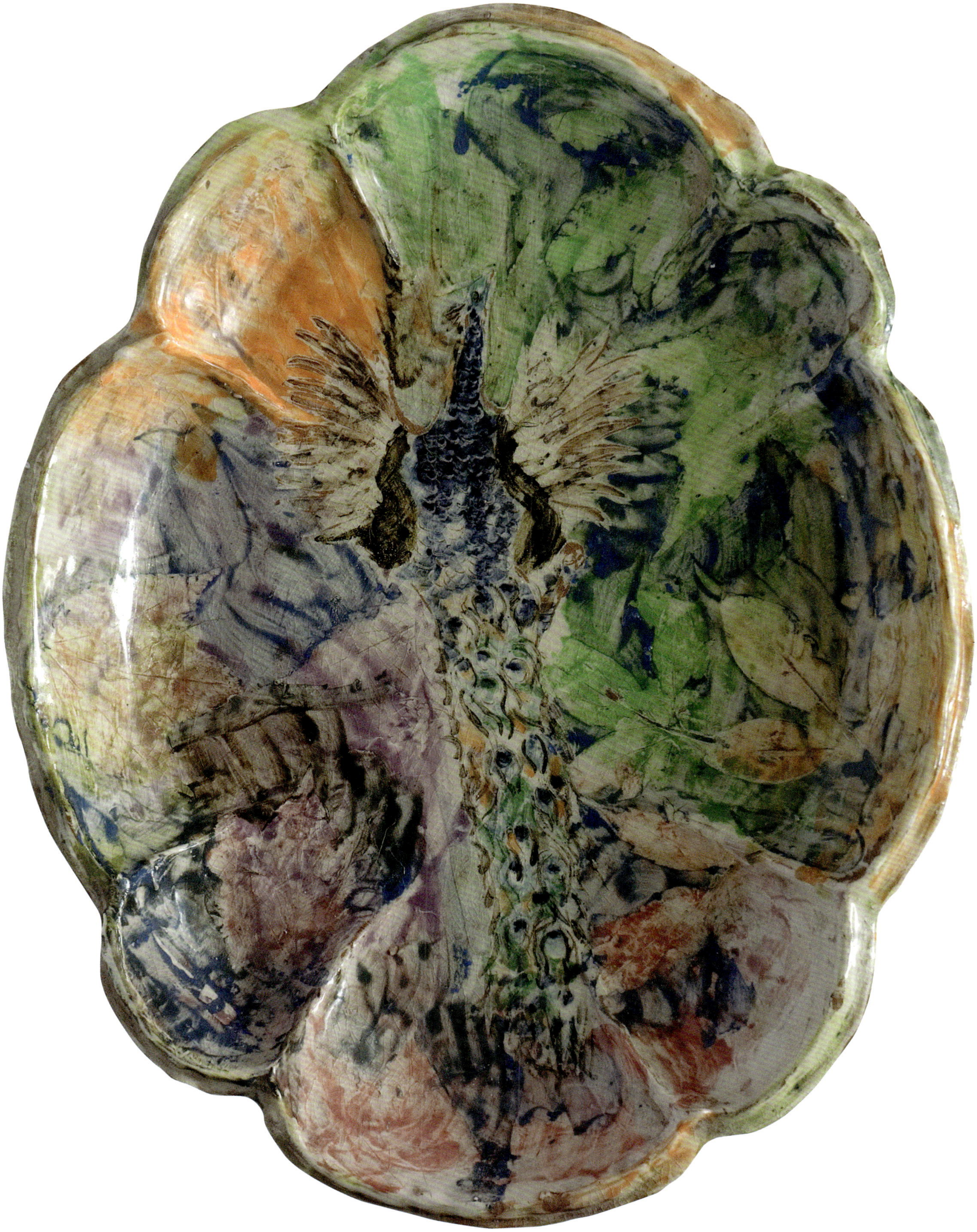

'The sauceboat and cover formed as a flat fish, the body somewhat unnaturally deepened and the mouth extended to make room for a spoon (missing).'

Michael Snodin (ed.), *Rococo: Art and Design in Hogarth's England*, Victoria and Albert Museum, London, 1984, p.247

In fruitful ways, Stokes' work has something of the ambitiousness displayed by children when they first manipulate clay. In his *Autobiography* the sculptor and printmaker Eric Gill recalled of his own first sculptures: 'I was really like the child who said, "first I think and then I draw my think" – in contrast with the art-student who must say: "First I look and then I draw my look".'[32] Each afternoon Ann Stokes takes a rest and during that time she sees in her mind's eye the objects she wants to make, complete and in every detail. This, she believes, is when she creates her pottery. As a result there are few limits to what she decides can be made in clay. As Stephenie Bergman, who worked in her studio in the 1970s, put it: 'I think of her half as a potter and half as a maker of objects ... someone who has images in her head of animals and the natural world and somehow she makes these images into real things regardless of formal judgement and aesthetic values and fashions.'[33]

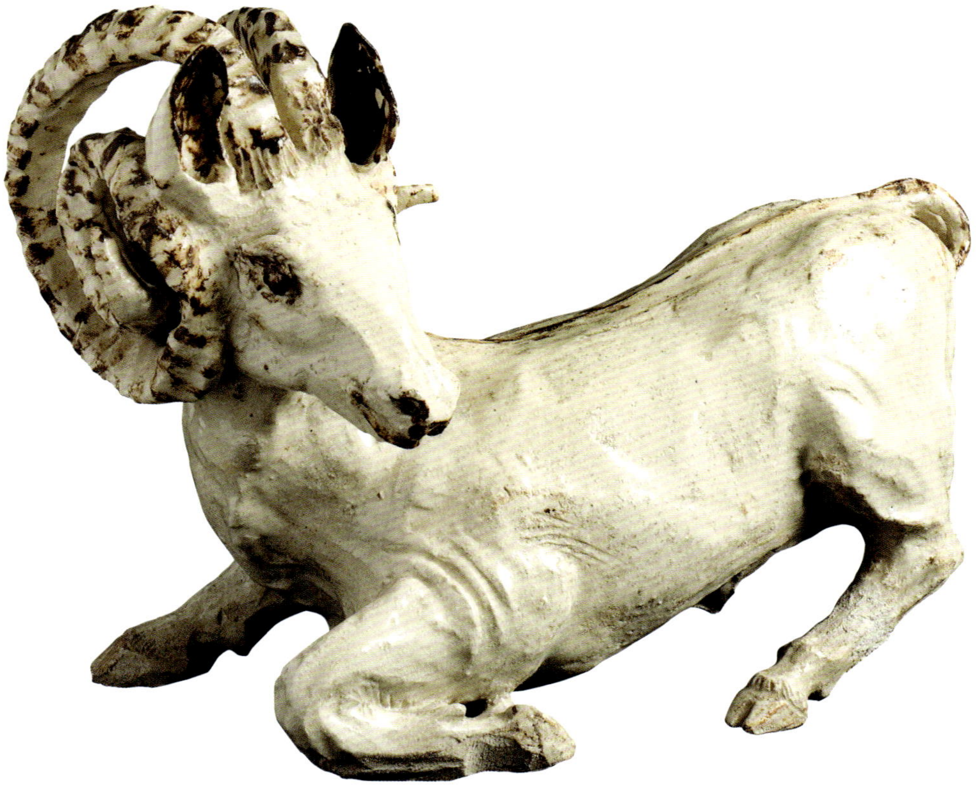

63 Goat, c.1979–80
Modelled
38 x 30 cm (15 x 11.8 in)
Collection: Lord Bragg
Photo: Stephen Brayne

First she thinks and then she makes her think. It is an intense kind of identification. Jennifer Anderson, who came to know Ann in about 1970, recalls walking with her in north Wales and looking back to see Ann gazing at a goat in a field, holding her hands to her head to make empathetic horns.[34] *(fig. 63)*

It is an approach that sets her apart from a studio pottery world that, until recently, was almost entirely focused on the abstraction of the vessel form. But by turning away from the representational, studio pottery relinquished what Philip Rawson described as ceramics' capacity for the 'primal interweaving of matter, human action, and symbol'.[35] The transformative nature of ceramics – in which wet clay is shaped and fired and given permanence – is an obvious birth and life metaphor. It goes some way to explaining potters' fondness for fashioning vessels, especially ritual vessels, in the form of animals or birds or, in the case of Peruvian Nazca pots, as portrait heads. The malleable nature of clay makes it possible to create a parallel world, fashioned out of ceramic.

Perhaps the most extreme example of this is the life-size terracotta army of infantrymen, crossbowmen, spearsmen, charioteers and horsemen unearthed at the tomb of the First Emperor at Mount Li in northern China. But in eighteenth-century Europe, the grand service had a comparable totalising quality, embodying entire miniaturised worlds and high-status pursuits in porcelain, creating a landscape of fountains, flowers and fruit, mountains and follies, temples and bridges. The grand service was further enlivened with every kind of figurine – from gods and goddesses, to nymphs, huntsmen, hunting dogs and animals. In the case of Frederick the Great of Prussia's gift to Catherine the Great, all the classes and races under Catherine's rule were created *in parvo*, with Catherine herself portrayed under a canopy as a table centrepiece. Truth to materials was hardly an issue here – the genesis of these extraordinary *Tafelzier* was a-ceramic. They originated as confectionery, masterpieces of sugary art.[36]

In the early twentieth century, ceramic zoomorphism and anthropomorphism became firmly equated with kitsch. In Britain, ceramicists who made figurative work between the wars – often women as it happens – dropped out of ceramic history. They were, for example, firmly excluded from the studio pottery canon in Muriel Rose's solemn 1955 study *Artist-Potters in England*. But the loss of status had already begun in the nineteenth century when the figurine left the dining table, and migrated to the mantelpiece. As a knick-knack or personal souvenir, such objects soon came under attack from taste-makers, culminating in Le Corbusier's furious denunciations of

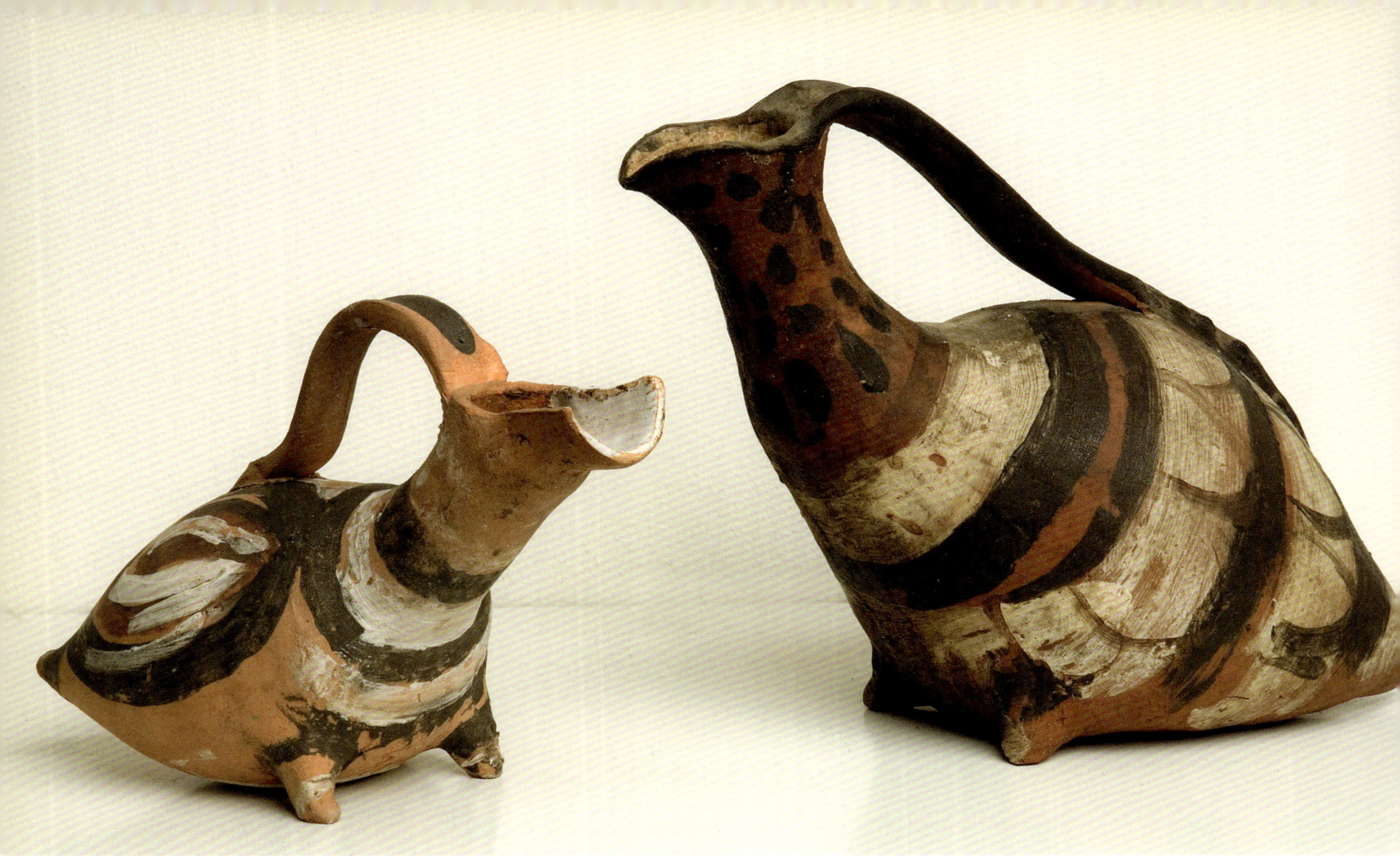

64 Oil jars, marked (left to right)
Σ 11/75; Σ 7/73
Thrown and modelled
(left to right) 9.5 x 15 cm (3.7 x 5.9 in);
14 x 16 cm (5.5 x 6.3 in)
Collection: Jennifer Anderson
Photo: Stephen Brayne

small decorative objects which, incidentally, he associated with women and, worse, shop-girls: 'Previously, decorative objects were rare and costly. Today they are commonplace and cheap.'[37] This horror of bibelots was to have a limiting effect on ceramics, with wit and narrative only properly re-emerging in the late 1970s amongst rebellious artists and studio potters eager to set aside the self-imposed limitations of Modernism.

By the late 1970s, tentative links can be made between Stokes' eclecticism and a generation who had graduated from the Royal College of Art and the Central School in London, including Alison Britton, Jill Crowley, Elizabeth Fritsch, Andrew Lord, Carol McNicoll, Jacqui Poncelet and Richard Slee. But their ceramics were highly self-conscious and self-referential. They made what Alison Britton called 'two-faced objects' with a 'double presence' – pots that commented on pots.[38] And their work shared one characteristic that is absent from Stokes' work – irony. The dark wing of Marcel Duchamp's thoughts on productive and artistic labour has never touched Ann Stokes. Enter folk art again with its forthrightness and gaiety – and images of Stokes herself in 1973. Taken for a book on his friends planned by the artist Jim

Dine, they show Ann climbing and swinging from a tree *(fig.7)*, and standing in her studio holding out a defiantly clay-covered hand.

As we have seen, in her earliest phase, Stokes chiefly sought inspiration from the ancient world. (The term 'early' in Stokes' career is, however, an elastic one. Her career falls into two parts, the first taking us up to the years just after the death of Adrian Stokes in 1972. From the mid 1970s Stokes was able to work longer and harder at her ceramics. Her domestic commitments were fewer and when she married the Orwell scholar Ian Angus in 1976, he whole-heartedly supported her work.) A striking example of her antique tendencies would be a series of oil jars with strap handles made around 1973–5 based on an eighth-century BC Syrian pot and taking the semi-abstract form of a bird with an extended neck *(fig.64)*. The exteriors were decorated but often unglazed, heightening the archaic echo. They are strongly reminiscent of Picasso's bird-like pitchers, which of course drew on similar antique sources.[39] But by 1967 Stokes was also creating zoomorphic vessels that have more in common with Baroque and Rococo faience. A little lidded bird pot of 1967, with a fan-tail forming a practical, pulled handle *(fig.65)*, leads on to a long line of lidded containers either of birds or fish, often brightly decorated and expressively formed, feathery or scaly, alive with movement. Some of these lids are integral, being simply sliced from the

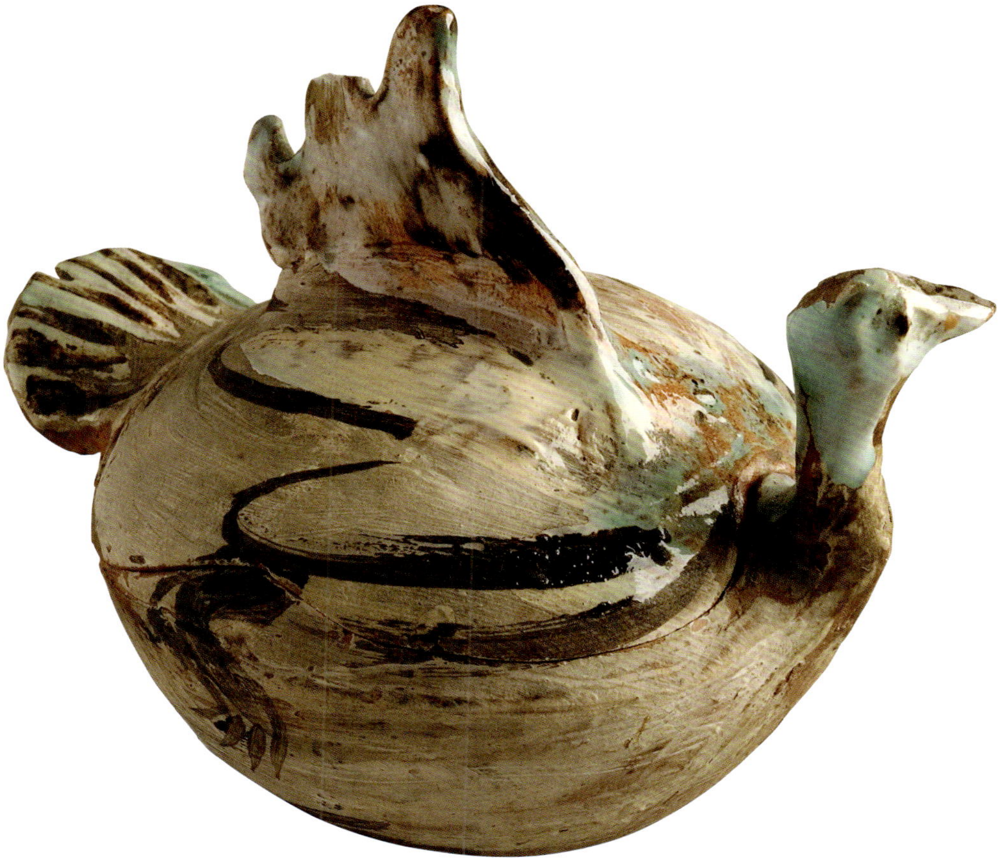

65 Salt pot in the form of a bird, marked 'This is for John 30/6/67'
Thrown and modelled
10 x 14 cm (3.9 x 5.5 in)
Collection: John Golding
Photo: Stephen Brayne

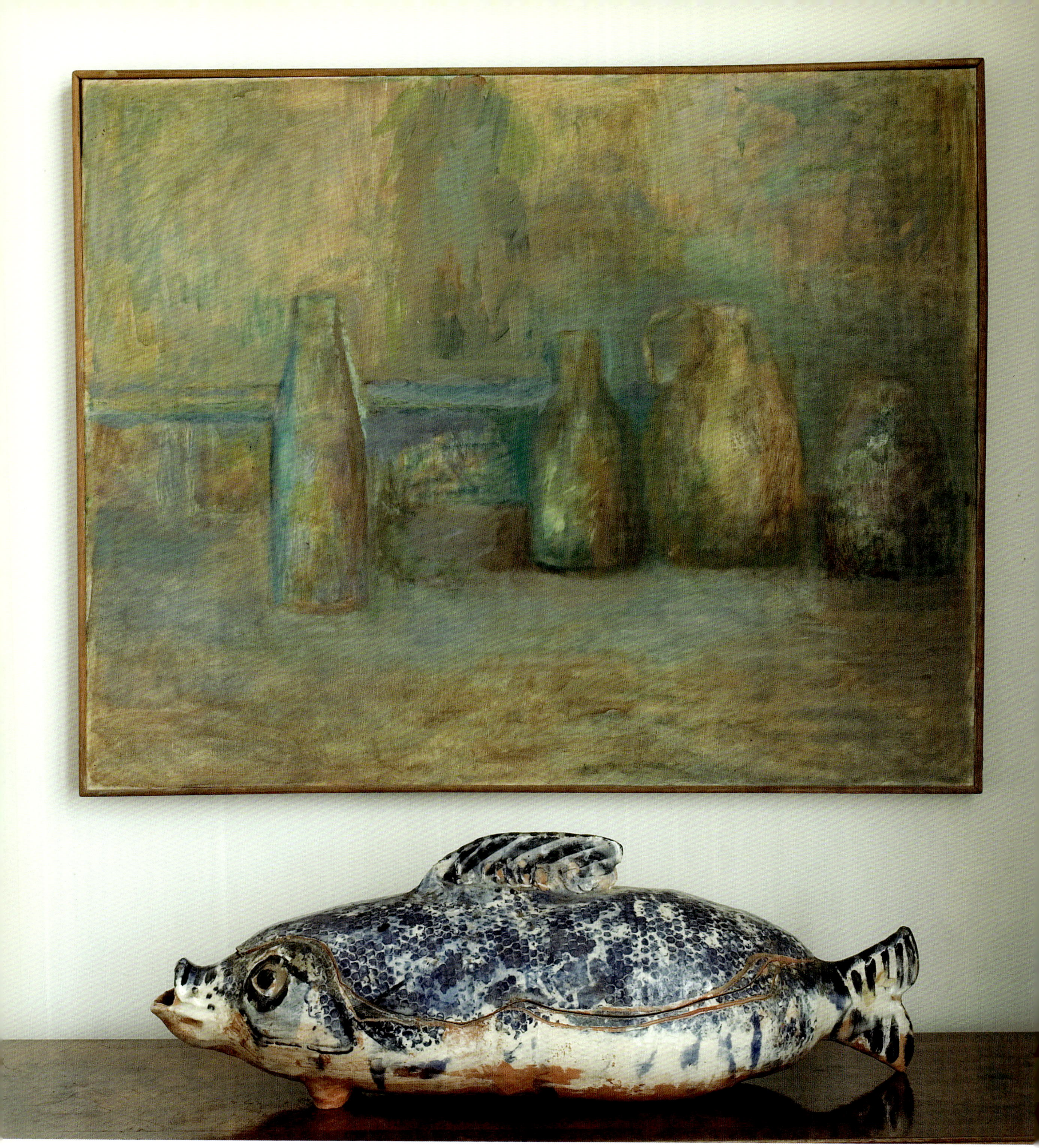

opposite:
66 (below) Fish tureen, unmarked, date unknown
Modelled
17 x 49 cm (6.7 x 19.3 in)
Collection: John Golding
(above) Adrian Stokes, Still Life, *1969–70*
Oil on canvas
50.9 x 63.5 cm (20 x 25 in)
Collection: John Golding
Photo: Stephen Brayne

67 Small sturgeon for caviar, unmarked, c.*1986*
Modelled
10 x 33 cm (3.9 x 13 in)
Collection: Dr Angela Hamilton
Photo: Stephen Brayne

upper part of the zoomorphic form and decorated and glazed separately. A series of rhinoceroses makes an impressive impact – massive, boldly modelled and conveying the essence of the beast with the élan of Dürer's famous woodcut. The Dürer-like exoticism reminds us of a significant part of her audience – art historians, psychoanalysts, artists and connoisseurs drawn initially into her circle by their admiration for her husband Adrian Stokes' writing. They remained loyal supporters after his death in 1972. Thus, the historian of Renaissance Italy Nicolai Rubenstein commissioned the first rhino in 1974 for the art historian Ernst Gombrich. Another was purchased by Dr Wolfgang Fischer, of Fischer Fine Art.[40] Surprisingly, they all turn out to be lidded soup tureens *(fig. 9)*. Here, perhaps, we can detect irony, or at least a joke on the part of Rubenstein. Her first rhinoceros was made shortly after T.H. Clarke's pioneering articles in *The Connoisseur* in which he tracked the various rhinoceroses imported into Europe in order to date and re-attribute works of art in which these great beasts appeared.[41]

Stokes' lidded fish vessels are also made as tureens, with smaller fish optimistically seen as potential repositories for caviar *(figs 66, 67, 69)*. But a more stylised series of fish is thrown as open dishes or bowls with modelled heads and tails. Birds, too, appear in this form, with cut and pierced

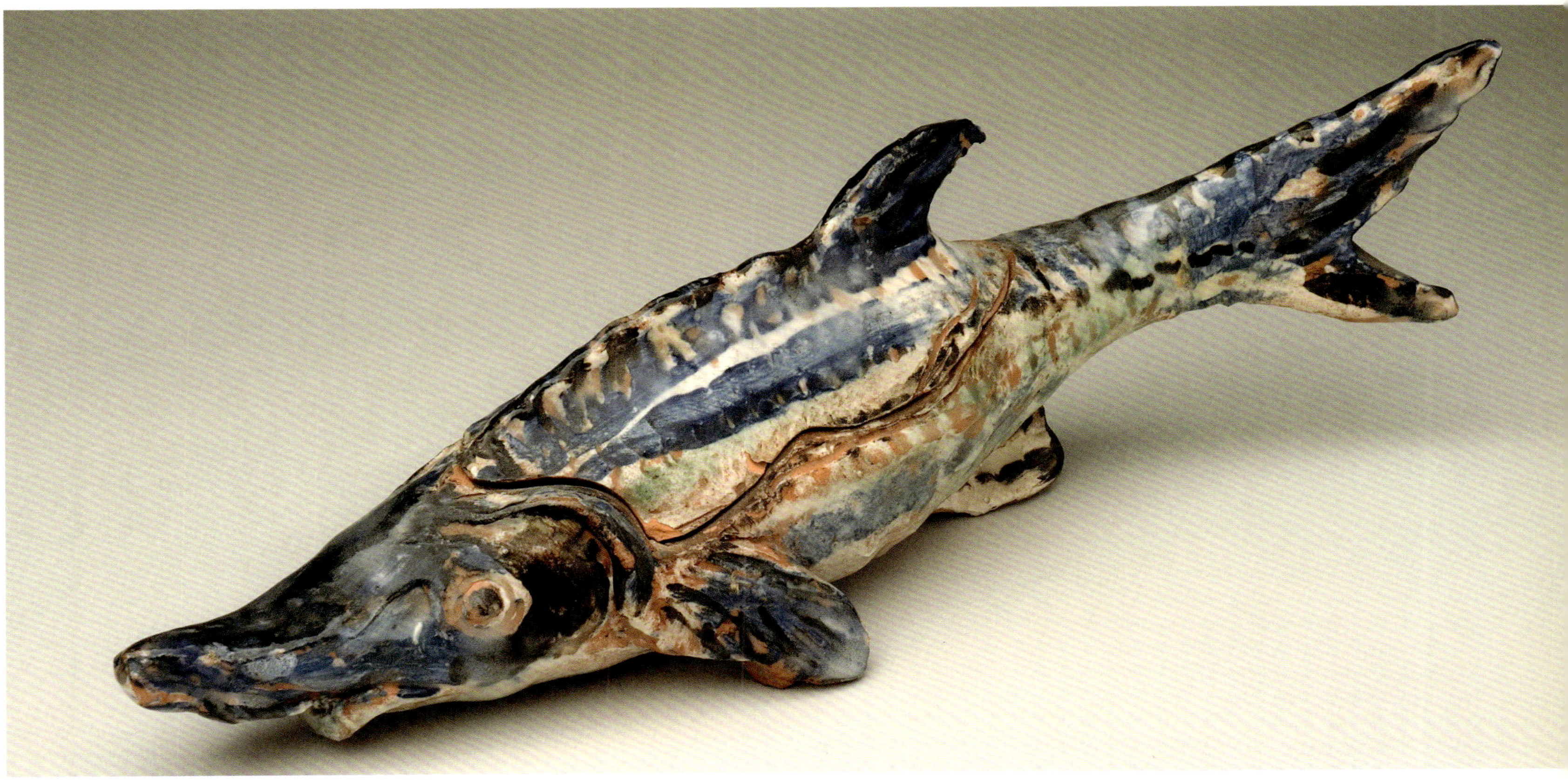

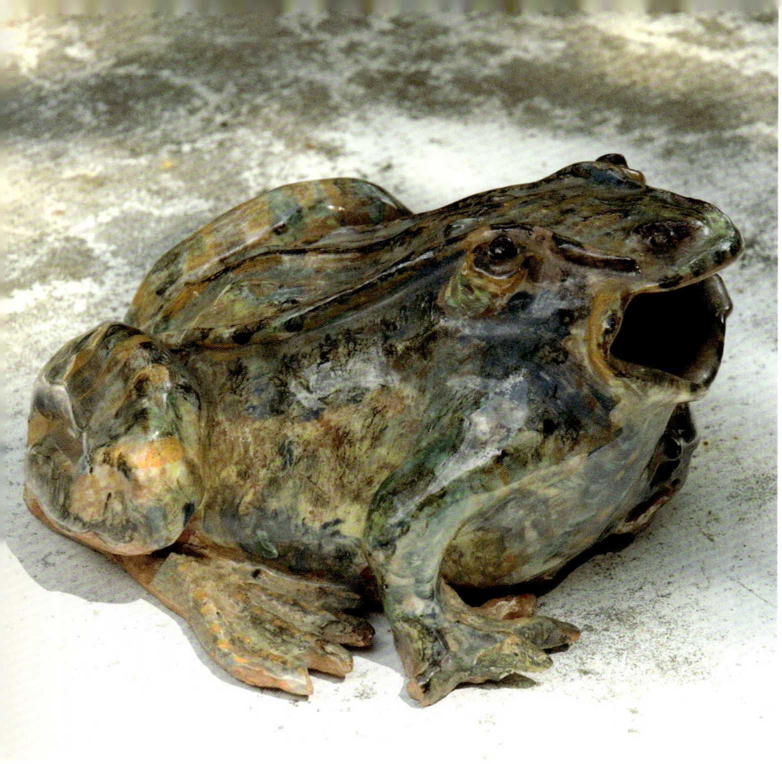

68 Toad, unmarked, early 1980s
Modelled
10 x 19 cm (3.9 x 7.5 in)
Collection: Richard Riley
Photo: Stephen Brayne

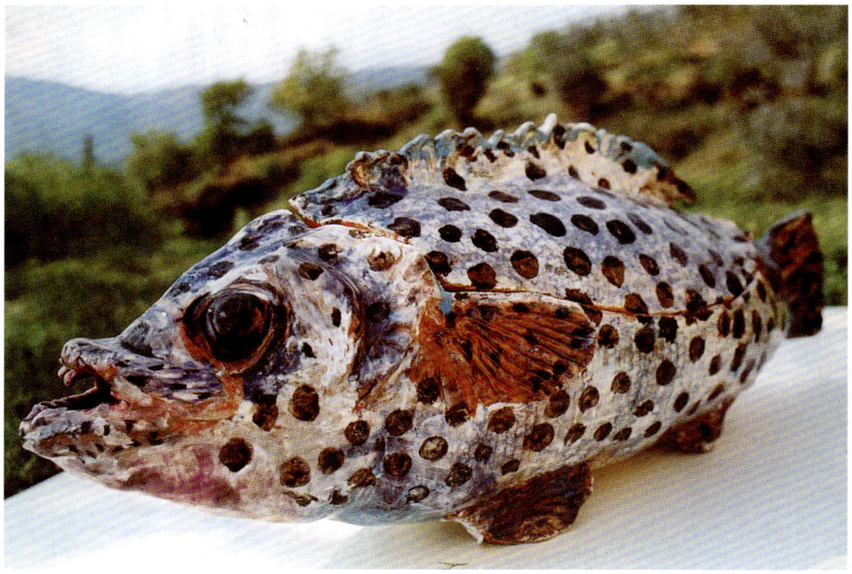

fluttering wings. Occasionally birds are luted on to a small thrown ceramic stand *(fig.70)*, poised with all the stylised grace of a dancer. Others, with fuller wings, are realised as displaying peacocks, made to conceal flower-pots. A series of ducks swim as lids on shallow casserole dishes. As Stokes noted helpfully on the back of one photograph of a lidded duck dish, the lid should be replaced by tin-foil when the dish is in the oven.[42] Stokes' fish and birds are usually thrown and then modelled – 'I bash it a bit and squeeze out a tail or a face'[43] – with empathetic skill.

More on Modelling

above right:
69 Spotted leopard fish, 1999, photographed in Italy for the invitation card to Ann Stokes: Soaring, Swooping, Leaping, *Charleston Gallery, Firle, Sussex, 1999*
Photo: John Ross

Some of Stokes' confidence as a modeller and hand-builder developed in classes that she began to attend in 1966–7 with Mary Day Lanier at the nearby Camden Arts Centre, as Richard Morphet mentions in his essay. Their teacher was a young Sudanese ceramicist, Mohammed Ahmed Abdulla *(fig.71)*, who had studied fine art and ceramics at Khartoum Technical Institute and won a scholarship to the Central School of Arts and Crafts in London, graduating in 1962.[44] His tutors at the Central included Gordon Baldwin, Dan Arbeid and William Newland (who taught him to throw), and William Turnbull who ran a pioneering Basic Design course modelled on the Bauhaus *Vorkurs*. Abdulla's work reflected the sculptural ethos of 1960s studio pottery. He worked in stoneware and porcelain, at that time making thrown and stacked sequences of columns, towers, mushroom forms and fragments of vernacular architecture, invariably combined with

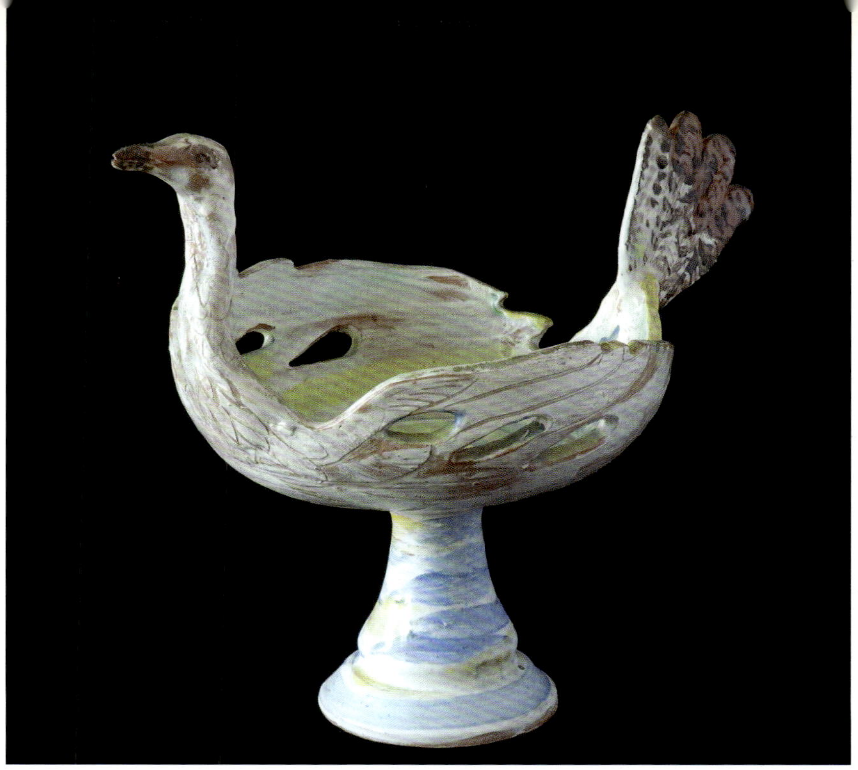

70 *Bird dish on a stand, marked Σ 8/86*
Thrown, modelled and pierced
23 x 30 x 18 cm (9 x 11.8 x 7 in)
Collection: Phoebe Greenwood
Photo: Stephen Brayne

sensitive hand-building. After graduating from the Central he had spent two years in Stoke-on-Trent, taking a postgraduate diploma in industrial pottery design and doing further research into the chemical analysis of ceramic materials. Arriving at Camden in 1966 he soon developed into a charismatic teacher. He attracted all kinds of students. There were middle-class married women for whom clay work proved a therapeutic outlet but also art students who found his informality created 'the right atmosphere to experiment and pursue personal ideas'.[45]

Altogether a remarkable person to be running part-time classes, Mo, as he was known, soon became friendly with Ann. He was struck by her energy and imagination, finding her 'excitable' and determined, learning what she needed to know with remarkable speed.[46] She began to work more three-dimensionally, modelling, as we have seen, thrown forms into fish and birds and stacking diverse components. Abdulla encouraged her foray into large coiled flowerpots, which she made for the interior decorator John Fowler's country retreat, The Hunting Lodge. Fowler kept her busy from 1967 into the early 1970s and he appears to have seen Ann as the embodiment of anti-industrialisation. He called on her to make 'heavy and chunky and not too smooth pots' for the garden, reflecting, 'I don't know how they got the clay so granular in the "old" days.'[47] Fowler also ordered double compartment vegetable dishes – 'very simple please' – and a jug with a golden brown glaze – 'very simple and a bit conventional as it's got to go with old things'.[48] He also suggested 'some trials of small blackish plates' – 'like the Bernard Leach plate I showed you'.[49]

71 *Ann Stokes and Mohammmed Abdulla, Church Row, Hampstead, late 1960s*
The artist's collection
Photographer unknown

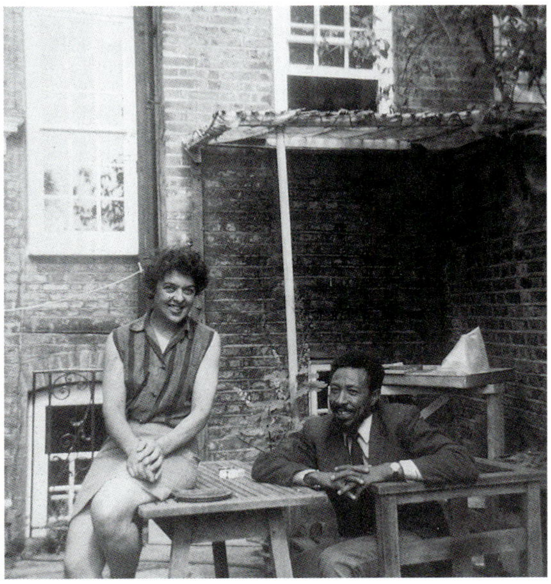

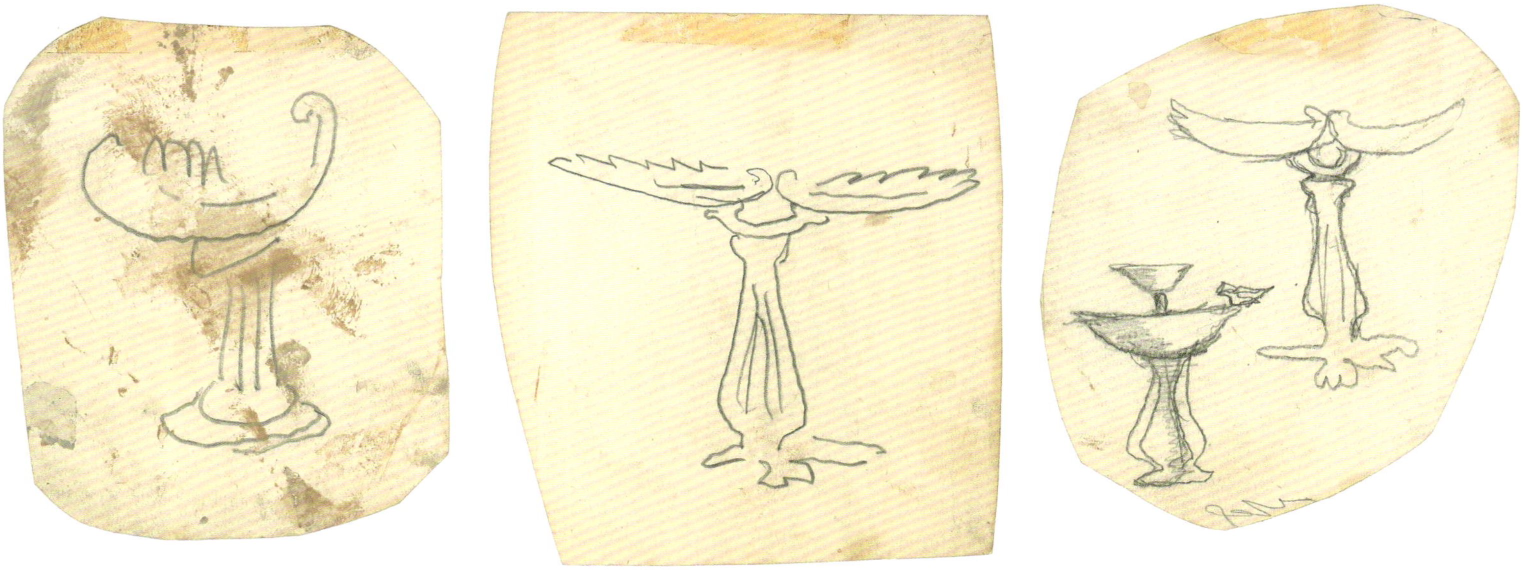

72 John Golding, drawings of birdbaths, c.1973
Pencil on paper
The artist's collection
Copyright: John Golding

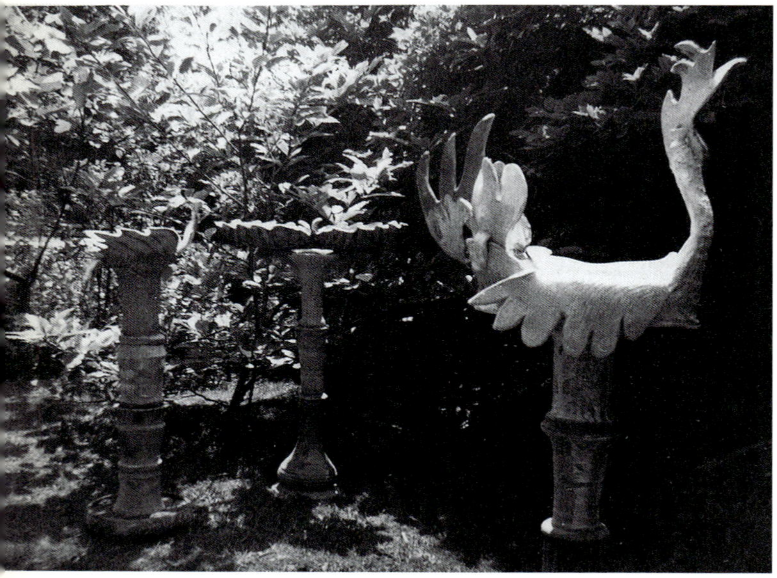

73 Birdbaths, early 1970s, 20 Church Row, Hampstead
The artist's collection
Photo: Ann Stokes

But if Stokes was ready to respond to Fowler's faux-pastoral vision, making her garden pots as chunky as possible, she was also experimenting, with Mo's encouragement, in other directions. There are some black and white photographs of Stokes' early birdbaths *(fig.73)*, perched on tall, stacked pedestals. These seem derived from the pierced pottery stands holding cult vessels in the Mesopotamian Galleries in the British Museum, or perhaps from the 'fruit stands' illustrated in her copy of A.D. Lacy's *Greek Pottery in the Bronze Age* (1967). Some fluent drawings were supplied by John Golding, and Ann followed them quite closely *(fig.72)*. She did not copy Golding's fluted classical or swelling baroque plinths, but she created a slab-built bird and a bivalve shell as birdbaths, and a more conventional fountain with descending basins. Golding's drawings also seem to have developed into strange bird lights, balanced on plinths *(fig.34)*. At first her fountain hydrology was crude, but by 1985 Stokes had several fountains in her garden, each surmounted by a fluttering bird. When the fountain played the bird appeared to beat its wings in the water, or, in another ensemble, the bird was revolved by a jet of water issuing from the mouth of a frog crouched at the fountain's base. At that time a life-sized ceramic eland also sat in the garden *(fig.74)*. The effect was strongly Italian, recalling, in miniaturised form, the *animalier* creations in the Parco dei Mostri at the Villa Orsini outside Bomarzo. By 1980 Ann and Ian were spending half the year in their house near Cortona, responsible for some 250 olive trees. Ann had a studio there and these long sojourns had an undoubted effect on her work.

Gaiety increased, in the form of fish lights, or ceiling lights made of a pierced, inverted bowl to which fluttering birds were luted *(fig.75)*. The

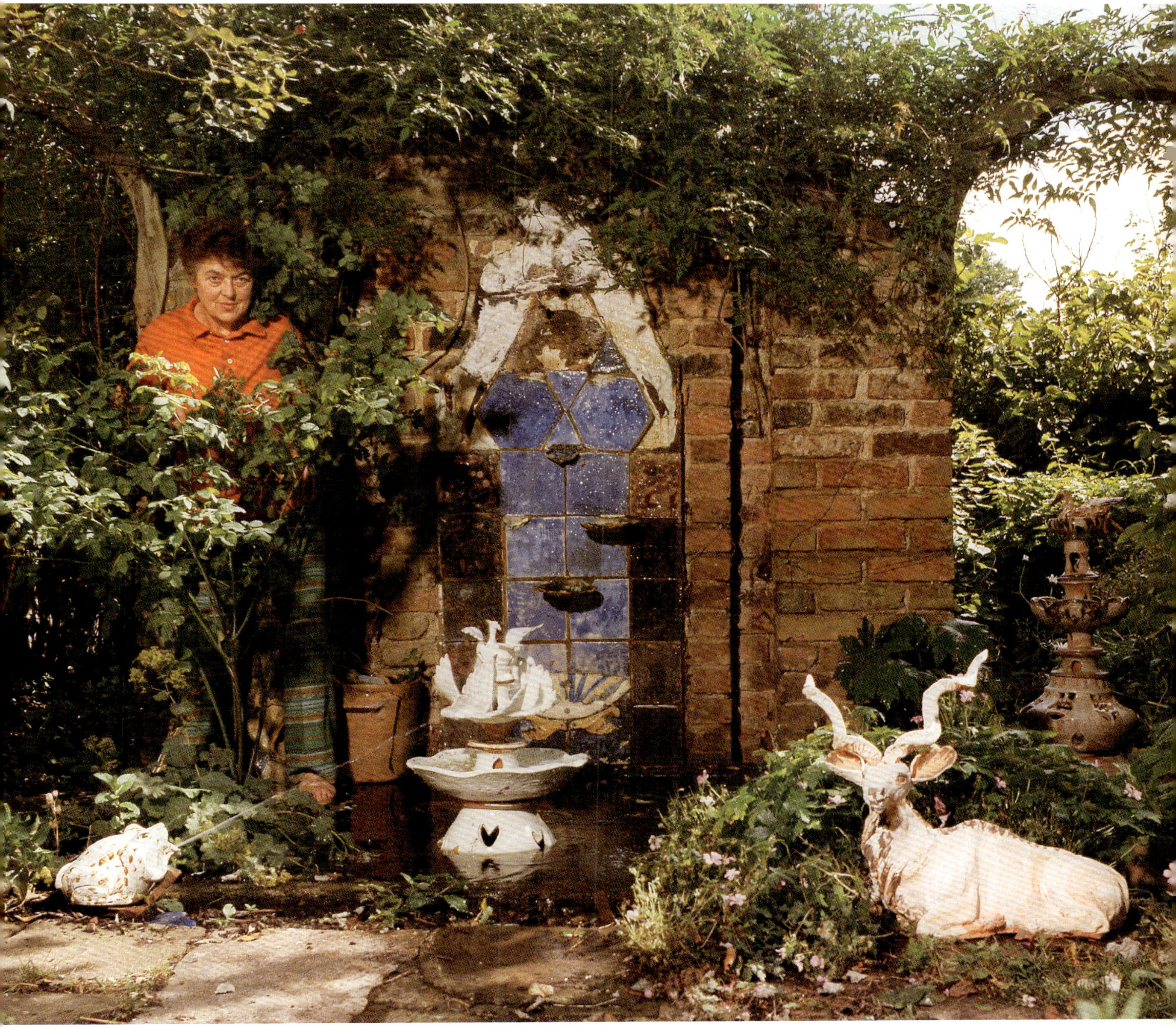

74 Ann Stokes with two fountains, a toad and an eland, in the garden at Church Row, Summer 1985
Photo: Ben Rice

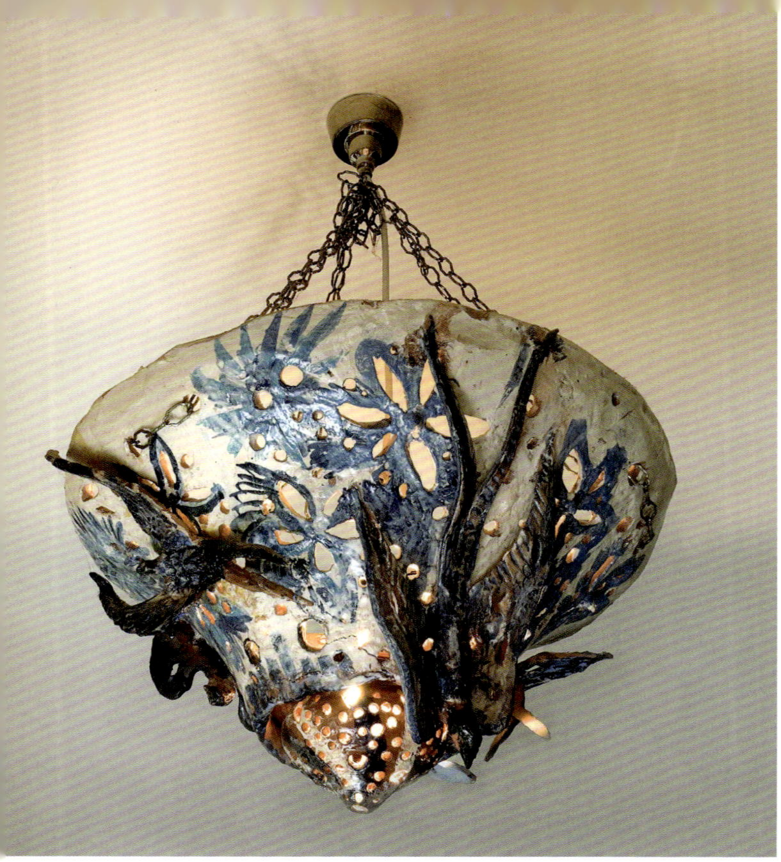

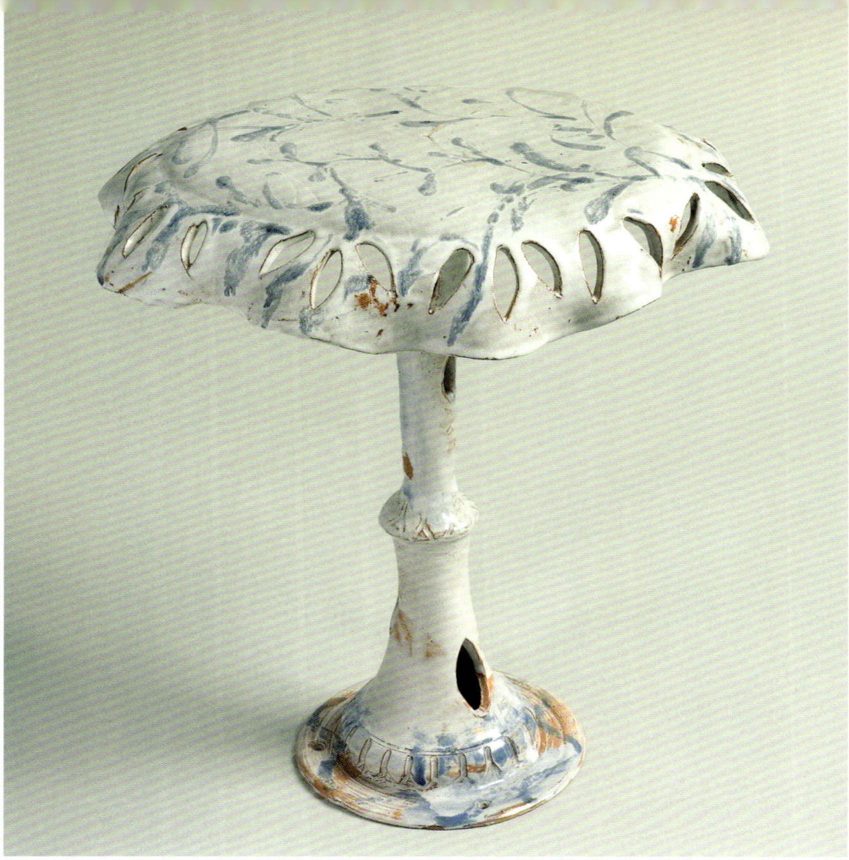

75 Chandelier, c.1995
Thrown and modelled
(height) 35.5 cm (14 in), (diameter at top) 55.9 cm (22 in)
Collection: Lord and Lady Ravensdale
Photo: Philip Stokes

76 Occasional table, unmarked, 1998
Thrown, moulded and slab-built
(height) 39 cm (15.4 in), (table-top) 40 x 30 cm (15.7 x 11.8 in)
The artist's collection
Photo: Stephen Brayne

opposite:
77 Occasional table, unmarked, 2002
Thrown, modelled and slab-built
(height) 43 cm (16.9 in), (table-top width at widest point) 43 cm (16.9 in)
The artist's collection
Photo: Stephen Brayne

78 Edging tiles in the garden at 20 Church Row, 1976
Photo: Philip Stokes

1990s saw the appearance of Ann's occasional tables, the top moulded like a tablecloth mounted on a pierced stand derived from Bronze Age pottery *(figs 76–7)*, and her distinctly Moroccan-looking stove-like lights in tin-glaze. Ann tends only to date her tableware, chiefly her plates. But the drive to make 'things' appears to have intensified in the late 1970s and 1980s. There are her edging tiles for flowerbeds in the form of tin-glazed horses' profiles *(fig.78)* and in the early 1980s the first of a series of letter racks, whose compartments were formed by lively horses, objects one might expect to be made in wood rather than clay. Her drive to turn dreams and events into ceramics had already led to some touching oddities, such as the tenderly made, slab-built tableau of her husband Ian Angus in the cramped bathroom under the stairs at Church Row *(fig.43)*, a toy-like ceramic bed with a mother and child lying under a real counter-pane *(fig.79)*, and a woman and child dancing made for Verity Ravensdale. Stokes rarely represents the human figure but when she does, her subjects look vulnerable – the exception being her *quattrocento* noblemen, gaily riding forth, taken from Benozzo Gozzoli's fresco of *The Journey of the Magi* (1459–61) in the Chapel of the Palazzo Medici-Riccardi in Florence *(fig.80)*. Her enthusiasm for the ancient world is reified in her well-researched clay models of Greek rowing and sailing ships, accurate enough to appear museological. Two, appropriately enough, were made in the late 1970s for the Greek restaurant owner Chris Dromedous, one to be submerged as a 'wreck' in a fish tank.[50]

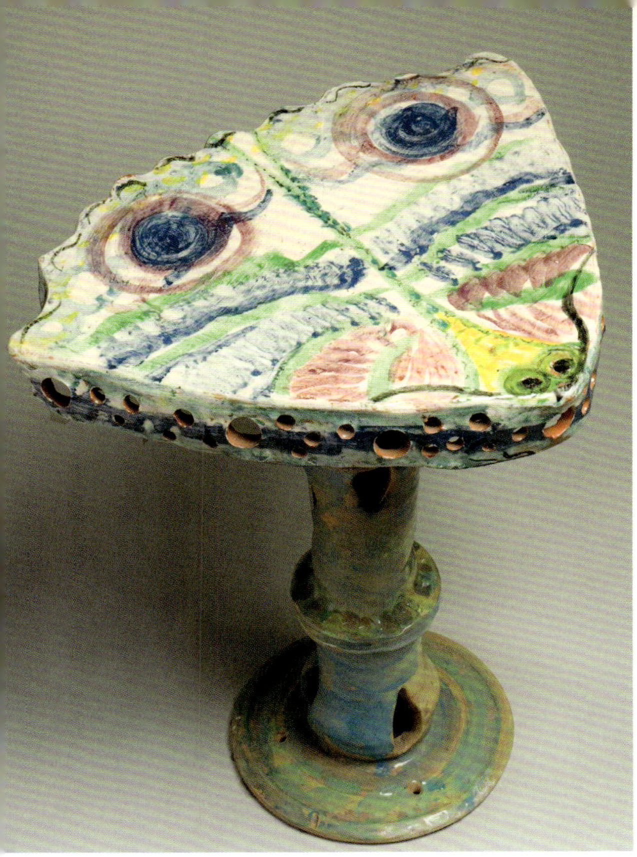

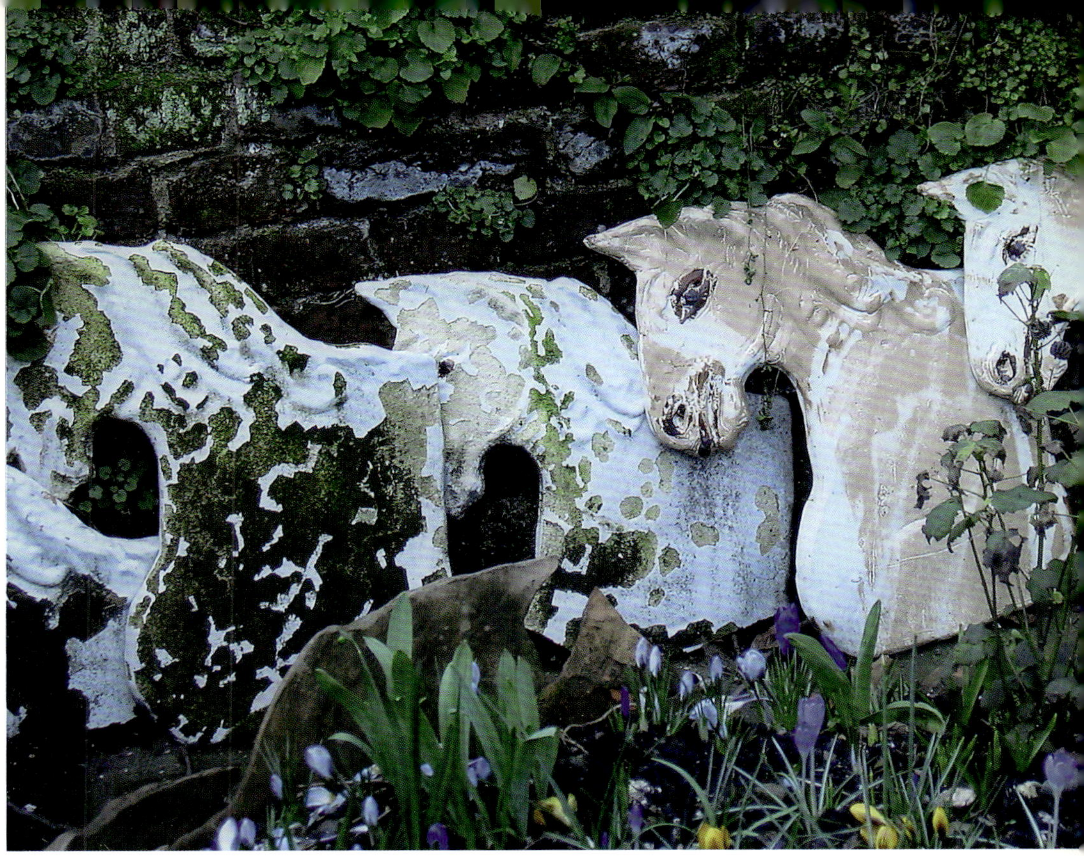

Myths and Legends – Tiles, Mirrors and Birds, Crocodiles and Trees

These clay models of Greek rowing vessels were preceded by an earlier work, a tile panel for the kitchen at Church Row, a bird's-eye seascape filled with triremes and sporting dolphins. Ann dates it to 1966 and remembers it was made to hide a damp patch. She began working confidently with tiles very early on – 'nothing daunted me in those days' – and they form an impressive, if more conventionally beautiful, part of her oeuvre, suggesting her skills as an illustrator and narrative artist. Several panels picture ancient oared Greek ships – one made in the mid 1990s showing rowers in a fierce storm, dolphins leaping *(fig.28)*. Another panel has a more stately ship entering a harbour, the sky and sea washed in atmospheric blues, framed by a rosette and swastika pattern taken from a 500 BC terracotta sarcophagus excavated near Smyrna, now in the British Museum *(fig.29)*. In 1973 Stokes began a series of tiles built into the risers of the stairs at Church Row from the basement to the ground floor – pastoral Aesopian narratives of birds and animals modelled in low relief, coloured in delicate blues and green and ochres *(fig.30)*. Two other tile panels at Church Row are strongly neo-Romantic in mood. A freestanding panel of great beauty in her studio, made around 1990 *(fig.81)*, depicts a flaming serpentine tree (neo-Romanticism at its most Blakean) with long tailed birds flying amongst the pattern of its branches against a Pompeian red background. It has some of the qualities

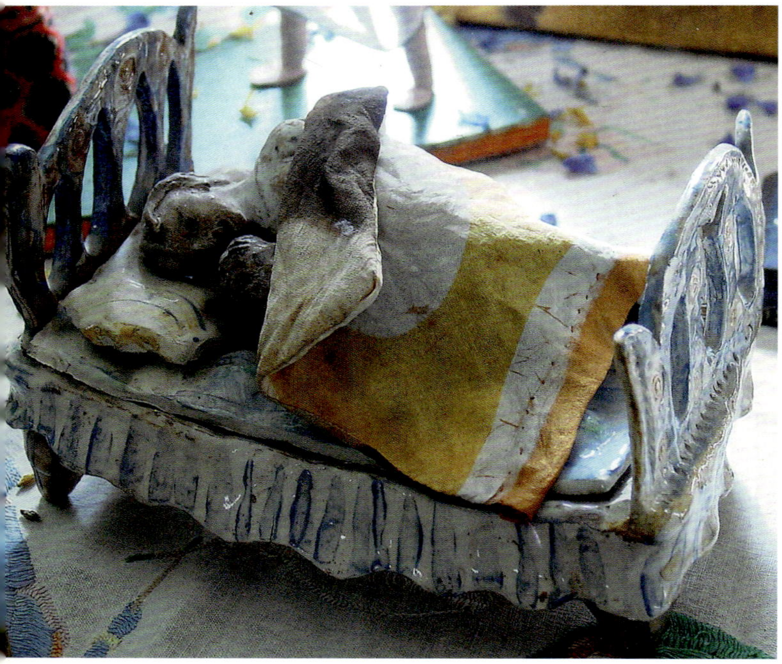

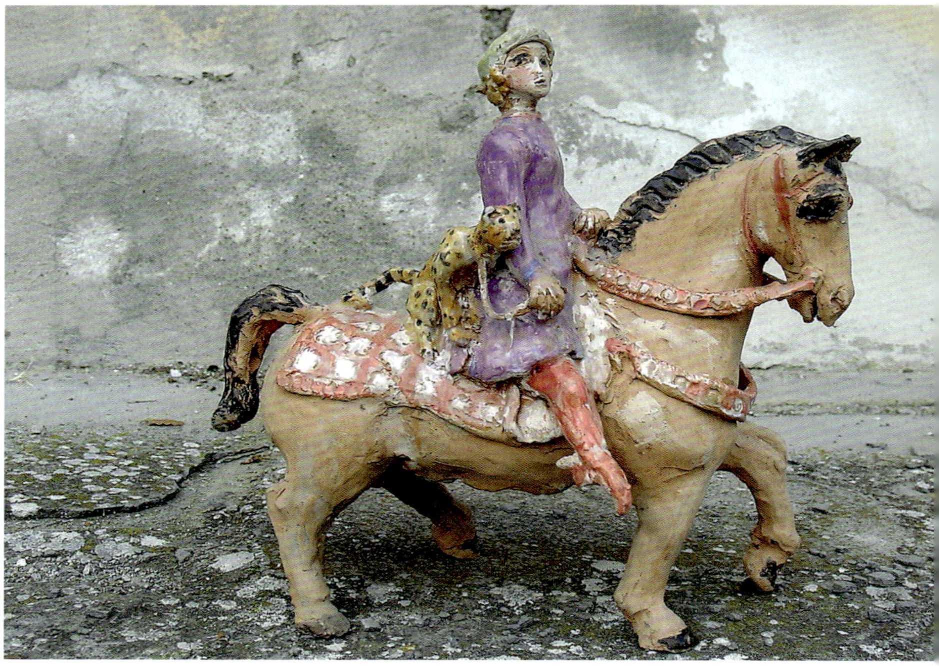

79 Mother and Child, *1985*
Modelled, cotton coverlet
10 x 42 x 33.5 cm (3.9 x 16.5 x 13.2 in)
Collection: Lord and Lady Ravensdale
Photo: Philip Stokes

80 *Horse and Rider, 1980s, one of three based on Benozzo Gozzoli's* Procession of the Three Kings, *Medici-Riccardi Palace, Florence*
Modelled
(height) 27 cm
The artist's collection
Photo: Philip Stokes

81 Forest Fire, *1990, made for Nigel Greenwood's New Burlington Street Gallery, London*
Carved relief glazed tiles
128 x 97 cm (50.4 x 38.2 in)
The artist's collection
Photo: Stephen Brayne

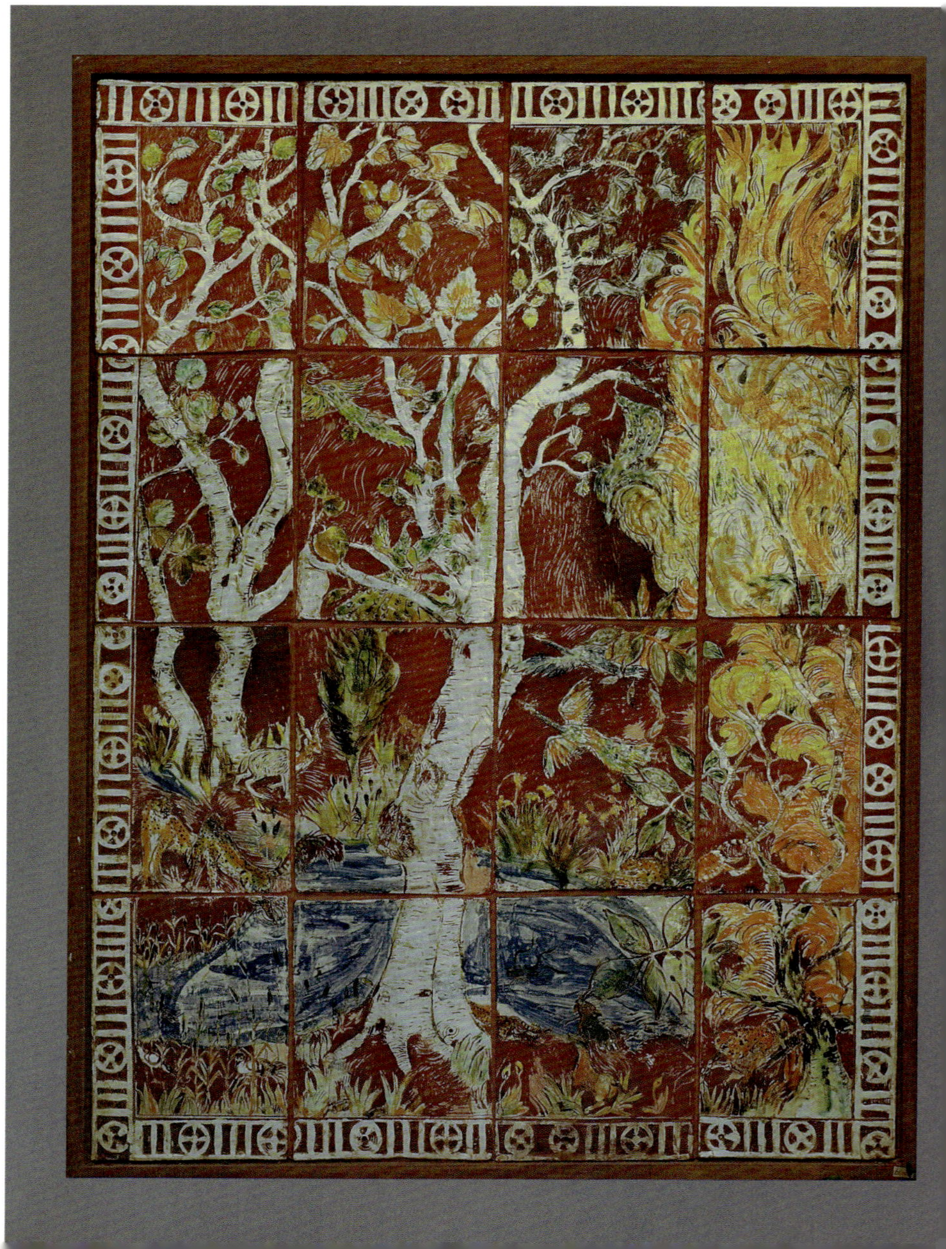

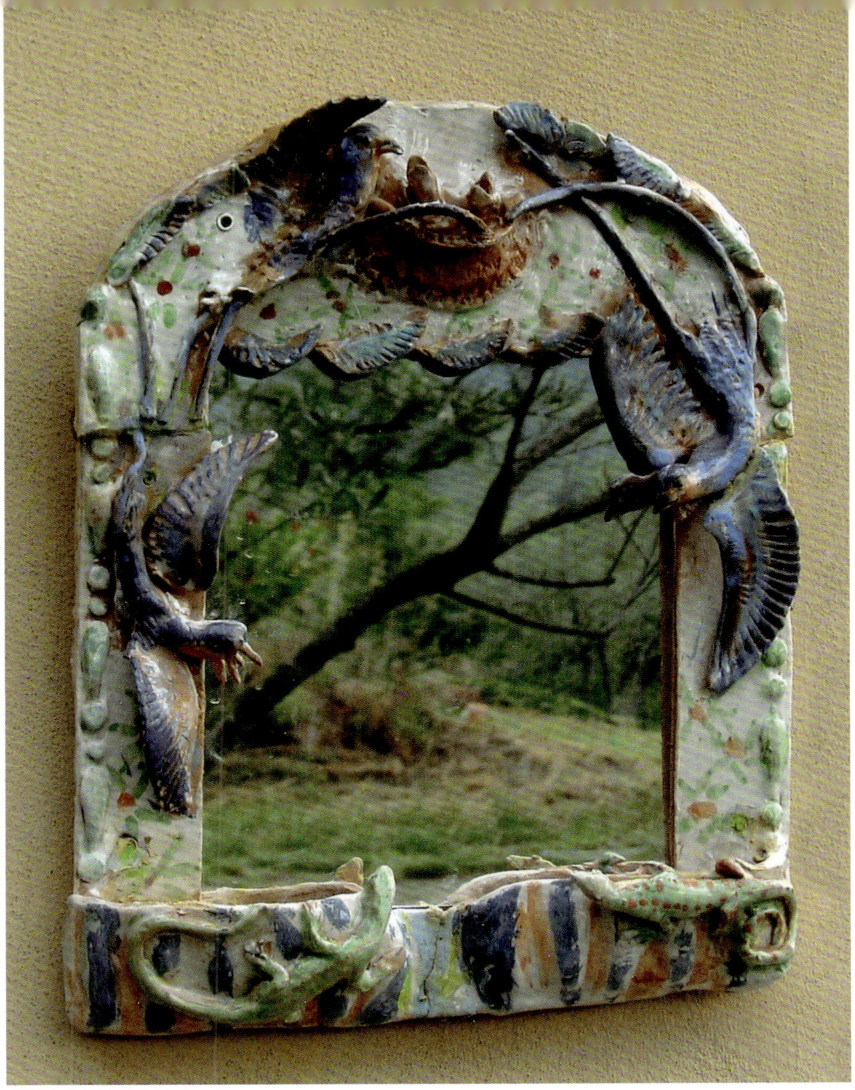

82 Mirror with swallows and lizards, 2000
Tiles, modelled birds, mirror glass on board
50 x 39 cm (19.7 x 15.4 in)
The artist's collection
Photo: Philip Stokes

of a backdrop for some piece of theatre or, more likely, ballet. Outside the house, built in above the area, there is another panel of a tree alive with swans.

From these versions of pastoral it was a short step to Stokes' great sequence of mirrors. She has made over eighty mirrors and believes the first were made as early as 1965. She remembers selling one to Sonia Orwell at a Christmas sale – which perhaps pushes the date forward to 1967. Certainly the mirrors went hand in hand with Stokes' facture of tiles – they are in effect tiles attached to a wooden support, framing the mirror glass. Mirror frames have a peculiar role. The job of the picture frame is to enhance a painting, to frame out the rest of the world. Arguably a picture needs a frame as much as a frame needs a picture.[51] In the case of mirrors there is potential for the supplemental *(figs 18, 82–3)* – the frame – to make witty play with the mirror's reflective role, to get right into the picture and curb the *vanitas* of the reflectee. As Stokes' mirrors became more ambitious she came to exploit the mirror and frame paradox to the full, by modelling birds and animals that peer into the glass, and in the case of her mirrors embellished

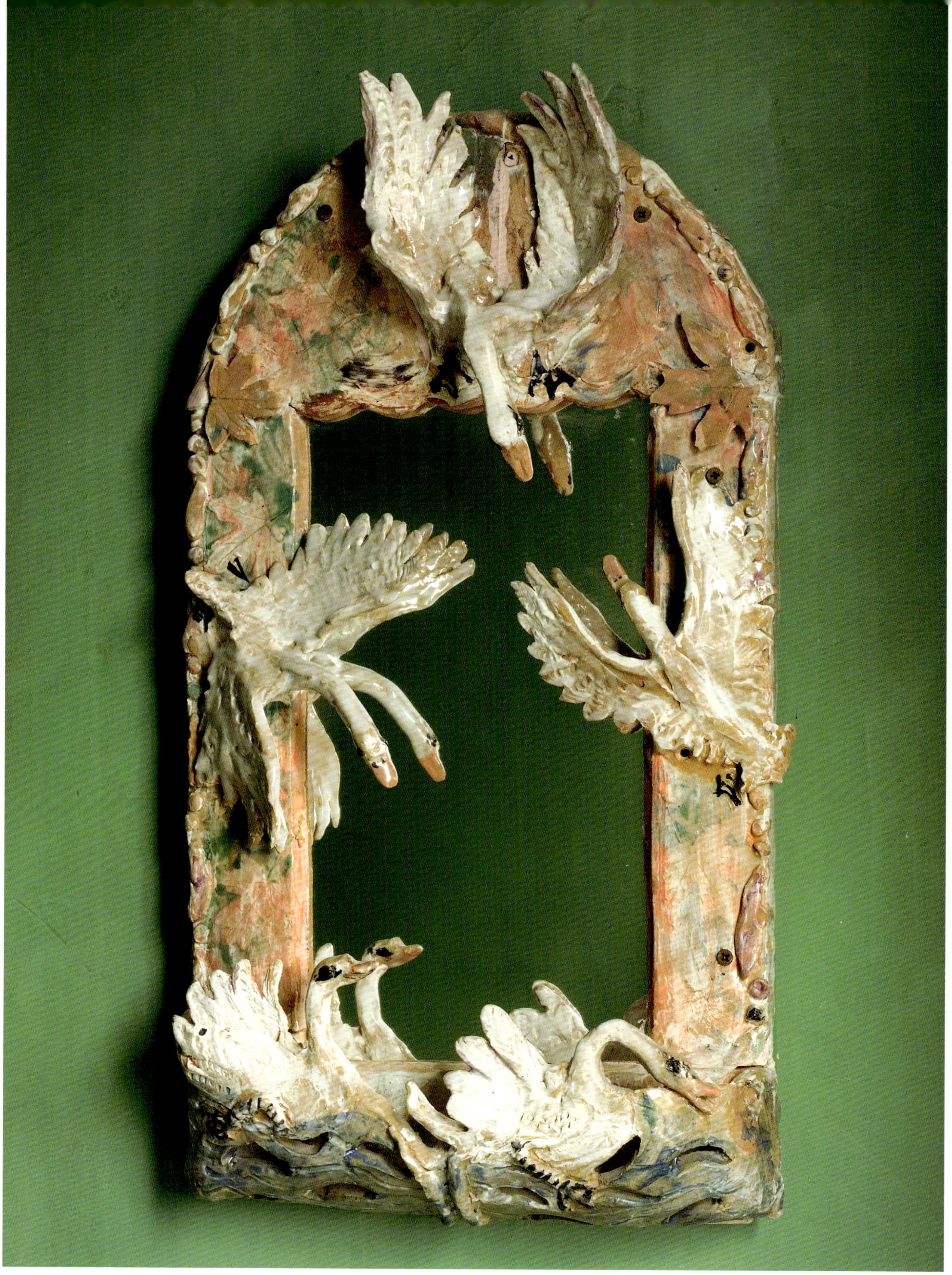

83 Swan mirror, 1992
Tiles, modelled birds, mirror glass on board
56 x 31 cm (22 x 12.2 in)
Collection: Niki and David Soskice
Photo: Stephen Brayne

84 Hummingbird, 2001, photographed for the invitation card to Ann Stokes: Retrospective, *11 September – 3 October 1998, Rebecca Hossack Gallery, Windmill Street, London*
Modelled
15 x 15 x 10 cm (5.9 x 5.9 x 3.9 in)
The artist's collection
Photo: Rebecca Hossack Gallery

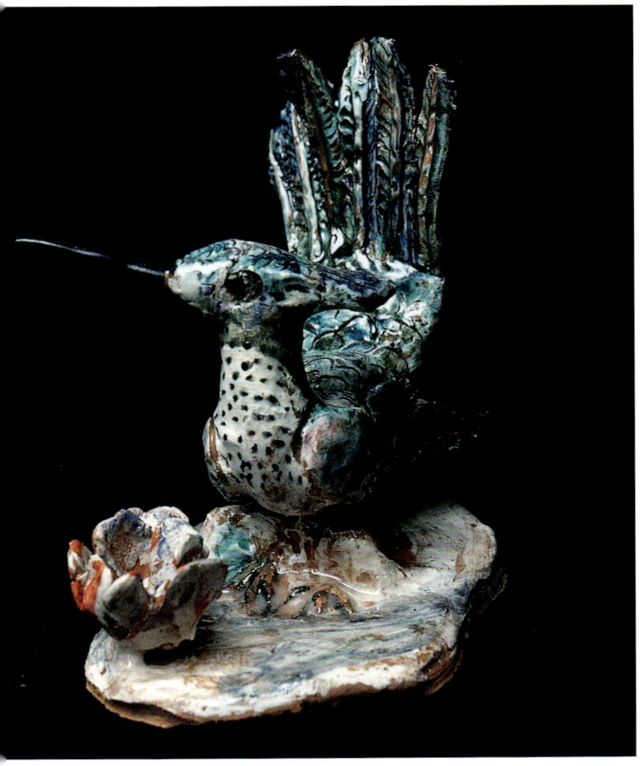

with magnificent swans, poised to go literally through the looking-glass. Her use of birds as a cresting at the top of the mirror and her fondness for candleholders have precedents in English mirrors and pier glasses, reaching a climacteric in eighteenth-century Rococo carved and gilt frames. But she has also taken Italian altarpieces as a model, with the lower part of the mirror frame resembling a *predella*, with a narrative tale to tell – one that would sometimes run round the whole frame, full of danger and excitement: nests are protected, birds fight with snakes *(fig.19)*, sea monsters threaten mer-babies, mermaids come to the rescue. Jennifer Anderson had such a mirror hanging in her study and as headmistress of London's Francis Holland School for Girls she found that simply pointing out the details would cheer up an unhappy student.[52]

Swans have long been favoured birds, made life-size as crestings over doorways, their great wingspan cut out of sections of rolled pierced clay. Their grandeur almost makes them ceramic equivalents of the Ho Ho birds carved in white painted wood by the mysterious Rococo designer Luke Lightfoot.[53] These swans appear to belong in the great saloon but are to be found, imperious, in Ann's studio, in north London kitchens and Greek restaurants *(figs 5–6)*. Stokes has also made flocks of smaller, freestanding birds *(fig.84)* – vital and expressive counterparts to the ceramic industry's naturalistic 'ranges', like Crown Staffordshire's 'British Garden Birds' and the 'Peter Scott Wildlife Series'. Some are perched in relief on slab-built boxes. We have grown blasé in a world of endless images and films recording the natural world. Stokes re-presents the wonder of small birds, fish, rhinos, wild swans and peacocks, and from 1979, crocodiles.

Her first crocodile appeared in 1979. It was small, inhabiting a freely modelled ceramic pool the size of a serving plate, the whole ensemble resembling Chinese Han dynasty tomb sculpture in the form of miniature pottery ponds with fish and frogs and trees, made to enjoy in the afterlife *(fig.90)*. These playful small crocodiles were also adapted as candlesticks holding candles in their jaws *(fig.14)*. But in 1981 she made her first life-sized crocodile, unglazed, with a massive threatening head. It is a sculpture of discrete parts, a diagrammatic piece rather than a purely representational one. The constituent parts of its long body and tail look very like curved Mediterranean ridge tiles, traditionally shaped by being draped over a mould the size of a man's thigh *(fig.89)*. Just as Picasso adapted bricks and kiln furniture to carry images of men and women and landscapes, Stokes quotes the roof-tile form and transforms it into something unexpected and exotic. Although, as we have seen, anything can be made of clay, this unexpected

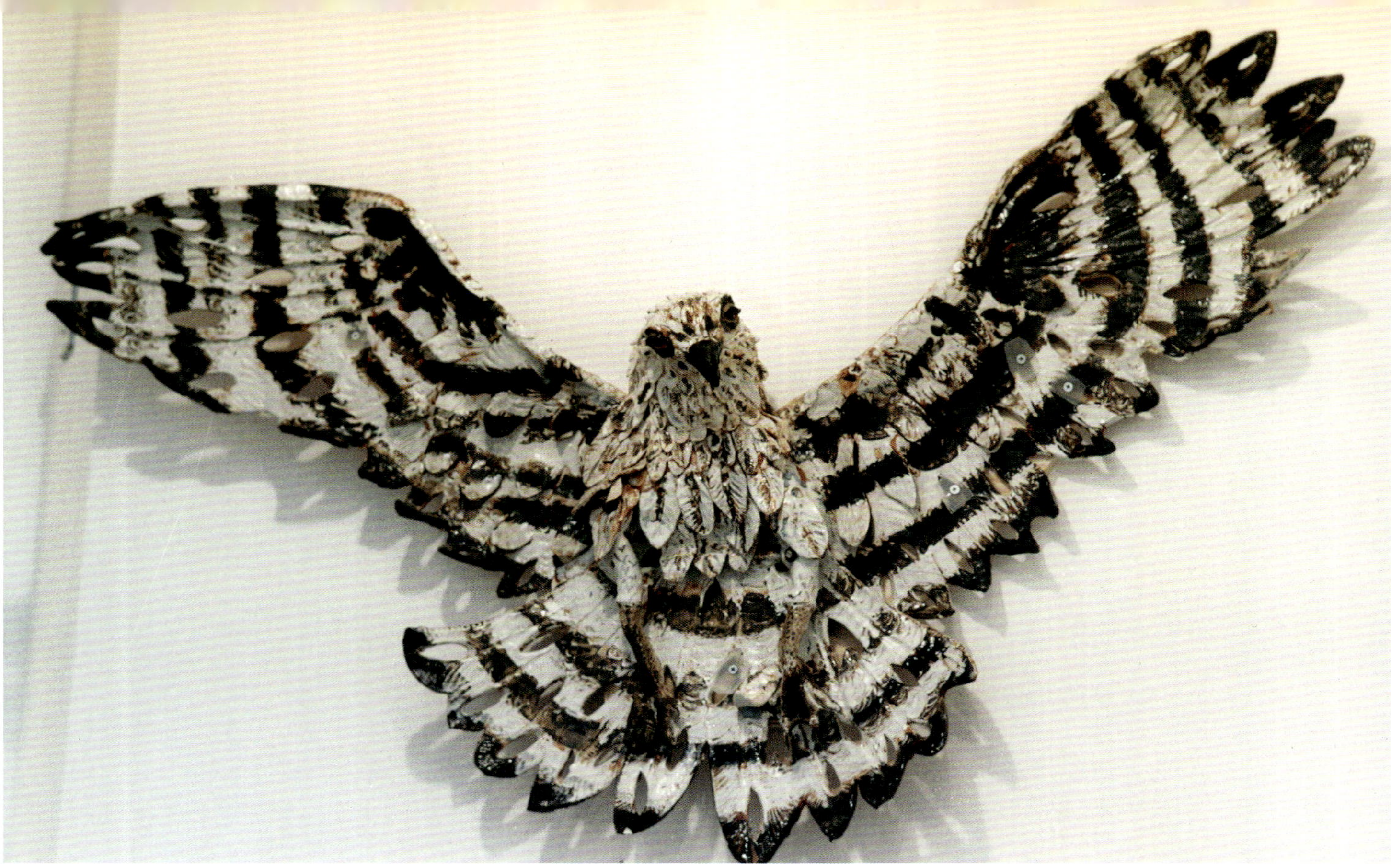

85 Osprey, 1990
Slab-built, modelled and assembled
145 x 55 cm (57 x 21.7 in)
Collection: George Farelly
Photo: Rebecca Hossack Gallery

86 Ann and Ian Angus with a Peacock, 2005
Assembled shaped tiles painted with slips and oxides
(height) 305 cm (120 in)
The artist's collection
Photo: Philip Stokes

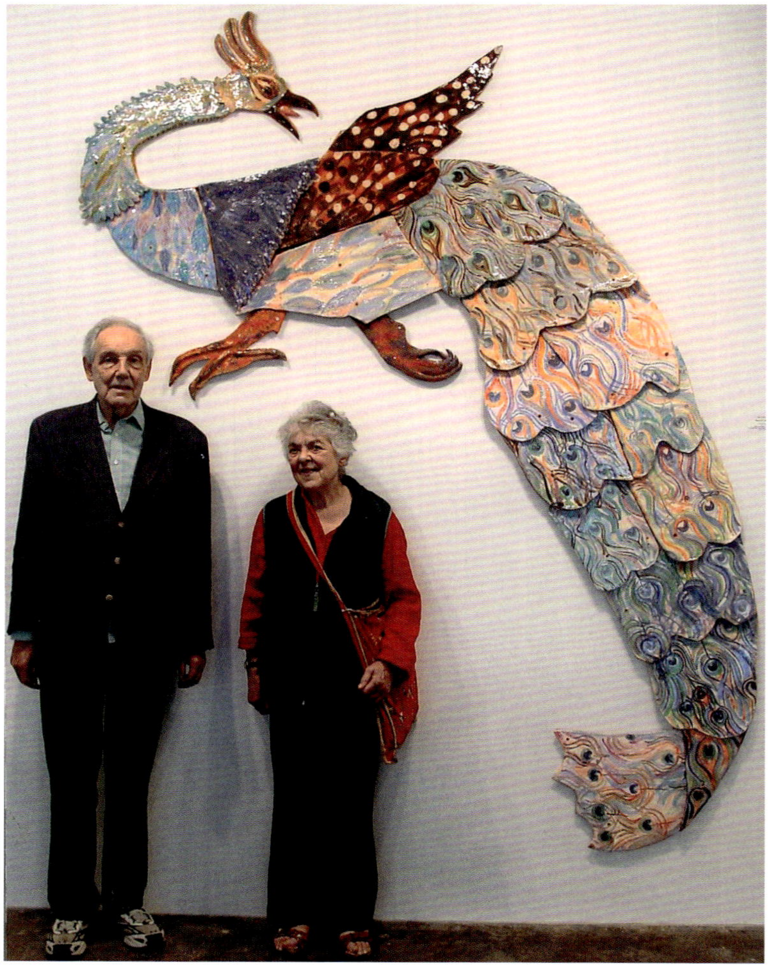

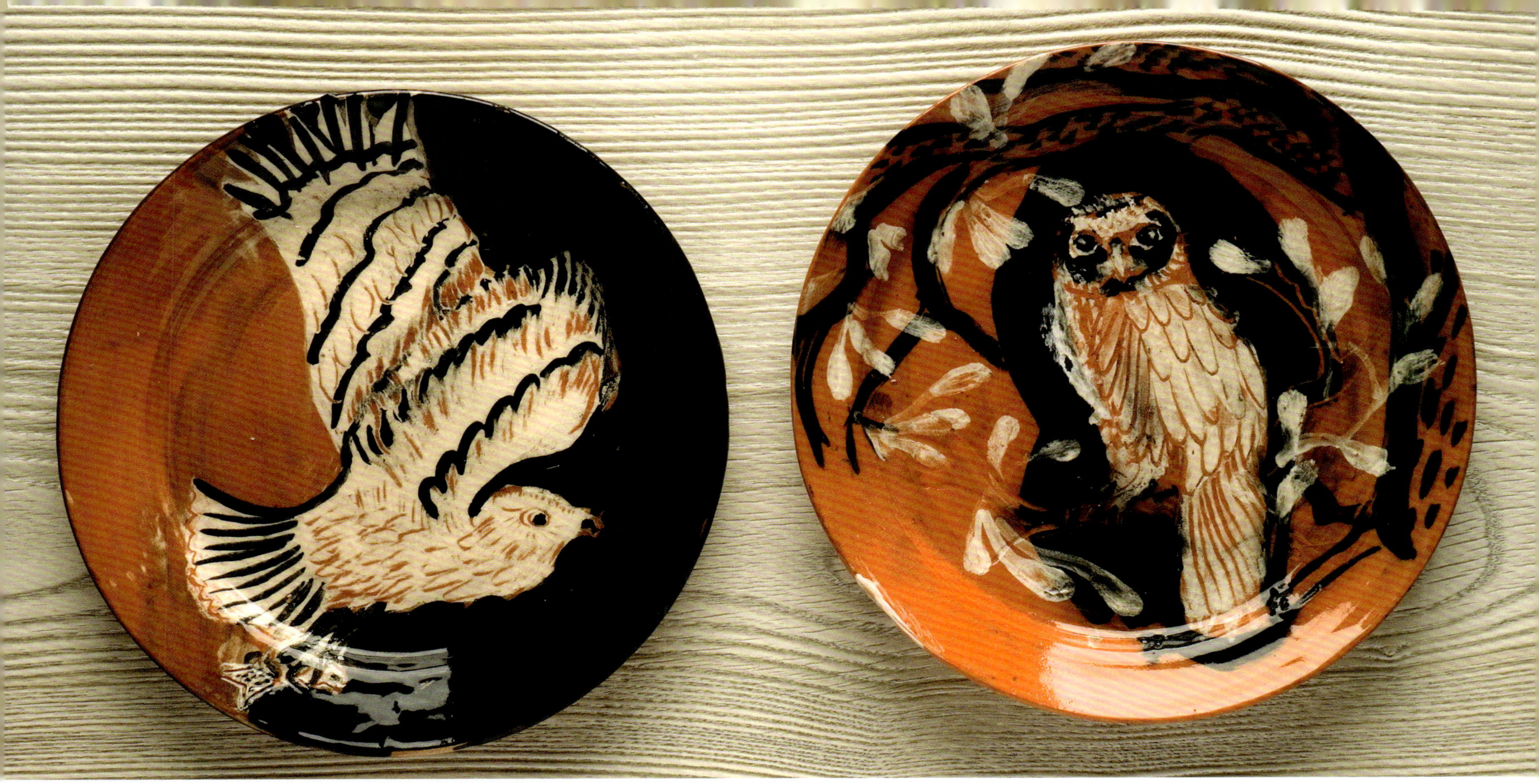

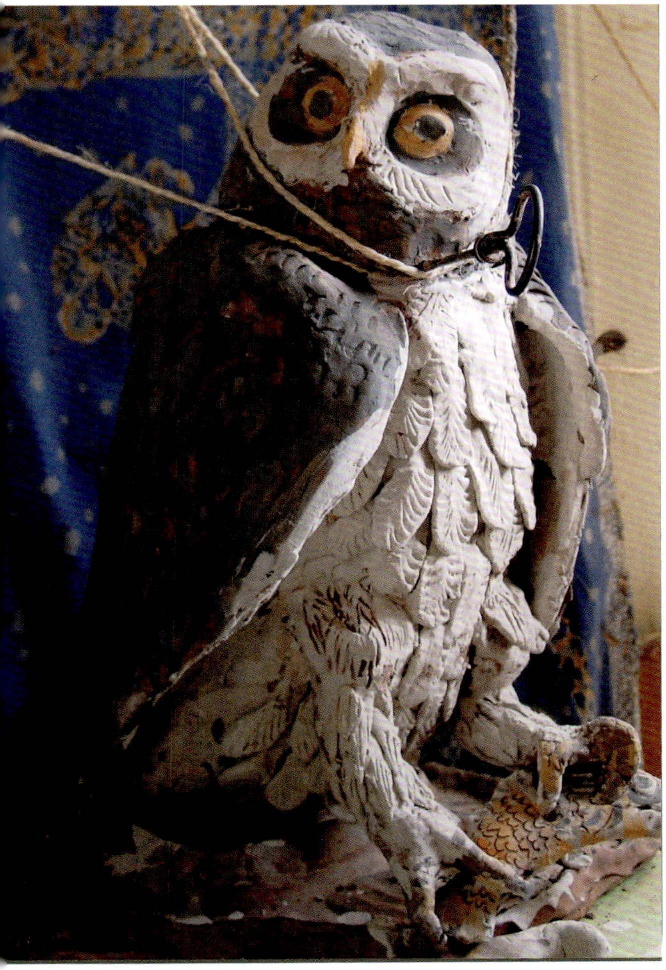

87 Owl plates, marked (left to right) 'Fish owl Σ 2/99'; 'Spectacled owl Σ 2/99'
(left to right) 19.5 cm (7.7 in); 20 cm (7.9 in)
Collection: John Golding
Photo: Stephen Brayne

88 Owl with fish (work in progress), supported in preparation for glaze firing, 1990s
Modelled
The artist's collection
Photo: Philip Stokes

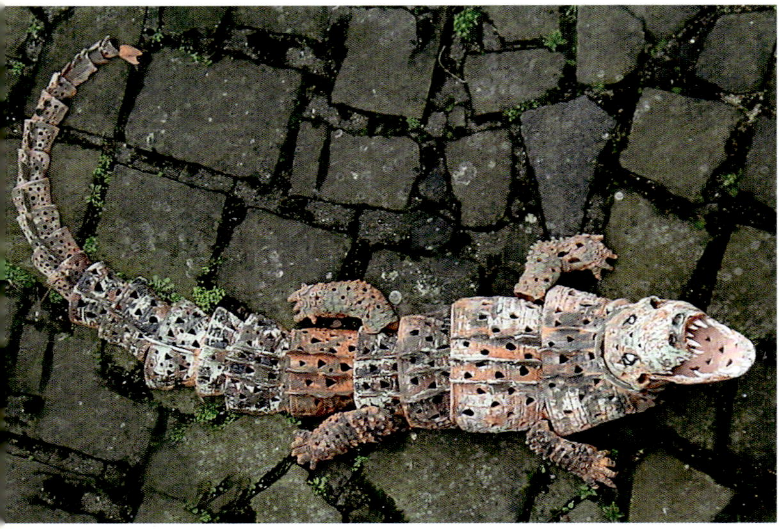

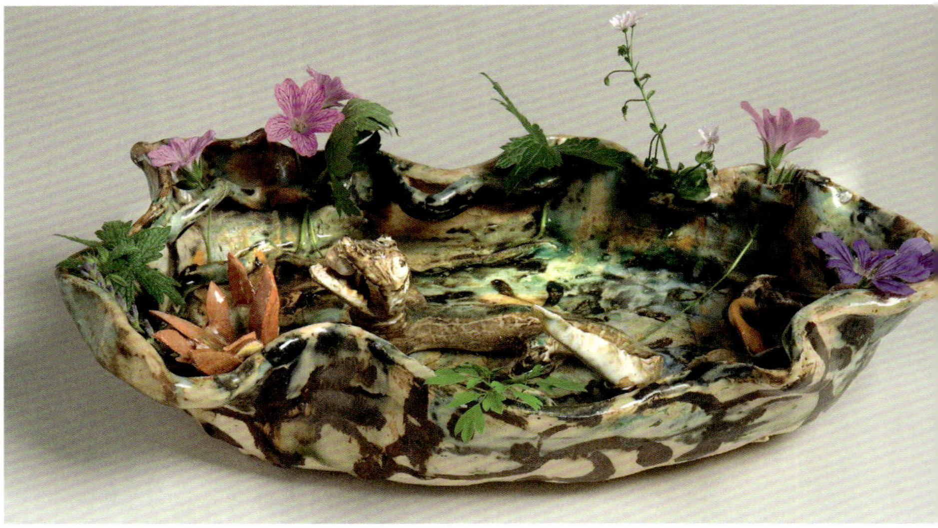

89 Crocodile photographed in the garden at Church Row, 2002
Photo: Philip Stokes

90 Crocodile, marked 'Σ 79 in pool'
Slab-built and modelled
(crocodile length) 8 cm (3.1 in), (pool length) 34 cm (13.4 in)
The artist's collection
Photo: Stephen Brayne

opposite:
91 Olive Tree*, 2003, photographed for the invitation card to* Giardino Incantevole: a mixed exhibition of pottery by Ann Stokes and paintings by Peter Bartlett*, Rebecca Hossack Gallery, Charlotte Street, London, November 2003–January 2004*
Modelled earthenware and plywood
(height) 15 cm (5.9 in)
Collection: Rebecca Hossack Gallery
Photo: Philip Stokes

92 Autumn Tree*, 2007*
Modelled earthenware and plywood
(height) 76 cm (30 in)
Collection: Rebecca Hossack Gallery
Photo: Philip Stokes

linkage with one of the most familiar architectural details of a traditional Italian skyline plays on our ceramic sensibility – another example of Stokes' skilful, and possibly unconscious, employment of ceramic echoes.[54]

These crocodiles were often lit from within *(fig. 15)*, part of an ongoing collaboration with her son Philip, whose electronic skills have led her work in increasingly kinetic directions. He helped to make clocks in the form of elephants and fish, and to install timepieces in some of her mirrors. Since 2003 her arboreal passions (so strong in her childhood when she spent much of her time up in the trees) have taken a startling new form. Initially she made a small ceramic tree, very fragile, which was bought by the artist Jim Farelly. Then she turned to her fretsaw to cut out extended plywood branches and leaves that are held in a branching ceramic base *(figs 91–4)*. Some directly record the olive culture of Tuscany while one has a metamorphic quality, its tips turned into dancing figures. Each tree, like her plates, has its own chromatic logic – mainly green or red, autumnal or spring-like in mood. Ceramic birds perch, ceramic olives hang among and from the branches. Wired for sound, sometimes placed in Victorian birdcages, these extraordinary objects emit birdsong. Like the swans they have grandeur of scale, being wayward, mannerist table pieces that condense Stokes' love of dance and of trees. A dancing figure and a fluttering tree become one and the same. Long ago her mother, learning of her love of ceramics, urged Stokes to avoid 'that awful heavy stuff'. The trees are the unexpected culmination of that advice. They also bring together, poetically, one of Ann's first practical interests – in fretsaw work – and her second, more sensuous engagement – with ceramics.

Tools for Conviviality

'The traces of the storyteller cling to the story the way the handprints of the potter cling to the clay vessel.'

Walter Benjamin, 'The Storyteller' (1936), *Illuminations*, Fontana/Collins, London, 1970, p.92

Ann Stokes remembers the potter Bernard Leach at St Ives. He and Adrian were in the Home Guard together and the household at Carbis Bay ate off 'seconds' from the Leach Pottery. To Ann he looked rather like a hare, and she remembers feeling sorry for him, trapped at his potter's wheel. Ceramics appeared to be a lonely business, not one that attracted her. But almost as soon as she became captivated by the craft, she saw its potential for conviviality.[55] Ann was to make her studio a safe haven for creative experimentation. Her cheerful assertion, 'I can teach anyone in three goes,'[56] explains why no one felt intimidated seeking her advice. Thus, the sculptor Barry Flanagan learnt simple coiling and made some haunting little Ur vessels. Ann taught the novelist David Plante to coil-build a garden pot and he went on to make three *pithoi*, one given to Natasha Spender – a great gardener. Some, like the art historian David Carrier, wrote regularly to Adrian.

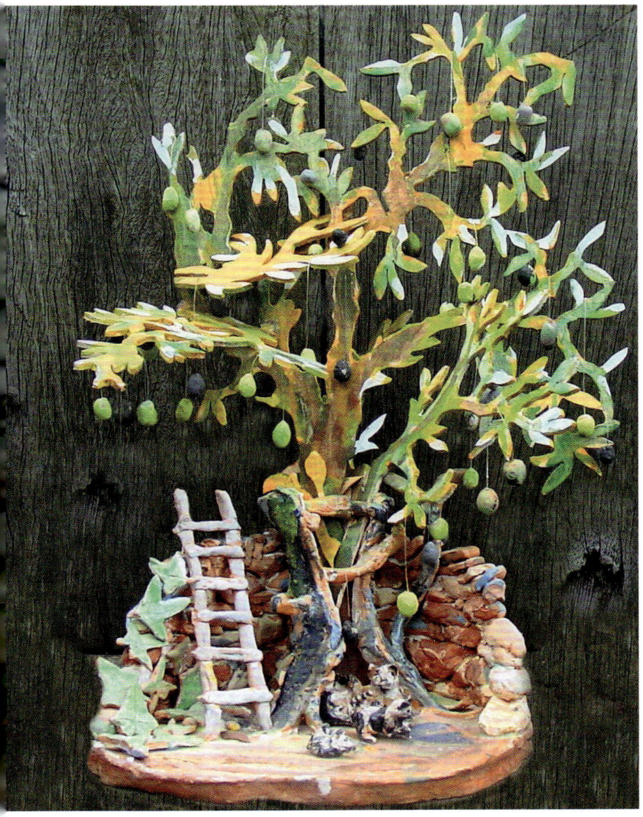

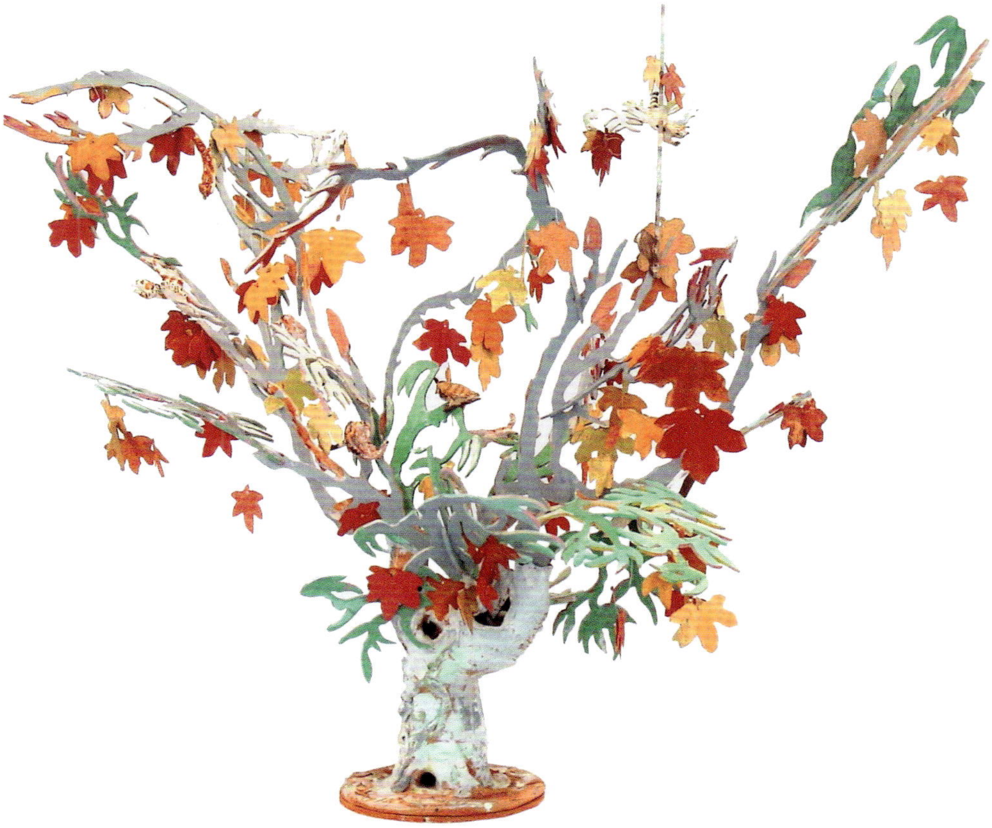

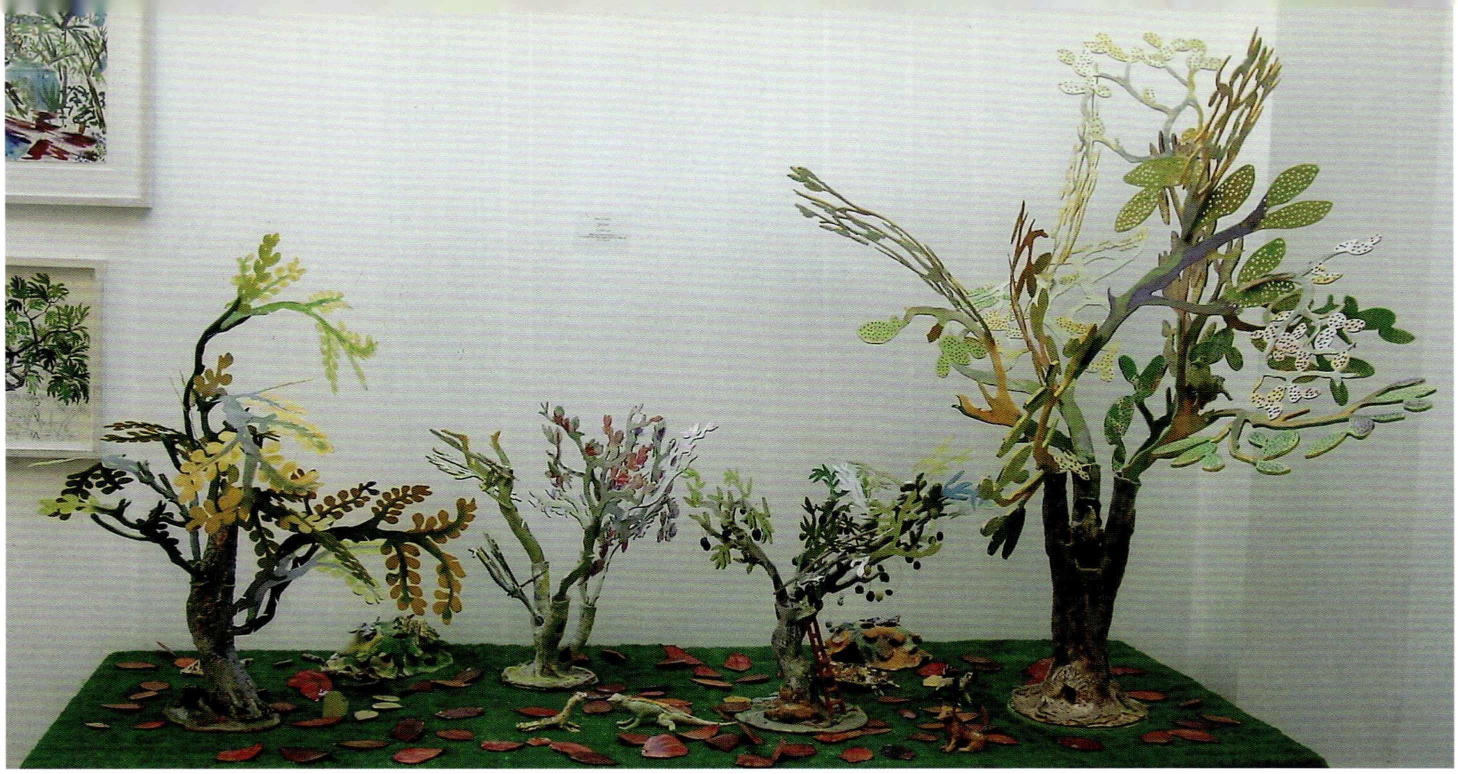

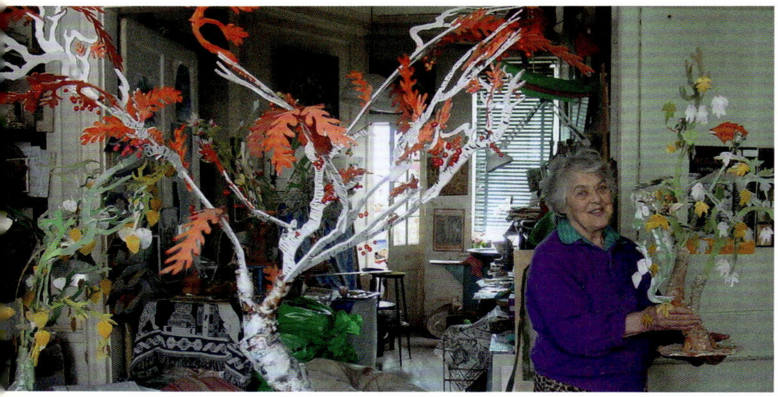

93 A Forest*, arranged by Philip Stokes, shown in* To Cage a Peacock: an exhibition of pottery by Ann Stokes with paintings by Johnny Dewe Mathews*, Rebecca Hossack Gallery, 2007*
Installation with bird and animal sounds
(length of table) 200 cm
Collection: Rebecca Hossack Gallery
Photo: Philip Stokes

94 Ann Stokes in her studio, 2006
Used as an invitation card for Ann Stokes: Trees are Life*, 2006*
Photo: Philip Stokes

95 Shelves in Ann Stokes' studio, June 2008
Photo: Stephen Brayne

He ended up meeting and loving Ann, doing odd jobs in her studio and paying her an unexpected tribute in a solemn review of Michael Fried's book *Courbet's Realism*.[57]

Much of this conviviality is less to do with the qualities of clay and more to do with a generosity of spirit, no better displayed than in her collaborations with the Dromedous family who owned a cafe round the corner in Heath Street, Hampstead. At the height of her 'Greek-Cretan' phase of the mid 1960s, Ann made them white shell-shaped ashtrays and much later, in 1978–9 she worked on an ambitious project for Chris Dromedous' *Primavera* restaurant in Hendon. The interior has now been demolished but a few rescued fragments – wall swans and distinctly Cretan-looking burnished oil jars – give a sense of its scale. The project was dominated by a major tile panel, a sylvan Mediterranean scene with a Laura-like woman entangled in a tree. This, surviving only as a blurry image in a brochure, was sited in the cocktail bar of Dromedous' *Melanie's Banqueting Suite* – above an incongruous tartan banquette on which sit a man and woman in evening dress, with Chris in a sharp white suit and dark glasses perched at the bar. *Et in Arcadia Ego*. The same touching whole-heartedness comes across in her collaborative work for her dealer, Rebecca Hossack, in particular for Hossack's house in London's Fitzrovia. Hossack exhibits some of the best of Aboriginal art and for Ann a new world, that of the Great Sandy Desert, opened up, partly inspired by a subsequent meeting with the Aboriginal artist Jimmy Pike in 2001. Ann bought one of his paintings and took an interest in Pike's drawings of his favoured subjects, which he was faxing to Hossack. In effect Ann

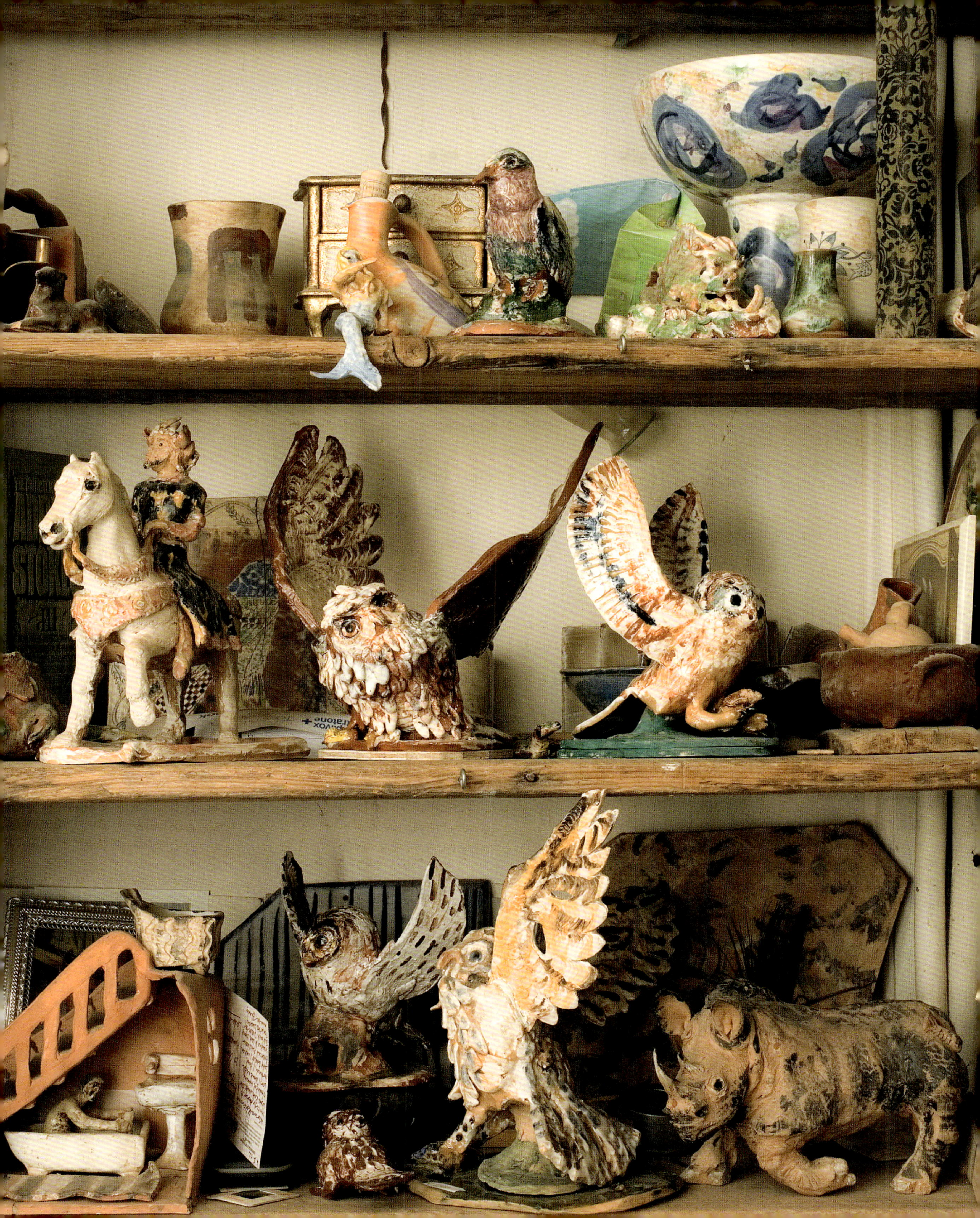

found a new chromatic and visual vocabulary inspired by the pigments used in Aboriginal art and by the fauna of the Australian desert; and these were the inspiration for plates and tiles made for Hossack's kitchen *(fig.45)*.

The Social Life of Things

In recent years – since 1995 – Stokes has had a 'gallery', like a conventionally successful artist. But until Stokes embarked on her relationship with Rebecca Hossack there was something unusual about the way in which her work was consumed. The designer Peggy Angus, who died in 1995,[58] and the sculptor and jeweller Andrew Logan,[59] are comparable figures, both generating a similar conviviality, both through their art and through access to their studios and way of life. As quintessentially British individualists, their work became known within a small circle (reminding us of the strict, if invisible, conventions of the 'proper' art world): to hang Angus' wallpapers or to wear Logan's jewellery (or to take part in his Alternative Miss World) were signs of possessing a certain kind of sensibility. This is also true of Stokes' ceramics. Their afterlife has an odd *samizdat* quality, with pieces passed from father to daughter, from friend to friend, lover to lover, bequeathed or entrusted, rarely re-released into the market place, inhabiting the world of the gift rather than that of the commodity. Owners worry about her work and wonder what might happen to it after they have gone – as if proper understanding might be in short supply. This is partly because her ceramics (while represented by a few cups and saucers in the collections of the Crafts Council in London, New Hall College in Cambridge and the Victoria and Albert Museum) demand a domestic context. Ann's plates and cups and her avian and fishy (and crocodilian and ceratorhine) vessels work powerfully in arrays, tightly packed on dressers, massed for display. Roughness of facture, a powerful design sensibility when it comes to colour and shape, together with an imagination steeped in invented mythologies, set these extraordinary objects apart from their commercially-made Mediterranean cousins – the fish platters and green-glazed, gurgling-fish water jugs to be found in tourist shops from Dubrovnik to Málaga. If the early classical Mediterranean echoes are the most powerful, her zoomorphic vessels also call up memories of objects long cherished in Albion's collective psyche – the homely beauties of cow creamers and Staffordshire flatbacks (which as Herbert Read put it, 'blunder into beauty')[60], egg dishes in the form of broody hens and the sophisticated playfulness of Chelsea porcelain tureens and sauceboats shaped as fish, crustacea and game. But if Stokes' ceramics appeal to a native fondness for 'Old China' her work is far more idiosyncratic than these vernacular and metropolitan examples, and more expressively made.

Displaying this work and knowing of her work is a sign – but a sign of what? That one belongs to a loose community of metropolitan writers, art historians, artists and critics with pastoral inclinations? Perhaps this is the case, although no one could be less elitist in her outlook than Stokes. Does admiring her work suggest a passionate anti-industrialism amongst educated men and women in Britain, with Stokes as reparation for Wedgwood's factories at Etruria in Staffordshire – where he vowed to make machines out of men? Ironically, to stand for the direct antithesis of industrial pottery had been the early aim of studio pottery. But after the Second World War many studio potters became well versed in ceramic technology, while those who made production pottery became almost too skilful, capable of throwing hundreds of identical forms at great speed. Beside them Bernard Leach appeared a mere amateur – and yet his pots remained recognisably superior; which is say that skill is contingent, particularly in the world of ceramics. To be an industry of one has never been Stokes' goal. Instead, she has put back on the table dreams, fantasy, childishness and sensuality – things that rationalism in design has ignored for too long.

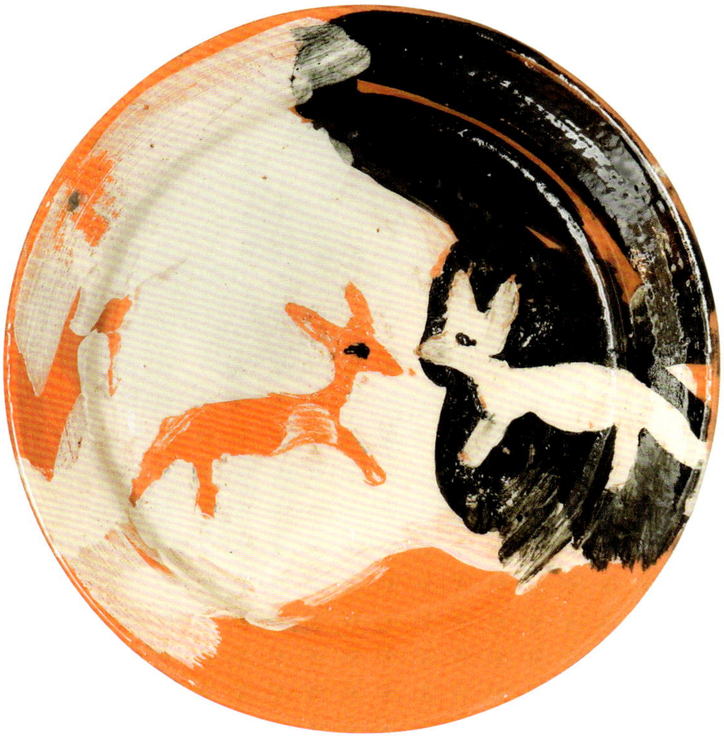

96 Plate with dogs stencilled from wooden models made by Philip Stokes as a child, marked Σ 8/02
19 cm (7.5 in)
Collection: Rebecca Hossack and Matthew Sturgis
Photo: Stephen Brayne

Notes

1. This apt phrase has been borrowed from Christopher Reed's *Bloomsbury Rooms*, Yale University Press, New Haven and London, 2004, where it is used to elucidate the 'domestic modernism' of the Bloomsbury Group.
2. John Ruskin, 'Of Queens' Gardens', *Sesame and Lilies* (1865), George Allen, Orpington Press, 1884, p.136. Ruskin goes on to develop a wife's role in a way that seems relevant: 'Her great function is Praise; she enters into no contest.'
3. Margaret Lambert and Enid Marx, *English Popular & Traditional Art*, Collins, London, 1946, p.8.
4. Adrian Stokes was interested in overturning high/low art categories too, speaking up for Mickey Mouse and finding in Disney cartoons 'the same evidence of intense observation' and 'the same exhaustiveness' that he admired in classical ballet. See *Tonight the Ballet*, Faber & Faber, London, 1934, p.21.
5. Ann Stokes interviewed by Linda Sandino, 2003, *Crafts Lives*, British Library Sound Archive.
6. Recorded conversation with Ann Stokes, 19 March 2008.
7. Adrian Stokes, *Stones of Rimini*, Faber & Faber, London, 1934, p.111.
8. ibid p.120.
9. Adrian Stokes, 'Mr Ben Nicholson's Painting' (1933), Lawrence Gowing (ed.), *The Critical Writings of Adrian Stokes, vol.i*, Thames & Hudson, London, 1978, 307–8. Also see Janet Sayers' essay on Adrian Stokes in her *Kleinians: Psychoanalysis Inside Out*, Polity, Cambridge, 2000, p.75.
10. Richard Wollheim, 'Adrian Stokes, critic, painter, poet', *Times Literary Supplement*, 17 February, 1978, pp 207–9.
11. See 'Memories of Adrian Stokes – presented by Eric Rhode', *The Listener*, 13 December 1973, p.815.
12. Adrian Stokes, 'The Painting of our Time' (1961), Lawrence Gowing (ed.), *The Critical Writing of Adrian Stokes, vol.iii*, Thames & Hudson, London, 1978, p.152.
13. Herbert Read, *The Meaning of Art* (1931), Pelican Books, Harmondsworth, 1949, p.33.
14. Clive Bell, *Art*, Chatto & Windus, London, 1914, p.8, p.58.
15. Herbert Read, *The Meaning of Art* (1931), op cit., p.33.
16. Charles Marriott, *British Handicrafts*, The British Council, London, 1943, p.33.
17. Craftsmen Potters Association, *Year Book 1966*, p.41.
18. Dora Billington, *The Art of the Potter*, Oxford University Press, London, 1937, p.110.
19. Jeffrey Jones, *Studio Pottery in Britain 1900–2005*, A. & C. Black, London, 2007, p.124; quoting Dora Billington, 'The Younger English Potters', *The Studio*, March 1953.
20. For a discussion of the Picassiettes see Tanya Harrod, *The Crafts in Britain in the 20th Century*, Yale University Press, London and New Haven, 1999, pp 266–70.
21. *Coper/Collingwood*, Victoria and Albert Museum, London, 1969, un-paginated.
22. Ann Stokes, email to the author, 22 April 2008.
23. ibid.
24. That they were bought and treasured by the art critic, connoisseur and collector David Sylvester is perhaps not surprising.

25. Ann Stokes interviewed by Linda Sandino, 2003, *Crafts Lives*, op.cit.
26. Henry Wilson, *Silverwork and Jewellery*, John Hogg, London, 1912, p.127.
27. Arts Council of Great Britain, *The Hayward Annual 1985: A Journey through Contemporary Art with Nigel Greenwood*, London, 1985, p.22.
28. Xavier Girard, Dominique Forest, *La Céramique Fauve*, exh.cat., Musée Matisse, Nice, 1996.
29. See Richard Morphet, pp.64–5; also Simon Watney, 'Quentin Bell, Potter', in Norbert Lynton et al, *Quentin Bell: A Man of Many Arts*, The Charleston Trust, 1999, p.19.
30. W.B. Honey, *The Art of the Potter: a Book for the Collector and Connoisseur*, Faber & Faber, London, 1946, p.37. Ann read several of Honey's books on ceramics while at Hurtwood House in the early 1950s.
31. On blue, see Philip Rawson, *Ceramics*, Oxford University Press, London, 1971, pp 139–42.
32. Eric Gill, *Autobiography*, Jonathan Cape, London, 1940, p.161.
33. Stephenie Bergman, email to the author, 27 March 2008.
34. Conversation with Jennifer Anderson, 9 April 2008.
35. Philip Rawson, *Ceramics*, op.cit. 1971, p.6.
36. For an overview of the grand service see Robert Schmidt, *Porcelain as an Art and a Mirror of Fashion*, W.A. Thorpe (trans.), George G. Harrap, London, 1932; and Stefan Bursche, *Tafelzier des Barock*, Editions Schneider, Munich, 1974.
37. Le Corbusier, *The Decorative Art of Today* (1925), James Dunnett (trans.), The Architectural Press, London, 1987, p.87.
38. Crafts Council, *The Maker's Eye*, London, 1981, p.16.
39. Paul Bourassa, Leopold Foulem, *Picasso and Ceramics*, exh.cat., Musée National des Beaux-Arts du Québec and Gardiner Museum of Ceramic Art, 2004, pp 200–1, pp 269–71.
40. Yet another found a home with Sir Joseph Lockwood, the chairman of EMI at the height of Beatlemania. Further rhinos were made for Jennifer Anderson, headmistress of Francis Holland School for Girls, and for Christopher Dromedous' *Melanie's Banqueting Suite* in Hendon. We can only wonder at the diversity of Stokes' friendships.
41. See T.H. Clarke, 'The Iconography of the Rhinoceros', *The Connoisseur*, vol.183, 1973, pp 2–13 and vol.184, 1974, no.744, pp 113–22.
42. Inscribed on a photograph, Rebecca Hossack Gallery archive.
43. Recorded conversation with Ann Stokes, 19 March 2008.
44. See Peter Carey, 'A New Potter in Camden', *Camden Journal*, vol.4, no.5, Feb/March 1969. Abdulla came from a long line of Koranic scholars who had founded madrasa schools throughout the Sudan. See Kenneth Okwesa, 'Abdulla, Sudanese Potter', *African Arts*, vol.3, no.2, Winter 1970, pp 29–31; and Salah M. Hassan, 'Khartoum Connections: the Sudanese Story', Clémentine Deliss (ed.), *Seven Stories about Modern Art in Africa*, exh.cat., Whitechapel Art Gallery, London, 1995, pp 123–4.
45. Catherine Lampert, email, 4 June 2004. Lampert went to Abdulla's classes during 1966–7 while at the Slade.
46. Conversation with Mohammed Abdulla, 2 May 2008.
47. John Fowler to Ann Stokes, 16 March (year omitted) *c.*1967–70, Ann Stokes'

personal archive.

48. John Fowler to Ann Stokes, 3 July (year omitted) *c.*1967–70, Ann Stokes' personal archive.

49. John Fowler to Ann Stokes, 26 April (year omitted) *c.*1967–70, Ann Stokes' personal archive.

50. For the Dromedous family, see p.114. My thanks to Philip Stokes for his exceptional help with this research.

51. For Jacques Derrida's discussion of frames in his *Truth in Painting*, see Glenn Adamson, *Thinking Through Craft*, Berg, Oxford, 2007, pp 11–13.

52. Conversation with Jennifer Anderson, op.cit.

53. See Lindsay Boynton, 'Luke Lightfoot (?1722–1789)', *Furniture History*, no.11, 1966, pp 7–17.

54. See Philip Rawson, 'Echoes: An Introduction', Garth Clark (ed.), *Ceramic Echoes: Historical References in Contemporary Ceramics*, The Contemporary Art Society, Nelson-Atkins Museum of Art, Kansas City, 1983.

55. On a tour of England in the 1930s J.B. Priestley found that potters were the most cheerful of industrial workers. See his *English Journey*, Heinemann Ltd, London, 1934, pp 204–34.

56. Recorded conversation with Ann Stokes, op.cit.

57. David Carrier, 'Review', *History and Theory*, vol.30, no.3, October 1991, p.373.

58. See Carolyn Trant, *Art for Life: The Story of Peggy Angus*, Incline Press, Oldham, 2004.

59. On Logan see Terence Maloon, 'Modes of Perception', *Artscribe*, 12 June 1978.

60. Herbert Read, *Staffordshire Pottery Figures*, Duckworth, London, 1929, p.22.

Chronology

Parents: Revd David Barclay Mellis (1875–1958), Presbyterian Minister and Margaret Mackenzie Mellis, née Mackenzie (1880–1970).

1914 Sister Margaret Nairn Mellis is born in Wu-Kung-Fu, China, where her father is a missionary.

1915 Parents and Margaret return to Edinburgh.
David Mellis enlists in the First World War and is wounded in action.
Brother David is born.

1918 Brother Duff is born.

1922 Ann Mellis is born on 21 September, Gullane, East Lothian.

1930 Ann is given a hand fretsaw by her brothers.

1935 Sees *Top Hat*, with Fred Astaire and Ginger Rogers, and decides to become a dancer.

1936 Joins St Leonard's School, St Andrews, Fife, in the autumn term.

1938 Margaret Mellis marries the writer, painter and critic Adrian Stokes on 14 July.

1939 Adrian Stokes buys Little Parc Owles, Carbis Bay, Cornwall, moving in on 3 April. Guests come and go, including Ben Nicholson, Barbara Hepworth and their triplets who arrive at the beginning of the war, staying until December. Adrian starts a market garden on two acres of land, supplying vegetables to two evacuated schools and a hotel. He joins the Home Guard.

1940 Ann leaves St Leonard's in the spring term, arriving in Carbis Bay in late summer to help Margaret prepare for the birth of her son, Telfer, in October. She reads Adrian Stokes' beguiling *Tonight the Ballet* (1934).
Naum Gabo endorses Stokes' plan for Ann to attend Phyllis Bedells' ballet school, evacuated to St Ives for the duration of the war. Ann goes to classes each weekday morning. She passes the Preliminary and Intermediate ballet exams.

1941 In June Ann goes to London and volunteers for the Women's Royal Naval Service (Wrens); trains as Morse code operator near Warrington.
Posted to the Isle of Man; an injured knee is treated by Sir Herbert Atkinson Barker, pioneer in osteopathy.
Sent to Liverpool and volunteers to go to France where she is billeted in the grounds of Hilaire Belloc's birthplace at La Celle-Saint-Cloud.
Occasional 'breathless' ballet classes in Paris with Madame Carlotta Zambelli.
Buys African sculptures in Paris.
Final posting to the 'snow-laden skies' north of Aberdeen.

1945 By the end of the year Ann is living in Highgate, London, staying with her aunt and her uncle Norman Wilkinson, the irrepressibly humorous marine painter, inventor of camouflage dazzle in World War 1 and War Artist 1939–45.
Prepares for Advanced ballet exam with Phyllis Bedells.
Adrian Stokes visits regularly when in London.

1947 Knee problems force Ann to abandon ballet. Takes up Spanish dancing.
Adrian Stokes divorces Ann's sister Margaret Mellis and marries Ann in Ascona, Switzerland on 22 May.

1948 Adrian rents Casa alla Motta in Ascona, Switzerland.
Son Philip Stokes is born on 18 February.
Adrian's analyst Melanie Klein visits Ascona; she asks Ann's opinion of her lecture *Love, Guilt and Reparation*. Ann replies, 'It is full of common sense.'

1949 Adrian Stokes publishes *Art and Science: A Study of Alberti, Piero della Francesca and Giorgione*, dedicated to Ann.
To Cap d'Antibes with Adrian Stokes to visit Telfer, her sister Margaret and second husband Francis Davison. Ann sees Picasso's ceramics at Vallauris.

1950 Adrian and Ann with Philip return to England to Heathgate, Bucklebury, Berkshire.

1951 Daughter Ariadne is born in Reading on 10 June.
The family move to Hurtwood House near Guildford, situated in woods northwest of Ewhurst. The architect A.T. Bolton had created 'a design like a Tuscan villa with a taller corner tower but the materials and detail those of an early Lutyens house, a queer hybrid' (Pevsner, *Surrey*, 1962, p.195).
Ann makes toys and trees with her fretsaw. She contributes articles on fretsaw projects to *Hobbies Weekly: the Fretworker's and Home Craftsman's Journal.*

1956 Moves to 20 Church Row, Hampstead, in September.
Adrian has a studio at the top of the house. A wide circle of friends become regular visitors, including Andrew Forge, John Golding, Lawrence Gowing, Derek Hill, David Sylvester and Richard Wollheim.

1957 Ann takes her son Philip to Well Walk Pottery, Hampstead, to be taught by Chris Magarshack, son of the translator and biographer David Magarshack, and receives instruction herself. 'I never got over the magic of it.'
Soon makes her own wheel adapting a weighted car wheel as the flywheel.

1960 Adrian Stokes is appointed a Trustee of the Tate Gallery.

1962 Buys her first kiln.

1963 Ann meets the Dromedous family, making ashtrays for their *Mykonos* restaurant on Heath Street, Hampstead, and *Olympus Taverna*, Finchley Road, and later in 1966 wedding presents for Chris Dromedous.

1965 Gives lessons to the Slade-trained sculptor Mary Day Lanier, beginning in December.

1966 Ann and Mary Day seek hand-building instruction from the Sudanese potter Mohammed Ahmed Abdulla at Camden Arts Centre.
Ann begins to learn Modern Greek. Completes a large tile panel of classical Greek sailing ships and dolphins for the kitchen at Church Row.
Installs a large kiln.

1967 In early December organises a 'sale' at 20 Church Row with Mary Day Lanier. Both artists make exactly £16 8 1/2d, part of which is donated to opponents of the military regime in Greece. These informal exhibitions at Church Row (which may have begun as early as 1965) become an eagerly awaited annual pre-Christmas event.
John Fowler becomes an enthusiastic client by the mid 1960s, buying garden pots and tableware for his Hampshire home, The Hunting Lodge.

1969 Mediterranean cruise with Adrian.
Mary Day Lanier marries philosopher Richard Wollheim.

1970 Second Mediterranean cruise trip with Adrian, 26 May–9 June.
Through John Fowler, exhibits in Rhoda, Lady Birley's Charleston Manor Festival, West Dean, East Sussex. Ann sends work annually in June and July for several years.

1971 Adrian has major operation for cancer.

1972 David Sylvester mounts the show *Islamic Carpets* at the Hayward Gallery, 19 October–10 December; Adrian and Ann visit and admire. A patron of Ann's work, Sylvester subsequently sells Ann a handsome two-handled Etruscan drinking cup.
On 15 December Adrian dies of a brain tumour at Church Row on the day of Ann's Christmas pottery sale.

1973 Ann attends consolatory tap-dancing classes three times a week followed by belly-dancing lessons.
Sells a Henry Moore sculpture and buys a flat in Cortona.
Begins a collaboration with John Craxton, making sets of dinner plates, from December 1973 to 1975. Craxton decorates them. 'I did all the work and he had all the fun.'

1974 Sculptor Barry Flanagan receives brief tutoring by Ann 'among her ceramic recipes'.

1976 Makes a hooked-rug stair carpet for 20 Church Row based on designs provided by John Golding, following his design (if not colour scheme) exactly for the first flight. (Later continuing the carpet to the second flight in 2005: 'I rather went my own way.')
Marries Ian Angus, George Orwell scholar and chief librarian at King's College, London, on 18 September.
Artist Stephenie Bergman works in Ann's studio, continuing for 3 to 4 years as a refuge from 'LCC evening class situations'.

1977 Exhibits at Chelsea Flower Show (also 1978 and 1979).

1978–9 Buys Andrew Lord's *Coffee service and tray (square, flat colour set)* from exhibition, *Andrew Lord: Pottery*, Anthony Stokes Ltd, 21 June–15 July 1978.
Embarks on major installation including a large tile panel, small framed panels and swan sculptures for the interior of Christopher Dromedous' *Melanie's Banqueting Suite* attached to his restaurant *La Primavera* on Hendon Way, London NW4.

1980 Ann and Ian buy a house at Pergo, near Cortona, with 250 olive trees.

1981 Installs large kiln at 20 Church Row in the cellar extending under the pavement.

1984 Dr Angela Hamilton starts learning pottery with Ann, inspired by white tin-glaze plates (by Ann Stokes and Mary Day Wollheim) seen at a dinner party given by Sonia Orwell.

1985 *A Journey through Contemporary Art with Nigel Greenwood*, Hayward Annual, includes a selection of plates by Ann. Greenwood writes: 'Elsewhere I may have voiced certain problems I have with craft when it is elevated to an art form, but with Ann Stokes' work I have no problems – she has a true artist's affinity with everything she touches.'

1991 Derek Hill brings the Prince of Wales and Oliver Hoare to Pergo, 11 May.

1994 *Light and Air Transformed*, 13–14 August, Burgh House, Hampstead, with Day Wollheim.

1995 *Pot & Paint*, Burgh House, Hampstead, 2–12 August.
Festive Fish, mixed show with Camilla Meddings and Katy Hackney, Rebecca Hossack Gallery, London, 27 November–23 December. Thereafter Ann regularly has work in the Rebecca Hossack Gallery but continues with her Christmas exhibitions until 2004.

1998 *Ann Stokes: A Retrospective*, Rebecca Hossack Gallery, Windmill Street, London, 11 September–3 October. Letter to Tanya Harrod: 'I am very excited to have a one-man show even if I have had to wait for my 76th B.' The catalogue includes words by the art historian John Golding – 'Ann Stokes: An Appreciation' – and also an anecdote from the artist: 'We visited Bernard Leach in the 1960s. He asked me what I did. I said loud and clear, as I felt he might be a little deaf – "I pot, I am a potter." There was a shocked silence. "That is I mean I try to be a potter," I ended blushing. All then went well.'

1999 *Ann Stokes: Soaring, Swooping, Leaping*, Charleston Gallery, Firle, Sussex, 4 July–29 August.

2000 *Ann Stokes: The Smile of the Crocodile*, 30 November–23 December, Rebecca Hossack Gallery, London.
Takes up salsa dancing.

2001 *Peter Bartlett, Ann Stokes*, Galleria d'Arte Gino Severini, Cortona.
Meets the Aboriginal artist Jimmy Pike through Rebecca Hossack.

2002 Exhibits a life-size crocodile together with paintings by Adrian Stokes and Margaret Mellis at an exhibition at Malatesta Castle, Montefiore Conca, near Rimini, held to celebrate the translation of Adrian Stokes' *Stones of Rimini* into Italian.

2003 Acquires two power-fretsaws for use in London and Italy.
Peter Bartlett, Ann Stokes, Gallerie d'Arte Gino Severini, Cortona, 10–16 May.
2003–4 *Giardino Incantevole*, a mixed exhibition of pottery by Ann Stokes and paintings by Peter Bartlett, Rebecca Hossack Gallery, Charlotte Street, London, 26 November–15 January.
Painter Johnny Dewe Mathews works in Ann's studio decorating tiles and plates.

2004 *Peter Bartlett, Ann Stokes*, Galleria Pentart, Rome, 16–23 April.
Pot and Paint, Ann Stokes' last Christmas show at 20 Church Row with Peter Bartlett, 11–12 December.

2005 Exhibits at the Gallerie Elle Arte, Palermo, Sicily, with Peter Bartlett.

2006 *Ann Stokes: Trees are Life*, Rebecca Hossack Gallery, Windmill Street, London, 23 June–8 July.

2007 *To Cage a Peacock*, exhibition of pottery by Ann Stokes with paintings by Johnny Dewe Mathews, Rebecca Hossack Art Gallery, 2 Conway Street, Fitzroy Square, London, 10–22 September

Public Collections

Crafts Council, London
International Museum of Ceramics, Faenza, Italy
New Hall College, Cambridge, UK
Victoria and Albert Museum, London

Bibliography

Boyer, Marie-France, 'Clay the Game', *The World of Interiors*, May 1990

Carrier, David, review of *Courbet's Realism* by Michael Fried in *History and Theory*, vol.30, no.3, October 1991, pp 368–81 (see p.372)

Freyberg, Annabel, 'The art of making a home', *Evening Standard*, October 26 2006
Freyberg, Annabel, 'Technicolour Dreamtime', *The World of Interiors*, November 2006
Freyberg, Annabel, 'Natural creativity takes wing', *The Independent*, 11 September 1998

Greenwood, Nigel, *A Journey through Contemporary Art with Nigel Greenwood: The Hayward Annual 1985*, Arts Council of Great Britain, London, 1985
Greenwood, Nigel, 'Avant Guardian', *The World of Interiors*, May 2004

Graves, Alun, *Studio Pottery: British Studio Ceramics in the Victorian and Albert Museum Collection*, Phaidon, London (forthcoming)

Harrod, Tanya, 'Lyrical Touch', *Crafts*, no.77, November/December 1985, pp 16–19
Harrod, Tanya, *The Crafts in Britain in the 20th Century*, Yale University Press, New Haven, 1999

Hossack, Rebecca, 'Ann Stokes', *Resurgence*, May/June 1999, no.194, p.15

May, Derwent, 'Birds in the hand', *The Times*, August 31 2005

McCarthy, Fiona, 'Dreaming in London: Rebecca Hossack's London Apartment', *Vogue Living Australia*, September/October 2008

Mosley, Nicholas, 'First Buy, Last Buy', *Sunday Telegraph*, May 7 2006

Neustatter, Angela, 'Cheap Chic', *The Guardian*, 3 August 1976

Schulenberg, Adelheid von der, 'Home is Where the Art is', *The World of Interiors*, March 1995

'Ann Stokes: La magia nelle ceramiche', *Corriere di Arezzo*, 19 October, 1997

Acknowledgements

Tanya Harrod

I would like to thank Ann Stokes for her kindness during the period of writing this book. Many visits were paid and many questions answered, always in a spirit of fun and good humour, often enlivened by the helpful presence of her husband Ian Angus. Throughout, Philip Stokes has been a kindly, patient guide. My two fellow authors, Richard Morphet and Hilary Spurling, were a constant inspiration. I thank all the owners of work by Ann Stokes who answered numerous questions and in many instances aided our photographic campaign and were unfailingly hospitable: Jennifer Anderson, John Craxton, Dr Angela Hamilton, Monica Humphries, François Gilles, John Golding, the Earl and Countess of Gowrie, Phoebe Greenwood, Jake Tilson and Jeff Lee, David Plante, Lord and Lady Ravensdale, Eric Rhode, Annie Weeks, Sarah and Saskia Whitfield. The artists Stephenie Bergman, Andrew Lord and Carol McNicoll contributed their usual keen insights. Glenn Adamson and Horatia Harrod provided new perspectives. Ann's former tutor Mohammed Ahmed Abdulla was gracious and generous with his time. Thanks also to Stephen Brayne (adaptable and indefatigable), to Maisie Hill and again to Philip Stokes for their photographs. Also many thanks to Rebecca Hossack and her gallery assistants for their help and support. Lucy Clark at Lund Humphries was consistently helpful. Above all, thanks to Josephine Batterham.

Richard Morphet

My keenest thanks are to Ann Stokes for her patience and kindness in answering so many questions over an extended period, and to her and Ian Angus for their warm hospitality. Philip Stokes has been consistently helpful and alert. I thank him and the many others with whom I have talked about Ann for their valuable insights. Many are named in my text, where I report what they told me, but I should also like to thank Jo Batterham, Jenny Gowing, Telfer Stokes, Matthew Sturgis, Naomi Sylvester, Lady Nolan and Sarah Whitfield; Cathy Courtney and Mary Stewart of National Life Stories at the British Library Sound Archive; and Sue Breakell and colleagues at the Hyman Kreitman Research Centre, Tate Britain.

Index

Page numbers in *italics* refer to illustration captions.